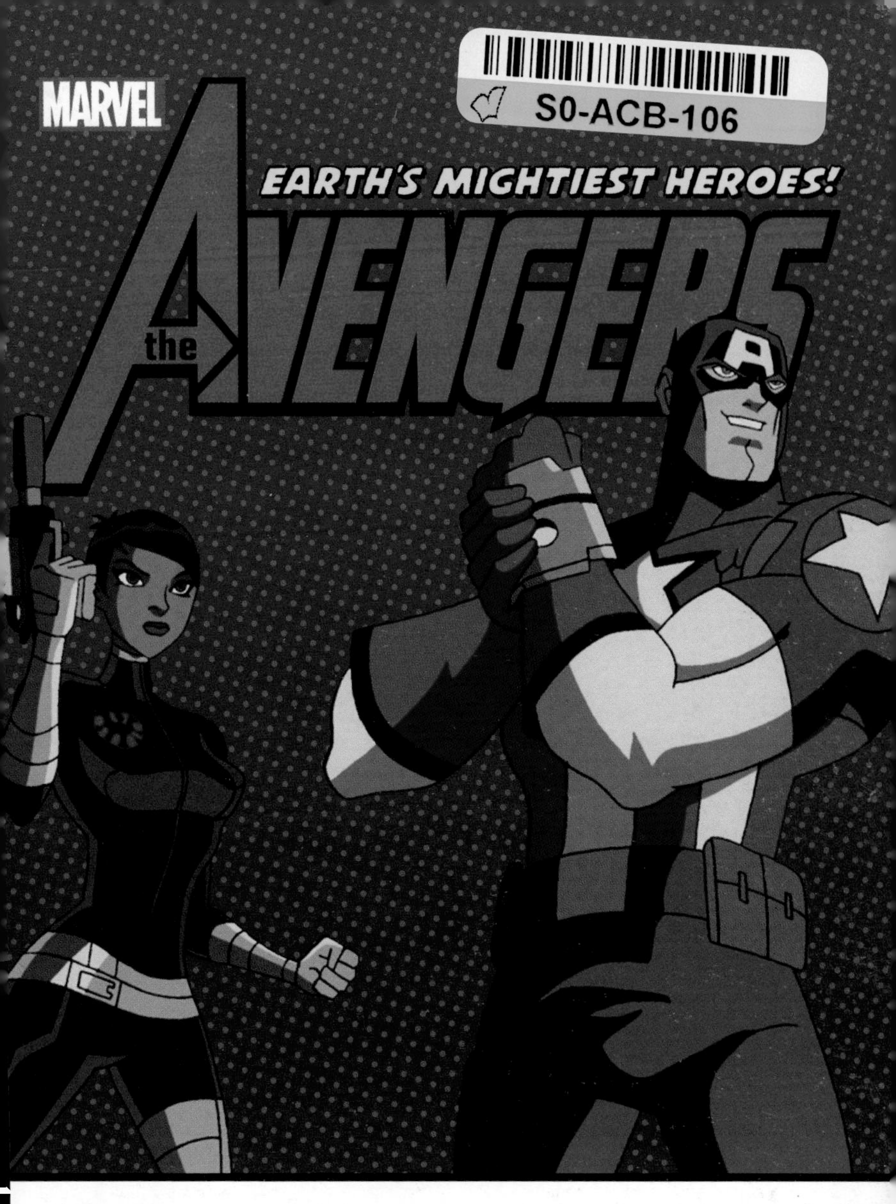
MARVEL
S0-ACB-106
EARTH'S MIGHTIEST HEROES!
the AVENGERS

MARVEL UNIVERSE AVENGERS EARTH'S MIGHTIEST HEROES VOL. 4. Contains material originally published in magazine form as MARVEL UNIVERSE AVENGERS EARTH'S MIGHTIEST HEROES #13-17. First printing 2013. ISBN# 978-0-7851-8421-8. Published by MARVEL WORLDWIDE, INC., a subsidiary of MARVEL ENTERTAINMENT, LLC. OFFICE OF PUBLICATION: 135 West 50th Street, New York, NY 10020. **Printed in the U.S.A.** ALAN FINE, EVP - Office of the President, Marvel Worldwide, Inc. and EVP & CMO Marvel Characters B.V.; DAN BUCKLEY, Publisher & President - Print, Animation & Digital Divisions; JOE QUESADA, Chief Creative Officer; TOM BREVOORT, SVP of Publishing; DAVID BOGART, SVP of Operations & Procurement, Publishing; C.B. CEBULSKI, SVP of Creator & Content Development; DAVID GABRIEL, SVP of Print & Digital Publishing Sales; JIM O'KEEFE, VP of Operations & Logistics; DAN CARR, Executive Director of Publishing Technology; SUSAN CRESPI, Editorial Operations Manager; ALEX MORALES, Publishing Operations Manager; STAN LEE, Chairman Emeritus. For information regarding advertising in Marvel Comics or on Marvel.com, please contact Niza Disla, Director of Marvel Partnerships, at ndisla@marvel.com. For Marvel subscription inquiries, please call 800-217-9158. **Manufactured between 9/20/2013 and 10/28/2013 by SHERIDAN BOOKS, INC., CHELSEA, MI, USA.**

10 9 8 7 6 5 4 3 2 1

MARVEL
EARTH'S MIGHTIEST HEROES!
the AVENGERS

Based on the TV series episodes by
**CHRIS YOST, KEVIN BURKE,
CHRIS WYATT, MICHAEL RYAN,
PAUL GIACOPPO** & **BRANDON AUMAN**

Adapted by
JOE CARAMAGNA

Cover Artists
KHOI PHAM & **CHRIS SOTOMAYOR** (#13),
TIM LEVINS & **CHRIS SOTOMAYOR** (#14),
and **CHRIS JONES** & **ANDREW DALHOUSE** (#15-17)

Editors
ELLIE PYLE & **SEBASTIAN GIRNER**

Consulting Editor
JON MOISAN

Senior Editor
MARK PANICCIA

Collection Editor
CORY LEVINE
Assistant Editors
ALEX STARBUCK & **NELSON RIBEIRO**
Editors, Special Projects
JENNIFER GRÜNWALD & **MARK D. BEAZLEY**
Senior Editor, Special Projects
JEFF YOUNGQUIST
SVP of Print & Digital Publishing Sales:
DAVID GABRIEL

Editor In Chief
AXEL ALONSO
Chief Creative Officer
JOE QUESADA
Publisher
DAN BUCKLEY
Executive Producer
ALAN FINE

AND THERE CAME A DAY...A DAY UNLIKE ANY OTHER, WHEN EARTH'S MIGHTIEST HEROES FOUND THEMSELVES UNITED AGAINST A COMMON THREAT...TO FIGHT THE FOES NO SINGLE SUPER HERO COULD WITHSTAND... ON THAT DAY WERE BORN...

EARTH'S MIGHTIEST HEROES! the AVENGERS

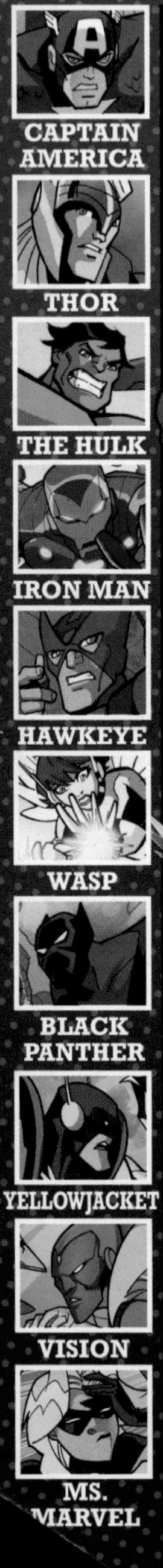
CAPTAIN AMERICA
THOR
THE HULK
IRON MAN
HAWKEYE
WASP
BLACK PANTHER
YELLOWJACKET
VISION
MS. MARVEL

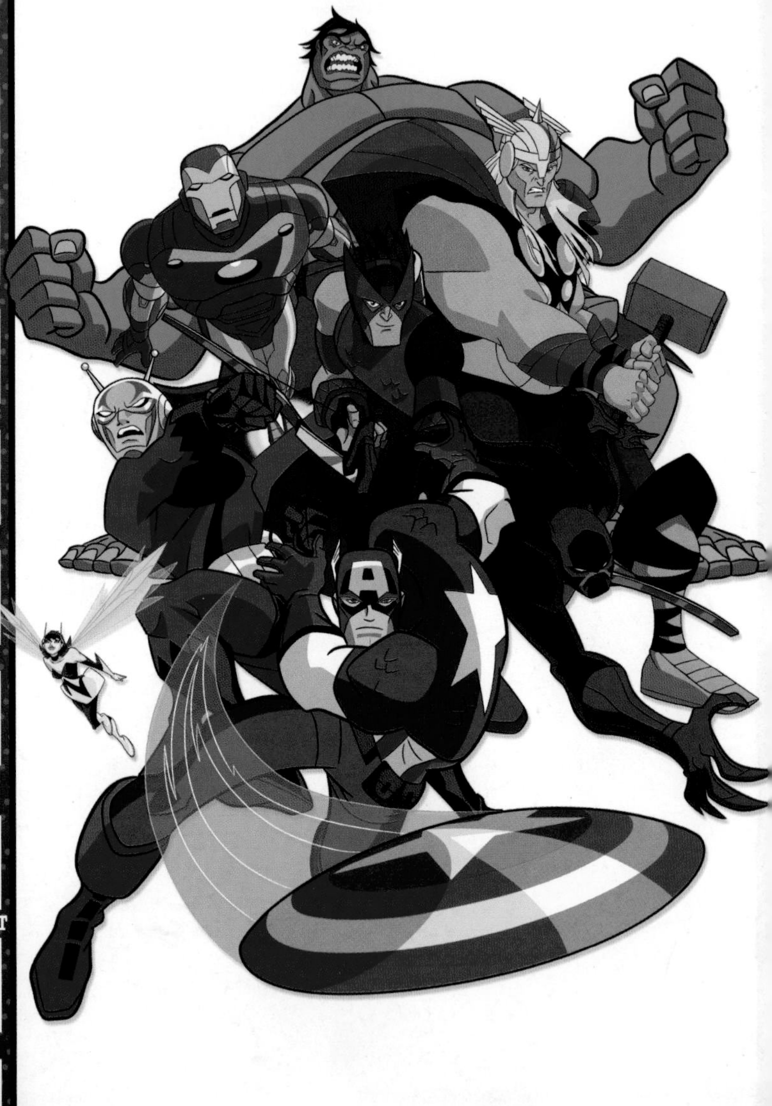

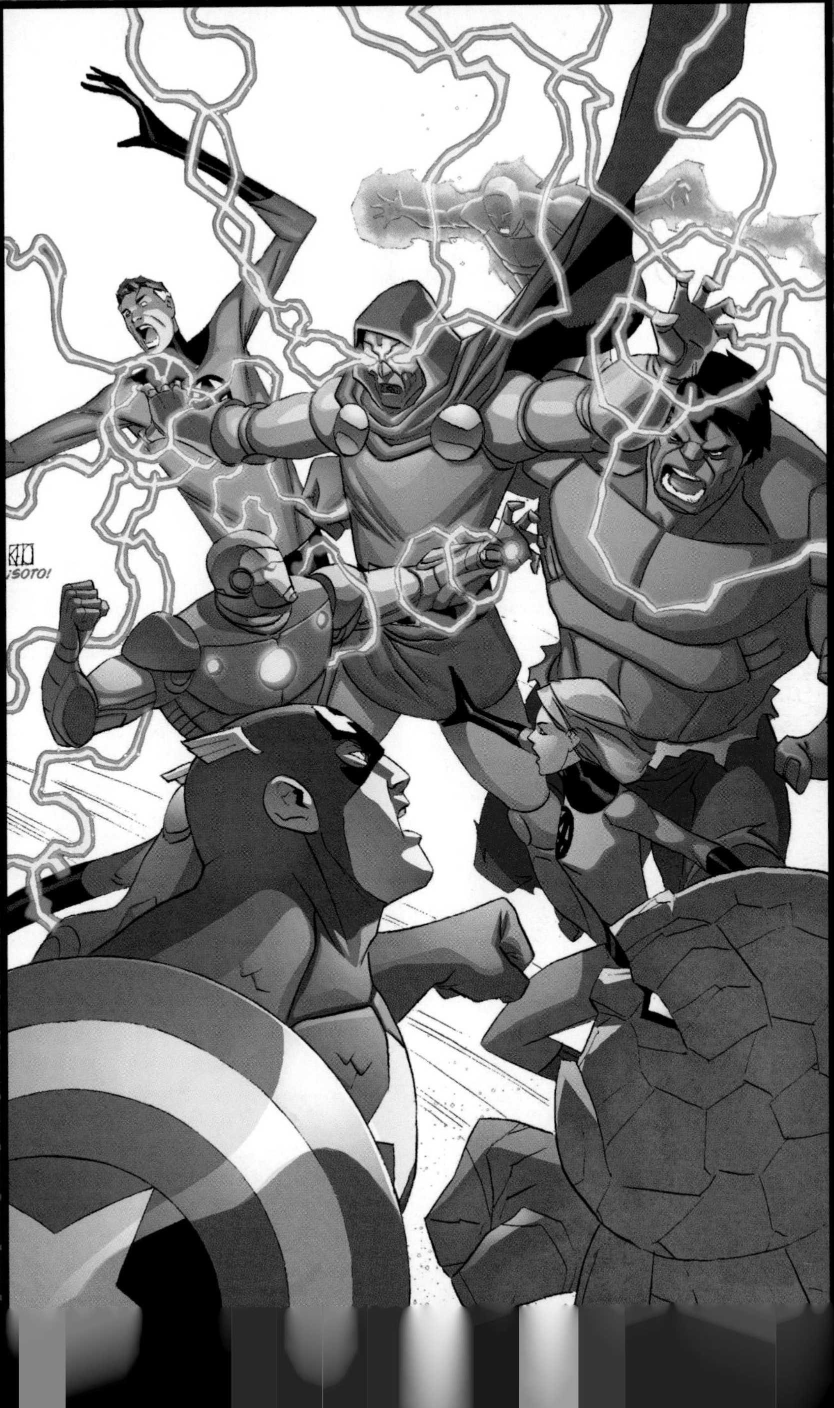
¡SOTO!

THE TARGET HAS BEEN LOCATED, BUT THERE HAS BEEN...A COMPLICATION.

ANTHONY STARK, A.K.A. **IRON MAN**. TEAM LEADER. ARMOR INCORPORATES ARC REACTOR AND REPULSOR TECHNOLOGY.

THREAT LEVEL: HIGH.

STEVE ROGERS, A.K.A. **CAPTAIN AMERICA**. ENHANCED STRENGTH AND SPEED. ARMED WITH A SHIELD MADE OF UNKNOWN MATERIAL.

THREAT LEVEL: MEDIUM.

JANET VAN DYNE, A.K.A. **THE WASP**. SUPERHUMAN ABILITIES INCLUDE SIZE ALTERATION, FLIGHT AND BIO-STINGS.

THREAT LEVEL: LOW.

KING T'CHALLA, A.K.A. THE **BLACK PANTHER**. HEIGHTENED SENSES, SPEED AND STRENGTH. ACCESS TO VIBRANIUM WEAPONS.

THREAT LEVEL: MEDIUM.

CLINT BARTON, A.K.A. **HAWKEYE**. SUBJECT CARRIES A BOW WITH A VARIETY OF WEAPONIZED ARROWS.

THREAT LEVEL: LOW.

BRUCE BANNER, A.K.A. **THE HULK**. STRENGTH ENHANCED BY GAMMA RADIATION, UPPER LIMIT.

THREAT LEVEL--

--EXTREME.

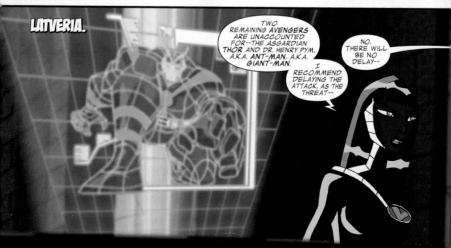

LATVERIA.

TWO REMAINING AVENGERS ARE UNACCOUNTED FOR--THE ASGARDIAN THOR AND DR. HENRY PYM, A.K.A. ANT-MAN, A.K.A. GIANT-MAN. I RECOMMEND DELAYING THE ATTACK, AS THE THREAT--

NO. THERE WILL BE NO DELAY--

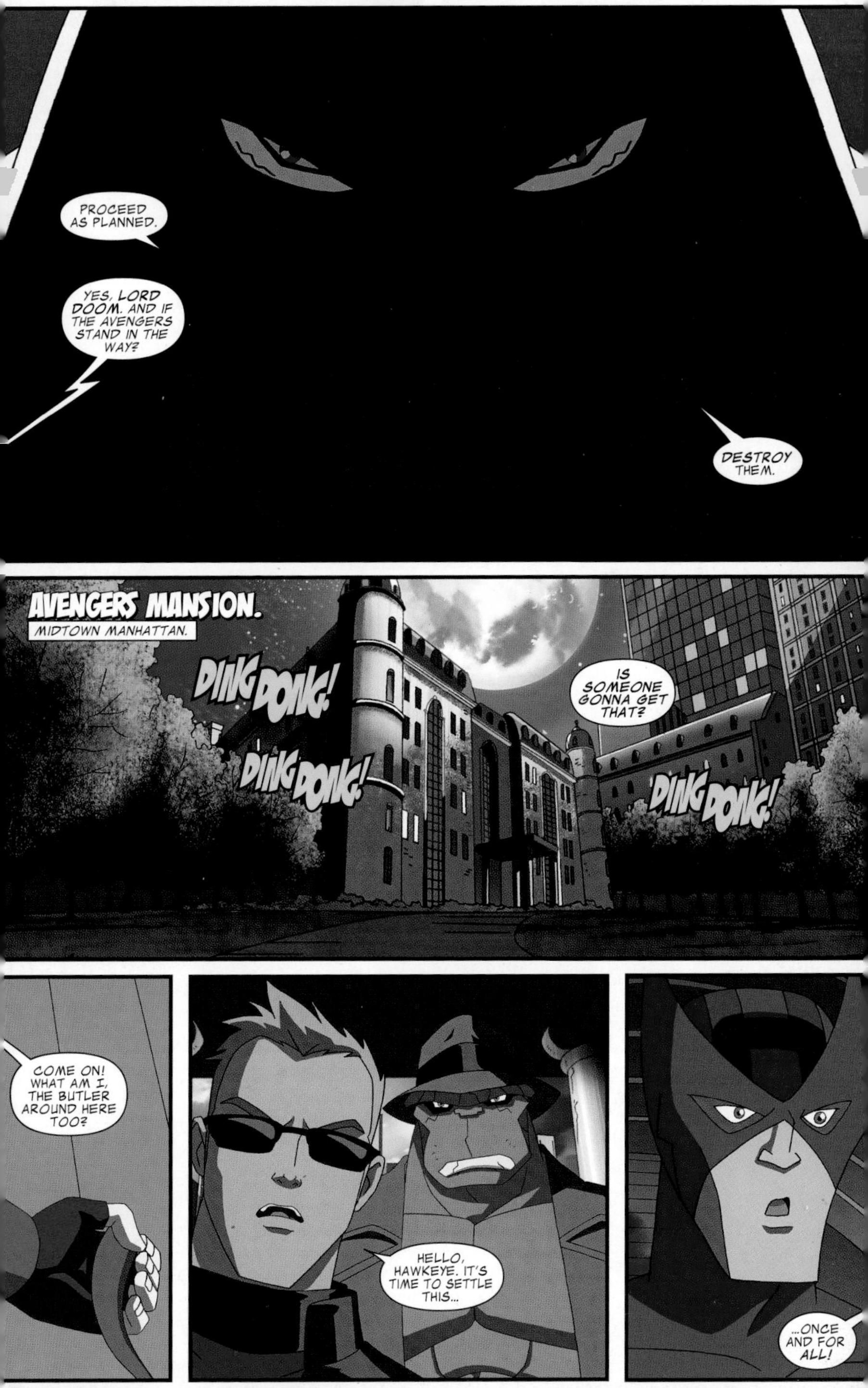
PROCEED AS PLANNED.
YES, LORD DOOM. AND IF THE AVENGERS STAND IN THE WAY?
DESTROY THEM.
AVENGERS MANSION.
MIDTOWN MANHATTAN.
DING DONG!
DING DONG!
IS SOMEONE GONNA GET THAT?
DING DONG!
COME ON! WHAT AM I, THE BUTLER AROUND HERE TOO?
HELLO, HAWKEYE. IT'S TIME TO SETTLE THIS...
...ONCE AND FOR ALL!

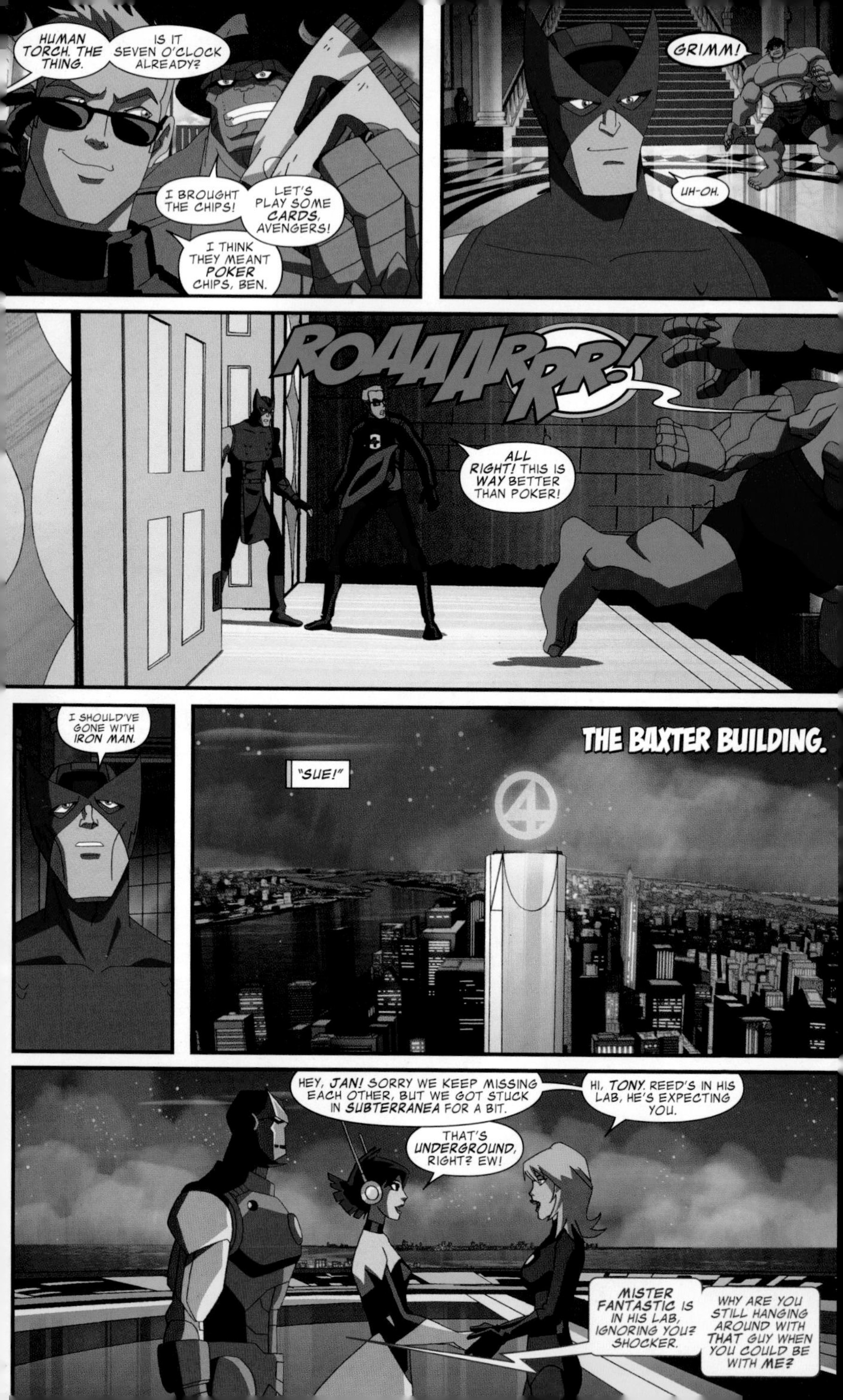
HUMAN TORCH. THE THING.
IS IT SEVEN O'CLOCK ALREADY?
I BROUGHT THE CHIPS!
LET'S PLAY SOME CARDS, AVENGERS!
I THINK THEY MEANT POKER CHIPS, BEN.
GRIMM!
UH-OH.
ROAAARRR!
ALL RIGHT! THIS IS WAY BETTER THAN POKER!
I SHOULD'VE GONE WITH IRON MAN.
THE BAXTER BUILDING.
"SUE!"
HEY, JAN! SORRY WE KEEP MISSING EACH OTHER, BUT WE GOT STUCK IN SUBTERRANEA FOR A BIT.
THAT'S UNDERGROUND, RIGHT? EW!
HI, TONY. REED'S IN HIS LAB, HE'S EXPECTING YOU.
MISTER FANTASTIC IS IN HIS LAB, IGNORING YOU? SHOCKER.
WHY ARE YOU STILL HANGING AROUND WITH THAT GUY WHEN YOU COULD BE WITH ME?

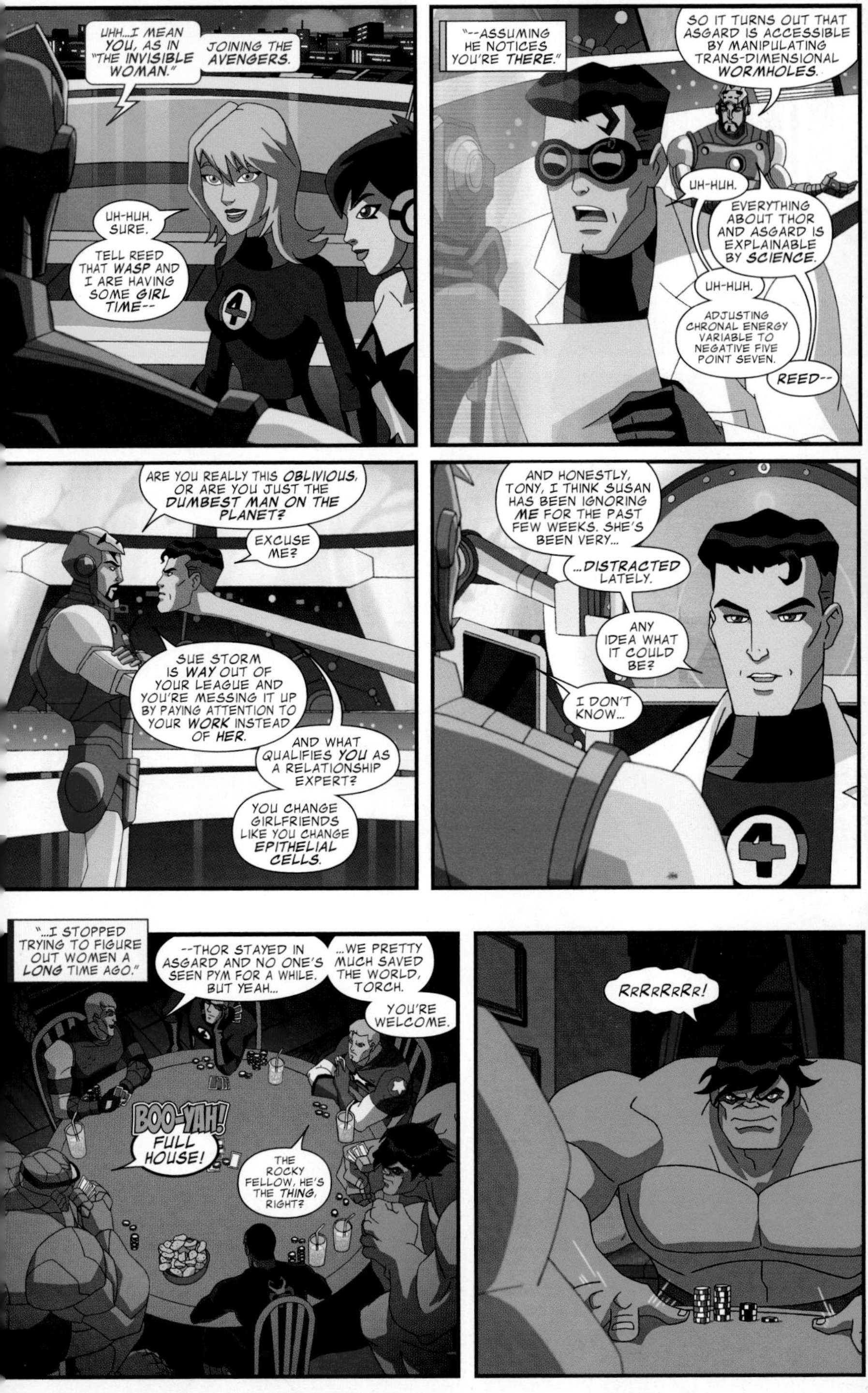
UHH...I MEAN YOU, AS IN "THE INVISIBLE WOMAN."
JOINING THE AVENGERS.
UH-HUH. SURE.
TELL REED THAT WASP AND I ARE HAVING SOME GIRL TIME--
"--ASSUMING HE NOTICES YOU'RE THERE."
SO IT TURNS OUT THAT ASGARD IS ACCESSIBLE BY MANIPULATING TRANS-DIMENSIONAL WORMHOLES.
UH-HUH.
EVERYTHING ABOUT THOR AND ASGARD IS EXPLAINABLE BY SCIENCE.
UH-HUH.
ADJUSTING CHRONAL ENERGY VARIABLE TO NEGATIVE FIVE POINT SEVEN.
REED--
ARE YOU REALLY THIS OBLIVIOUS, OR ARE YOU JUST THE DUMBEST MAN ON THE PLANET?
EXCUSE ME?
SUE STORM IS WAY OUT OF YOUR LEAGUE AND YOU'RE MESSING IT UP BY PAYING ATTENTION TO YOUR WORK INSTEAD OF HER.
AND WHAT QUALIFIES YOU AS A RELATIONSHIP EXPERT?
YOU CHANGE GIRLFRIENDS LIKE YOU CHANGE EPITHELIAL CELLS.
AND HONESTLY, TONY, I THINK SUSAN HAS BEEN IGNORING ME FOR THE PAST FEW WEEKS. SHE'S BEEN VERY...
...DISTRACTED LATELY.
ANY IDEA WHAT IT COULD BE?
I DON'T KNOW...
"...I STOPPED TRYING TO FIGURE OUT WOMEN A LONG TIME AGO."
--THOR STAYED IN ASGARD AND NO ONE'S SEEN PYM FOR A WHILE. BUT YEAH...
...WE PRETTY MUCH SAVED THE WORLD, TORCH.
YOU'RE WELCOME.
BOO-YAH! FULL HOUSE!
THE ROCKY FELLOW, HE'S THE THING, RIGHT?
RRRRRRRR!

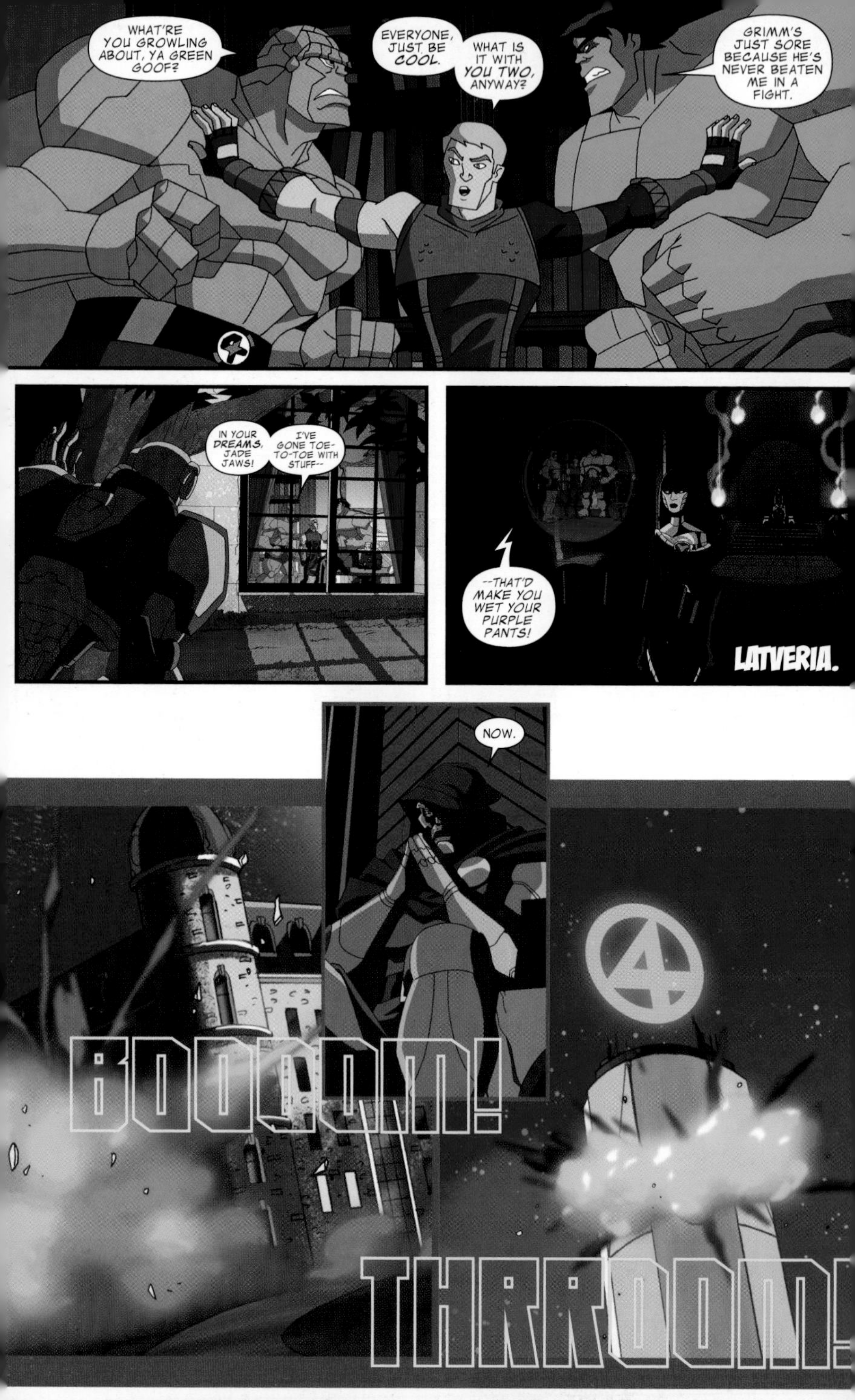

WHAT'RE YOU GROWLING ABOUT, YA GREEN GOOF?
EVERYONE, JUST BE COOL.
WHAT IS IT WITH YOU TWO, ANYWAY?
GRIMM'S JUST SORE BECAUSE HE'S NEVER BEATEN ME IN A FIGHT.
IN YOUR DREAMS, JADE JAWS!
I'VE GONE TOE-TO-TOE WITH STUFF--
--THAT'D MAKE YOU WET YOUR PURPLE PANTS!
LATVERIA.
NOW.
BOOOOM!
THRROOM!

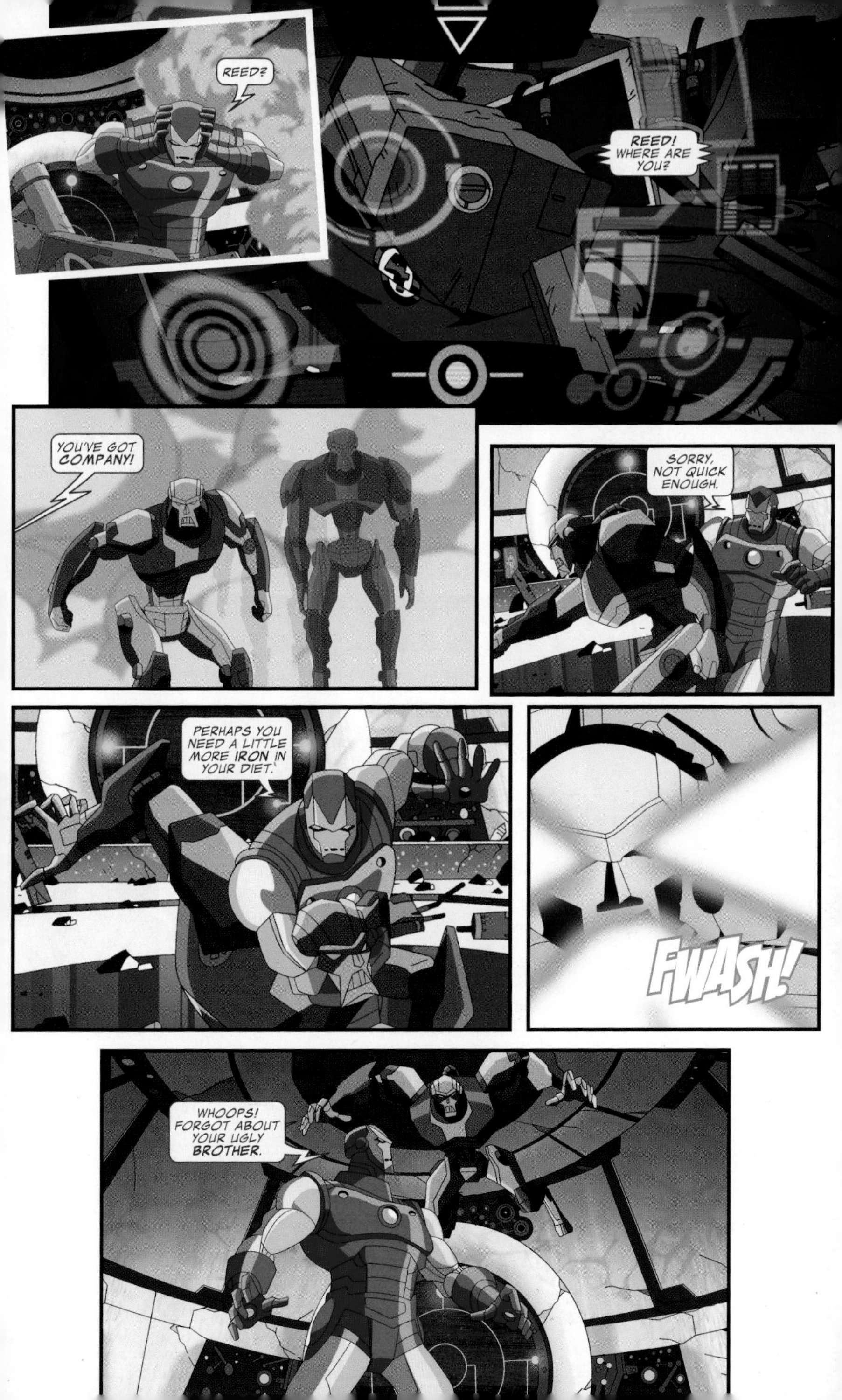
REED?
REED! WHERE ARE YOU?
YOU'VE GOT COMPANY!
SORRY, NOT QUICK ENOUGH.
PERHAPS YOU NEED A LITTLE MORE IRON IN YOUR DIET.
FWASH!
WHOOPS! FORGOT ABOUT YOUR UGLY BROTHER.

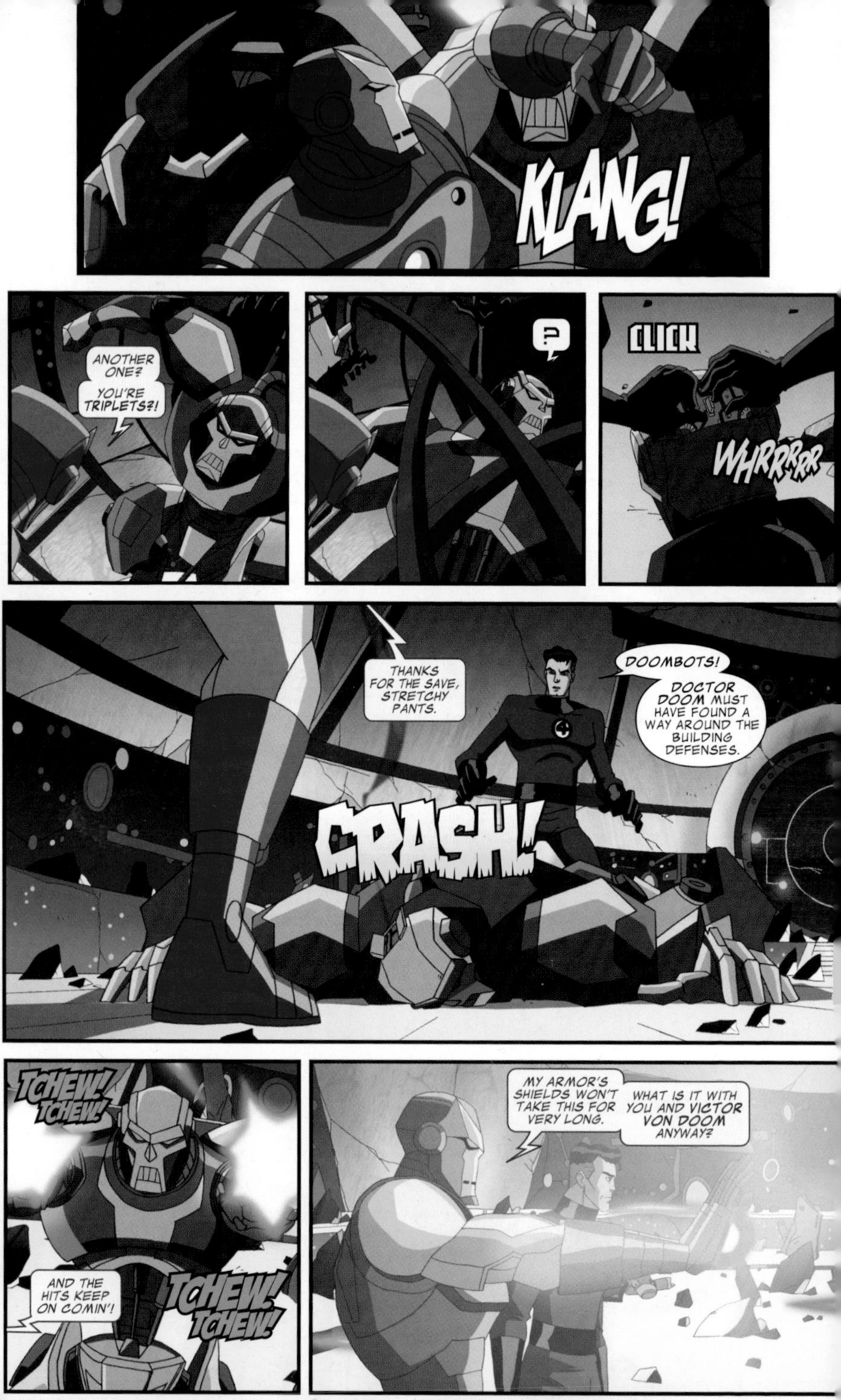
KLANG!
ANOTHER ONE? YOU'RE TRIPLETS?!
?
CLICK
WHRRRRR
THANKS FOR THE SAVE, STRETCHY PANTS.
DOOMBOTS!
DOCTOR DOOM MUST HAVE FOUND A WAY AROUND THE BUILDING DEFENSES.
CRASH!
TCHEW! TCHEW!
AND THE HITS KEEP ON COMIN'!
TCHEW! TCHEW!
MY ARMOR'S SHIELDS WON'T TAKE THIS FOR VERY LONG.
WHAT IS IT WITH YOU AND VICTOR VON DOOM ANYWAY?

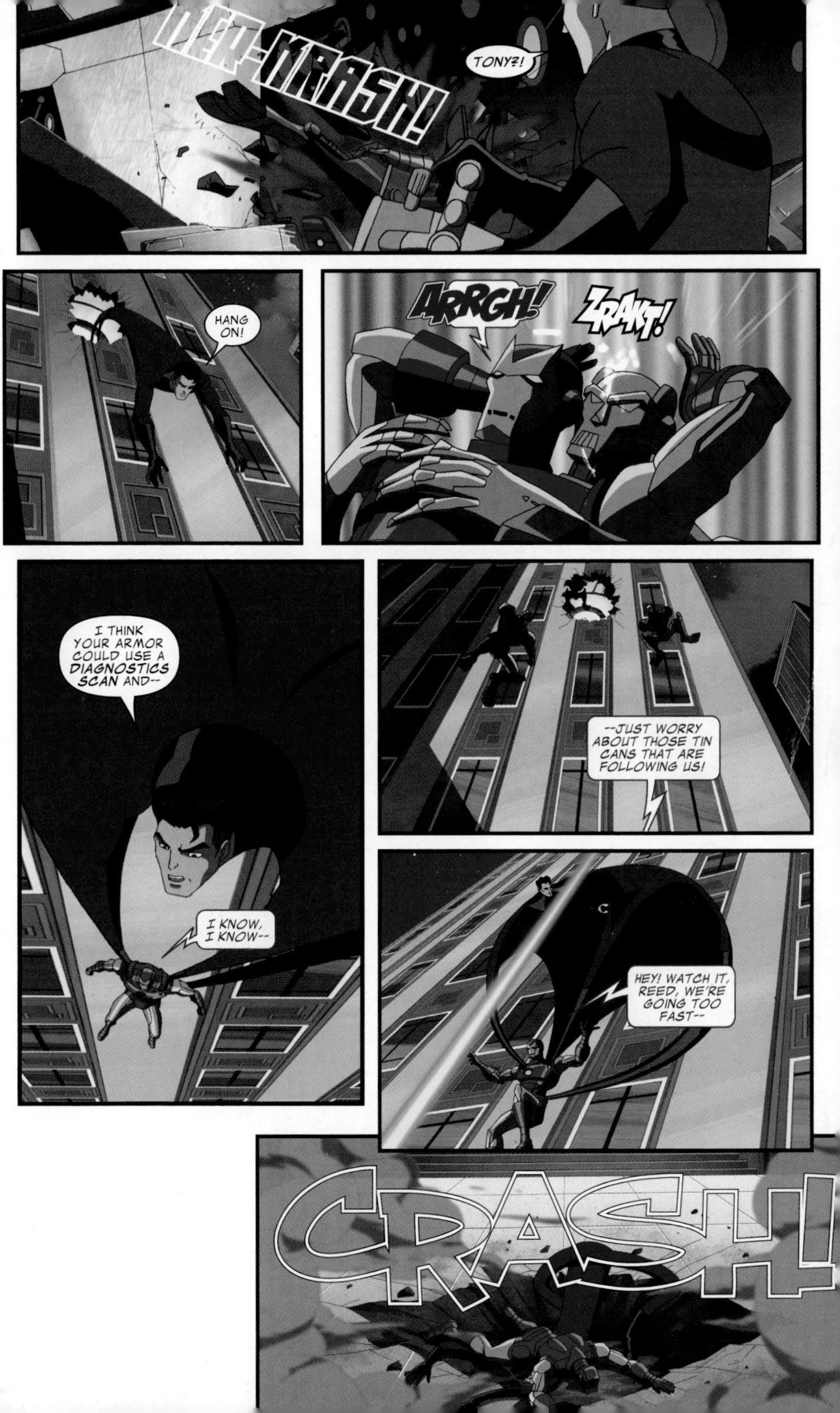
KRASH!
TONY?!
HANG ON!
ARRGH!
ZRAKT!
I THINK YOUR ARMOR COULD USE A DIAGNOSTICS SCAN AND--
I KNOW, I KNOW--
--JUST WORRY ABOUT THOSE TIN CANS THAT ARE FOLLOWING US!
HEY! WATCH IT, REED, WE'RE GOING TOO FAST--
CRASH!

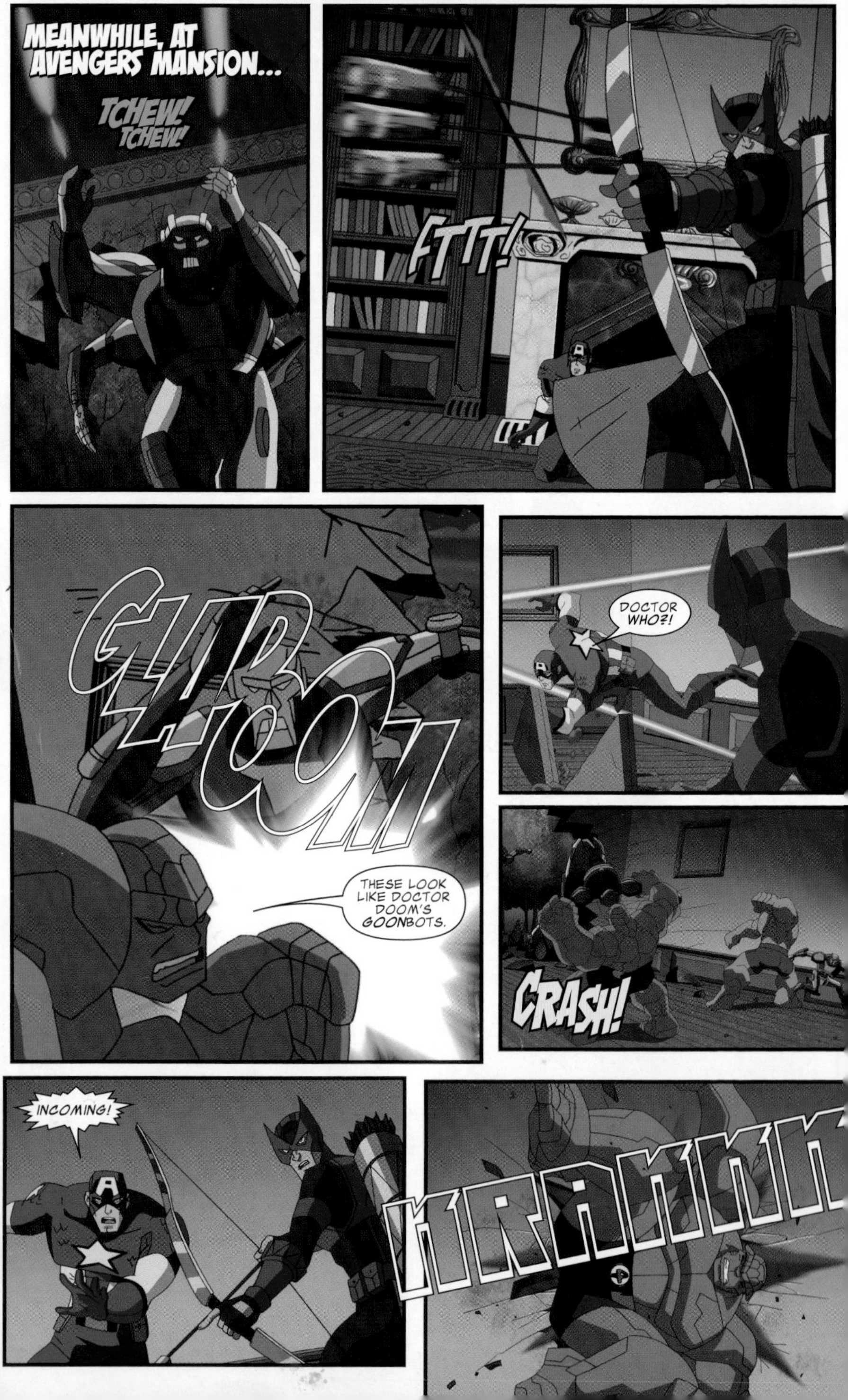
MEANWHILE, AT AVENGERS MANSION...
TCHEW! TCHEW!
FTTT!
GLADOOM
THESE LOOK LIKE DOCTOR DOOM'S GOONBOTS.
DOCTOR WHO?!
CRASH!
INCOMING!
KRANNN

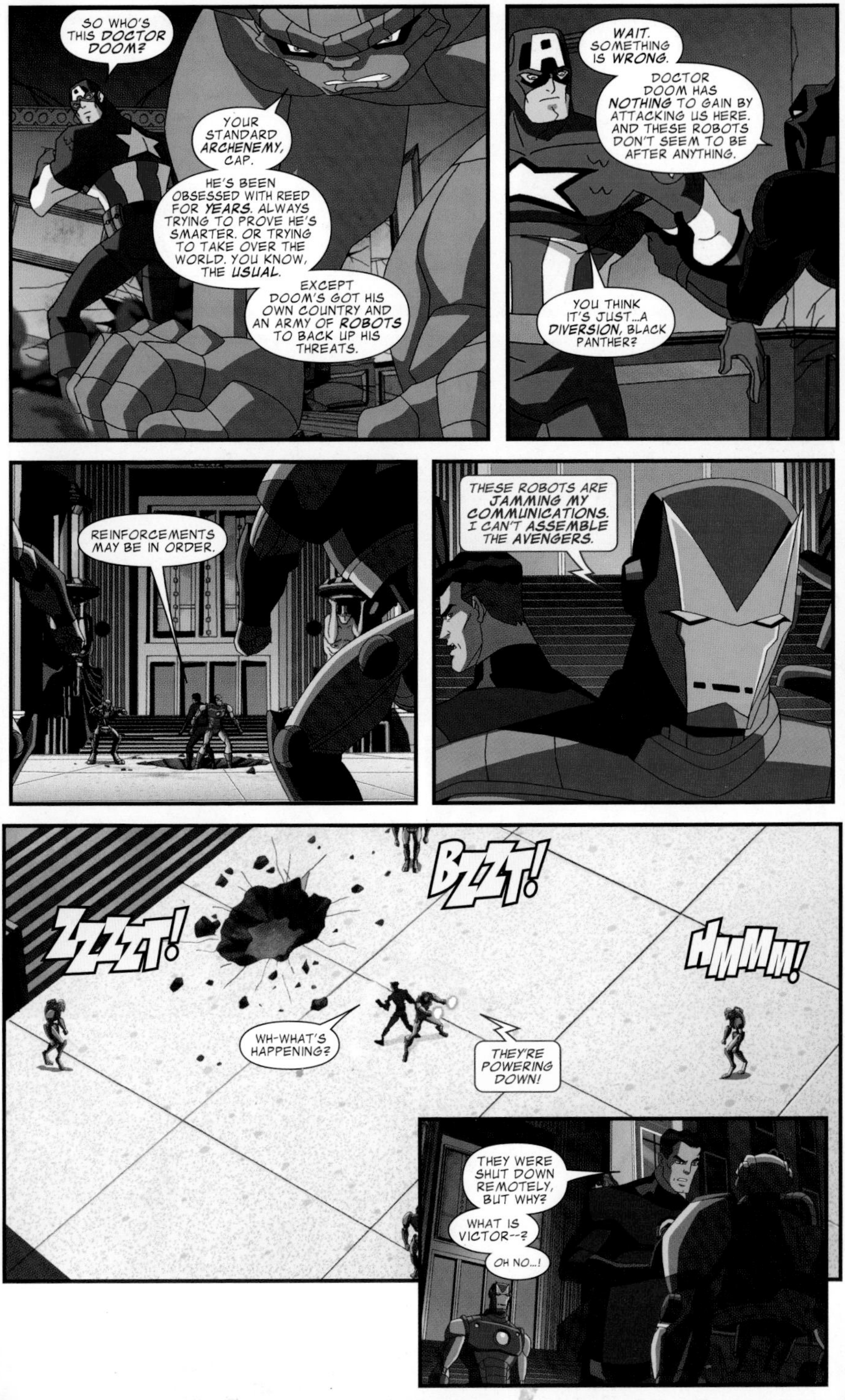
SO WHO'S THIS DOCTOR DOOM?
YOUR STANDARD ARCHENEMY, CAP.
HE'S BEEN OBSESSED WITH REED FOR YEARS. ALWAYS TRYING TO PROVE HE'S SMARTER. OR TRYING TO TAKE OVER THE WORLD. YOU KNOW, THE USUAL.
EXCEPT DOOM'S GOT HIS OWN COUNTRY AND AN ARMY OF ROBOTS TO BACK UP HIS THREATS.
WAIT. SOMETHING IS WRONG.
DOCTOR DOOM HAS NOTHING TO GAIN BY ATTACKING US HERE. AND THESE ROBOTS DON'T SEEM TO BE AFTER ANYTHING.
YOU THINK IT'S JUST...A DIVERSION, BLACK PANTHER?
REINFORCEMENTS MAY BE IN ORDER.
THESE ROBOTS ARE JAMMING MY COMMUNICATIONS. I CAN'T ASSEMBLE THE AVENGERS.
ZZZZT!
BZZT!
HMMM!
WH-WHAT'S HAPPENING?
THEY'RE POWERING DOWN!
THEY WERE SHUT DOWN REMOTELY, BUT WHY?
WHAT IS VICTOR--?
OH NO...!

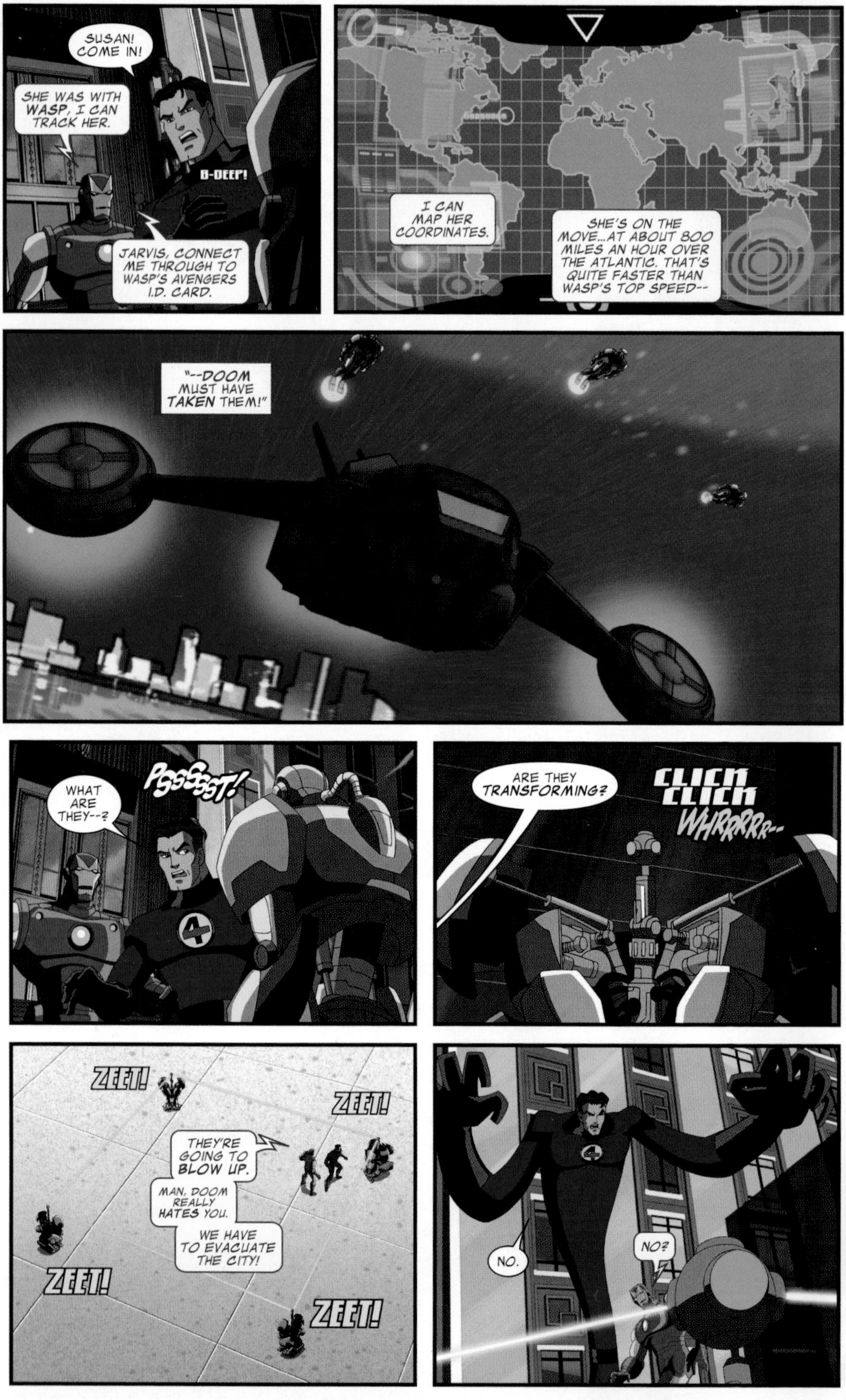

SUSAN! COME IN!
SHE WAS WITH WASP, I CAN TRACK HER.
B-DEEP!
JARVIS, CONNECT ME THROUGH TO WASP'S AVENGERS I.D. CARD.
I CAN MAP HER COORDINATES.
SHE'S ON THE MOVE...AT ABOUT 800 MILES AN HOUR OVER THE ATLANTIC. THAT'S QUITE FASTER THAN WASP'S TOP SPEED--
"--DOOM MUST HAVE TAKEN THEM!"
WHAT ARE THEY--?
PSSSSST!
ARE THEY TRANSFORMING?
CLICK CLICK WHRRRR--
ZEET!
ZEET!
THEY'RE GOING TO BLOW UP.
MAN, DOOM REALLY HATES YOU.
WE HAVE TO EVACUATE THE CITY!
ZEET!
ZEET!
NO.
NO?

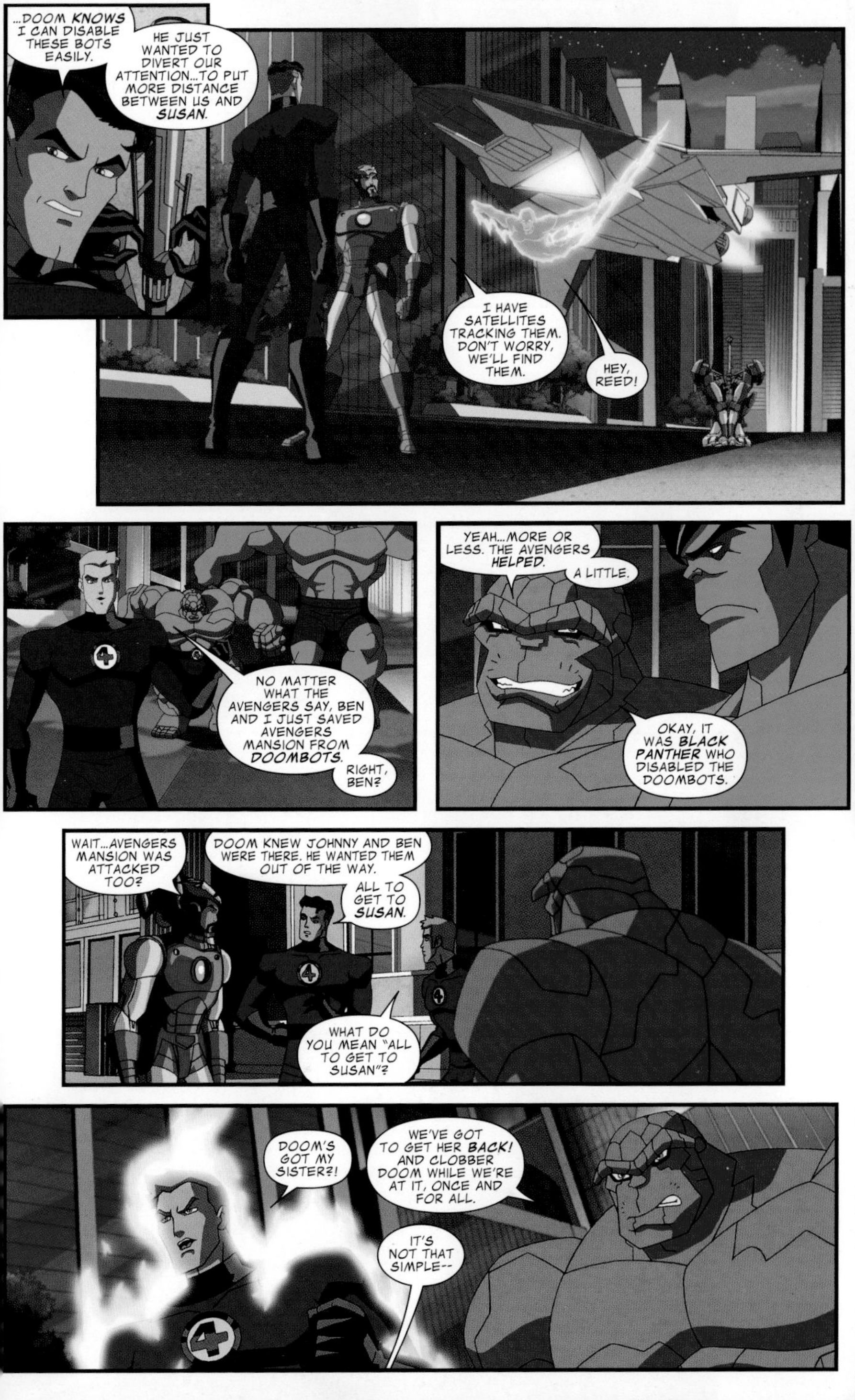
...DOOM KNOWS I CAN DISABLE THESE BOTS EASILY.
HE JUST WANTED TO DIVERT OUR ATTENTION...TO PUT MORE DISTANCE BETWEEN US AND SUSAN.
I HAVE SATELLITES TRACKING THEM. DON'T WORRY, WE'LL FIND THEM.
HEY, REED!
NO MATTER WHAT THE AVENGERS SAY, BEN AND I JUST SAVED AVENGERS MANSION FROM DOOMBOTS.
RIGHT, BEN?
YEAH...MORE OR LESS. THE AVENGERS HELPED.
A LITTLE.
OKAY, IT WAS BLACK PANTHER WHO DISABLED THE DOOMBOTS.
WAIT...AVENGERS MANSION WAS ATTACKED TOO?
DOOM KNEW JOHNNY AND BEN WERE THERE. HE WANTED THEM OUT OF THE WAY.
ALL TO GET TO SUSAN.
WHAT DO YOU MEAN "ALL TO GET TO SUSAN"?
DOOM'S GOT MY SISTER?!
WE'VE GOT TO GET HER BACK! AND CLOBBER DOOM WHILE WE'RE AT IT, ONCE AND FOR ALL.
IT'S NOT THAT SIMPLE--

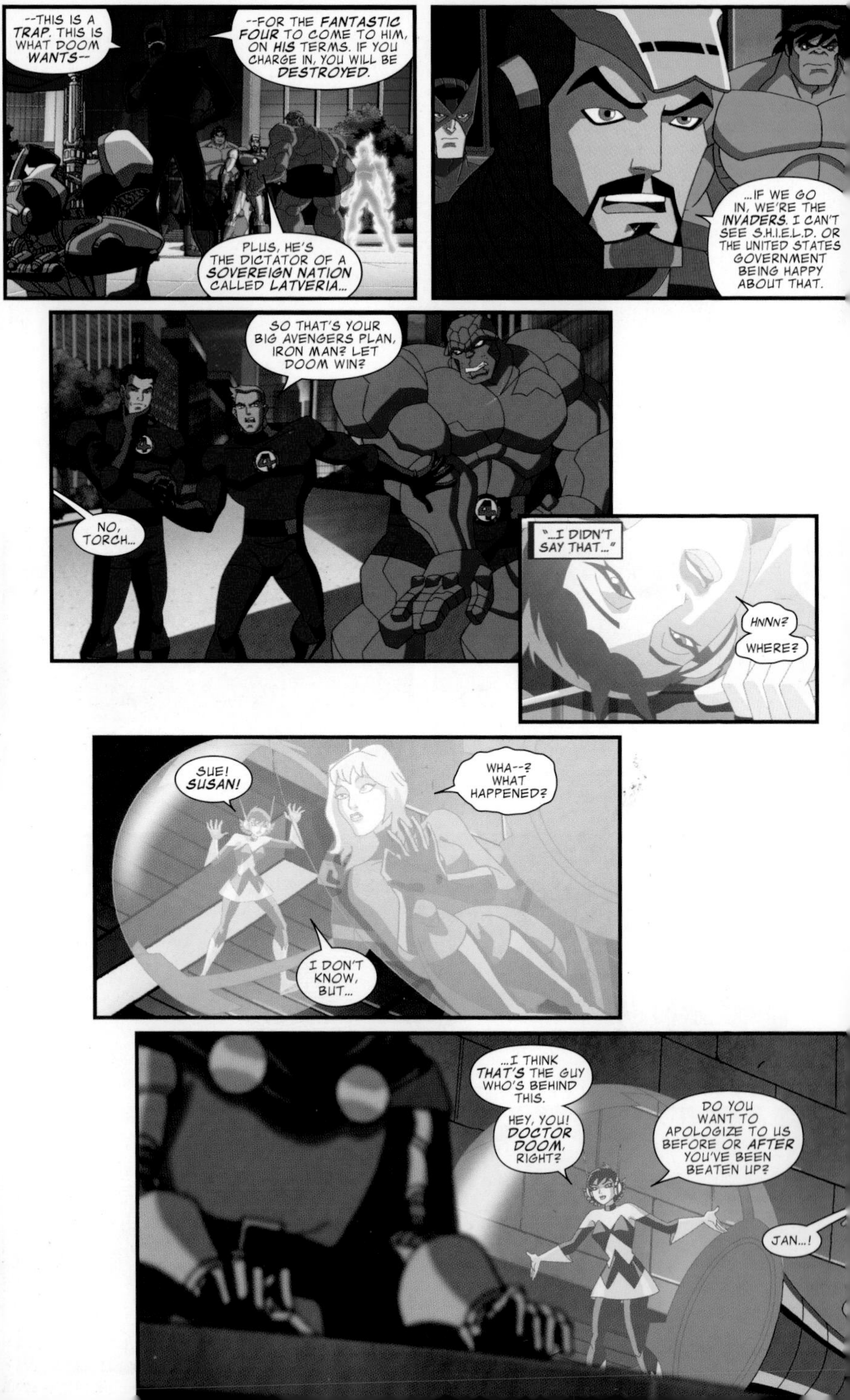
--THIS IS A TRAP. THIS IS WHAT DOOM WANTS--
--FOR THE FANTASTIC FOUR TO COME TO HIM, ON HIS TERMS. IF YOU CHARGE IN, YOU WILL BE DESTROYED.
PLUS, HE'S THE DICTATOR OF A SOVEREIGN NATION CALLED LATVERIA...
...IF WE GO IN, WE'RE THE INVADERS. I CAN'T SEE S.H.I.E.L.D. OR THE UNITED STATES GOVERNMENT BEING HAPPY ABOUT THAT.
SO THAT'S YOUR BIG AVENGERS PLAN, IRON MAN? LET DOOM WIN?
NO, TORCH...
"...I DIDN'T SAY THAT..."
HNNN?
WHERE?
SUE! SUSAN!
WHA--? WHAT HAPPENED?
I DON'T KNOW, BUT...
...I THINK THAT'S THE GUY WHO'S BEHIND THIS.
HEY, YOU! DOCTOR DOOM, RIGHT?
DO YOU WANT TO APOLOGIZE TO US BEFORE OR AFTER YOU'VE BEEN BEATEN UP?
JAN...!

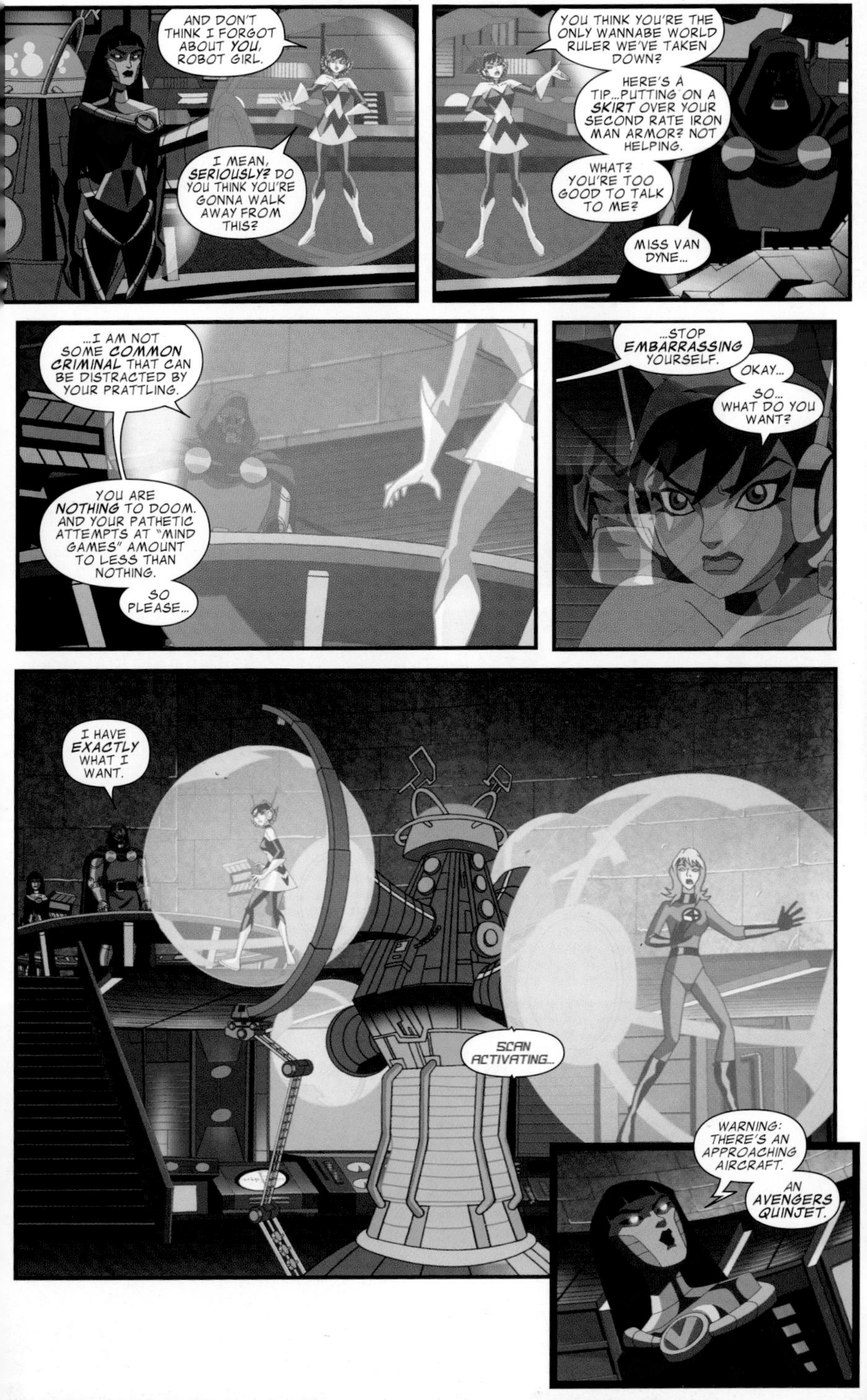
AND DON'T THINK I FORGOT ABOUT YOU, ROBOT GIRL.
I MEAN, SERIOUSLY? DO YOU THINK YOU'RE GONNA WALK AWAY FROM THIS?
YOU THINK YOU'RE THE ONLY WANNABE WORLD RULER WE'VE TAKEN DOWN?
HERE'S A TIP...PUTTING ON A SKIRT OVER YOUR SECOND RATE IRON MAN ARMOR? NOT HELPING.
WHAT? YOU'RE TOO GOOD TO TALK TO ME?
MISS VAN DYNE...
...I AM NOT SOME COMMON CRIMINAL THAT CAN BE DISTRACTED BY YOUR PRATTLING.
YOU ARE NOTHING TO DOOM. AND YOUR PATHETIC ATTEMPTS AT "MIND GAMES" AMOUNT TO LESS THAN NOTHING.
SO PLEASE...
...STOP EMBARRASSING YOURSELF.
OKAY...
SO... WHAT DO YOU WANT?
I HAVE EXACTLY WHAT I WANT.
SCAN ACTIVATING...
WARNING: THERE'S AN APPROACHING AIRCRAFT.
AN AVENGERS QUINJET.

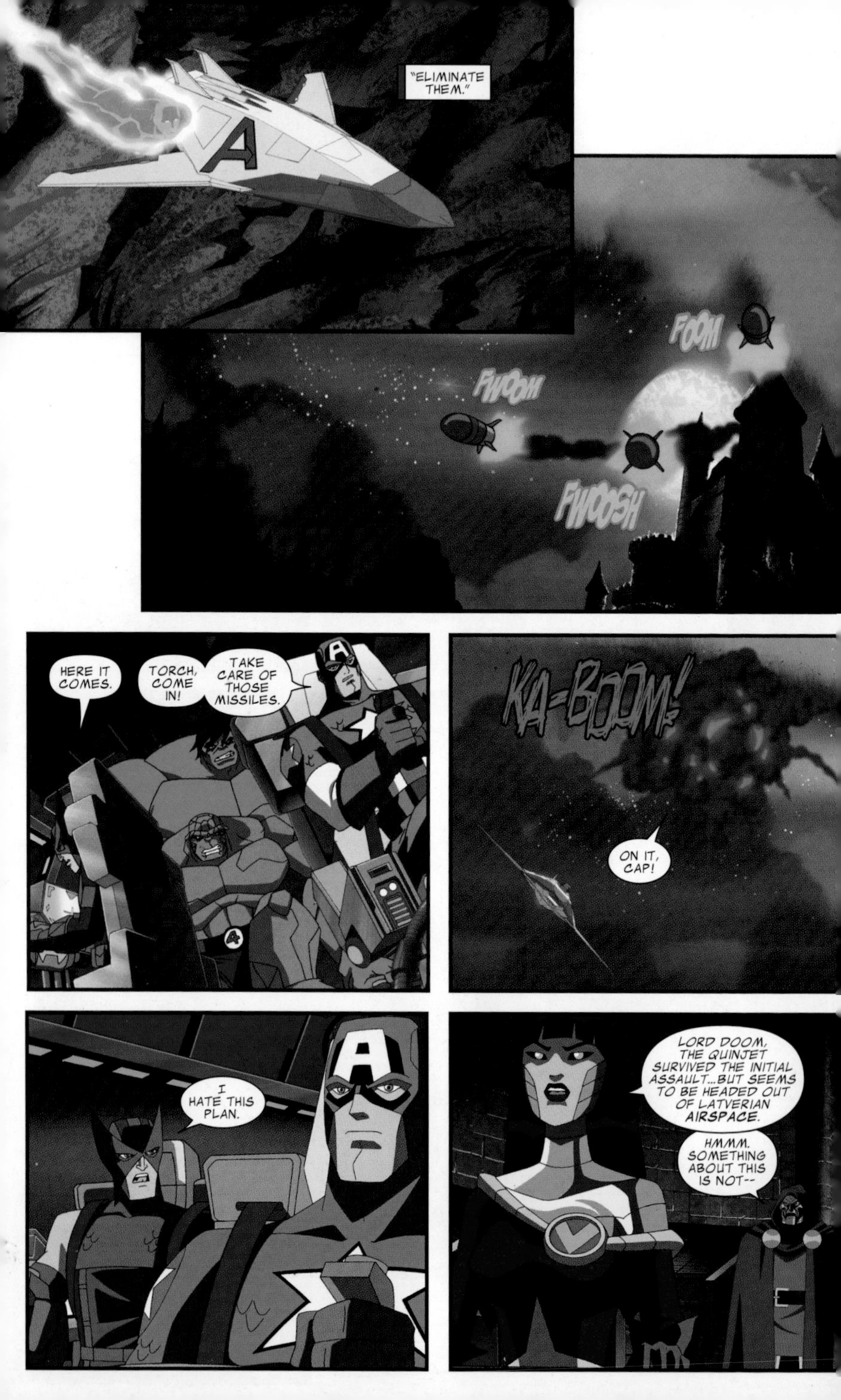
"ELIMINATE THEM."
FOOM
FWOOM
FWOOSH
HERE IT COMES.
TORCH, COME IN!
TAKE CARE OF THOSE MISSILES.
KA-BOOM!
ON IT, CAP!
I HATE THIS PLAN.
LORD DOOM, THE QUINJET SURVIVED THE INITIAL ASSAULT...BUT SEEMS TO BE HEADED OUT OF LATVERIAN AIRSPACE.
HMMM. SOMETHING ABOUT THIS IS NOT--

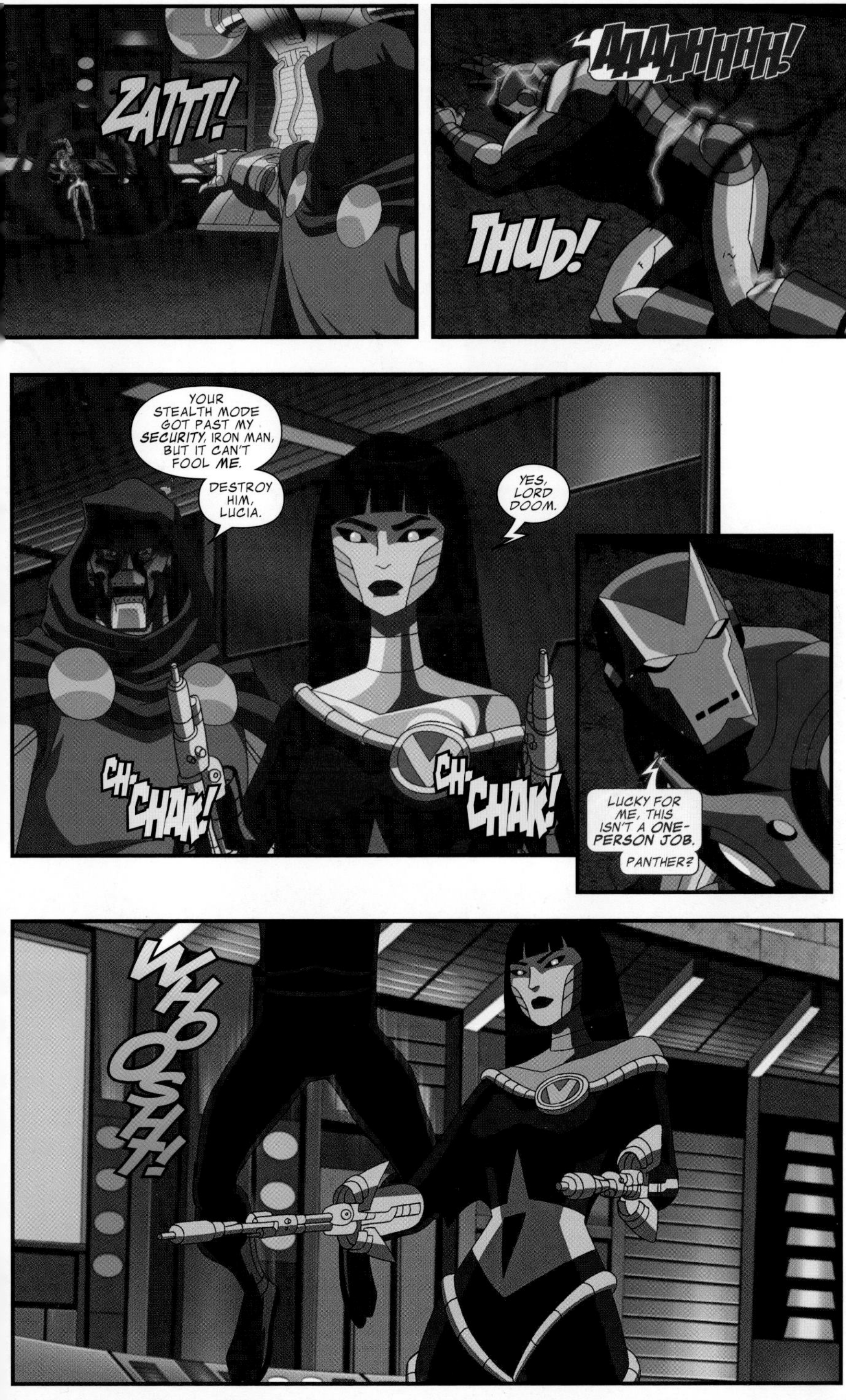
ZATTT!
AAAAHHHH!
THUD!
YOUR STEALTH MODE GOT PAST MY SECURITY, IRON MAN, BUT IT CAN'T FOOL ME.
DESTROY HIM, LUCIA.
YES, LORD DOOM.
CH-CHAK!
CH-CHAK!
LUCKY FOR ME, THIS ISN'T A ONE-PERSON JOB.
PANTHER?
WHOOSH!

...YOU MUST WATCH WHERE YOU POINT THAT THING.

BEEP!

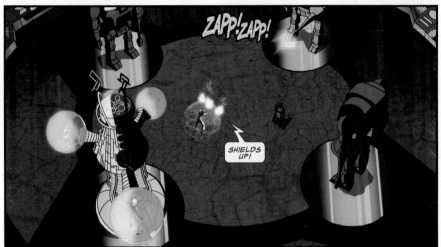

ZAPP! ZAPP!

SHIELDS UP!

OKAY, SO MUCH FOR AVOIDING AN INTERNATIONAL INCIDENT...

AVENGERS-- AND FANTASTIC FOUR--

"...ASSEMBLE!"

IT'S CLOBBERIN' TIME!

CRUNCH!

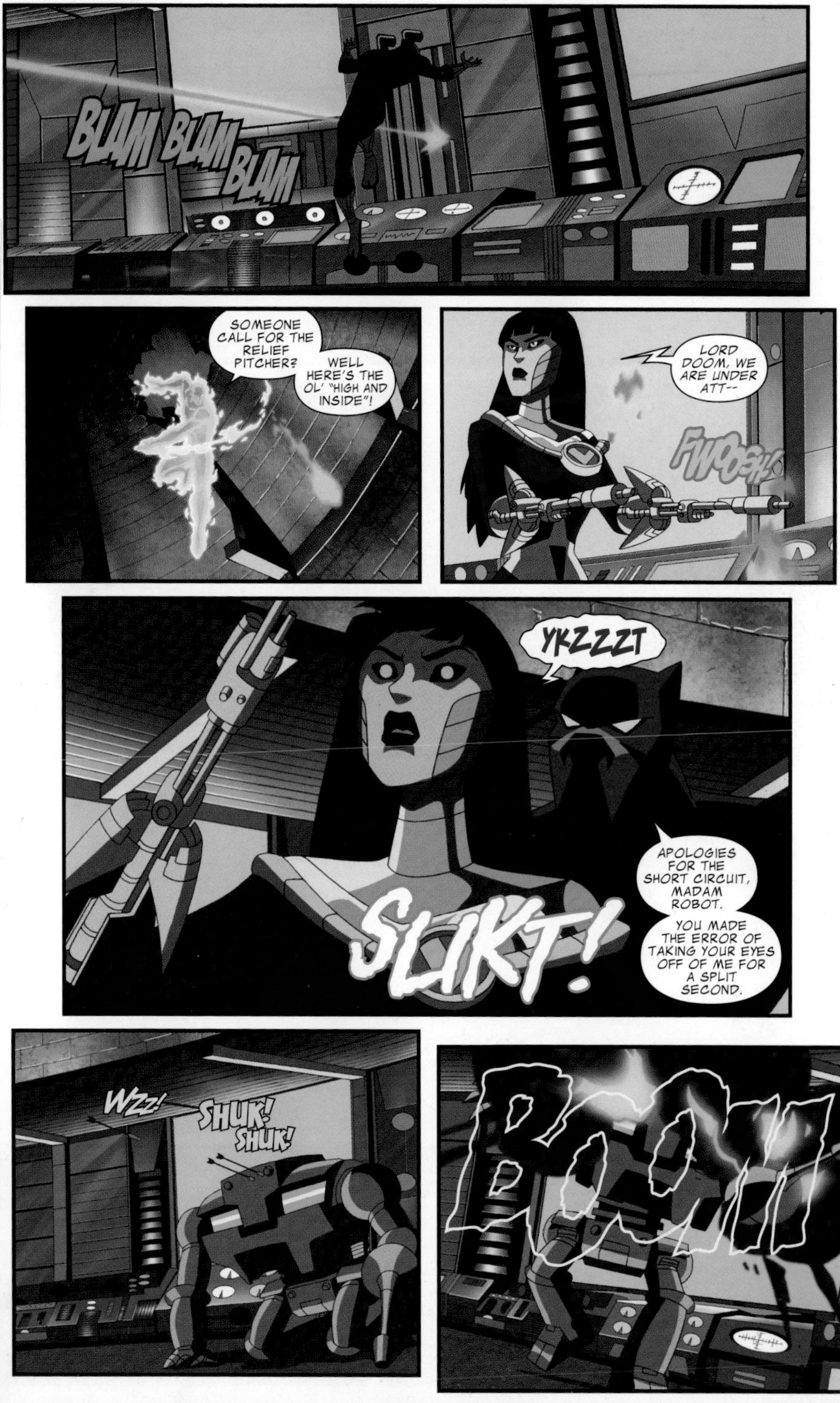

BLAM BLAM BLAM
SOMEONE CALL FOR THE RELIEF PITCHER?
WELL HERE'S THE OL' "HIGH AND INSIDE"!
LORD DOOM, WE ARE UNDER ATT--
FWOOSH!
YKZZZT
APOLOGIES FOR THE SHORT CIRCUIT, MADAM ROBOT.
YOU MADE THE ERROR OF TAKING YOUR EYES OFF OF ME FOR A SPLIT SECOND.
SLIKT!
WZZ!
SHUK! SHUK!
BOOM

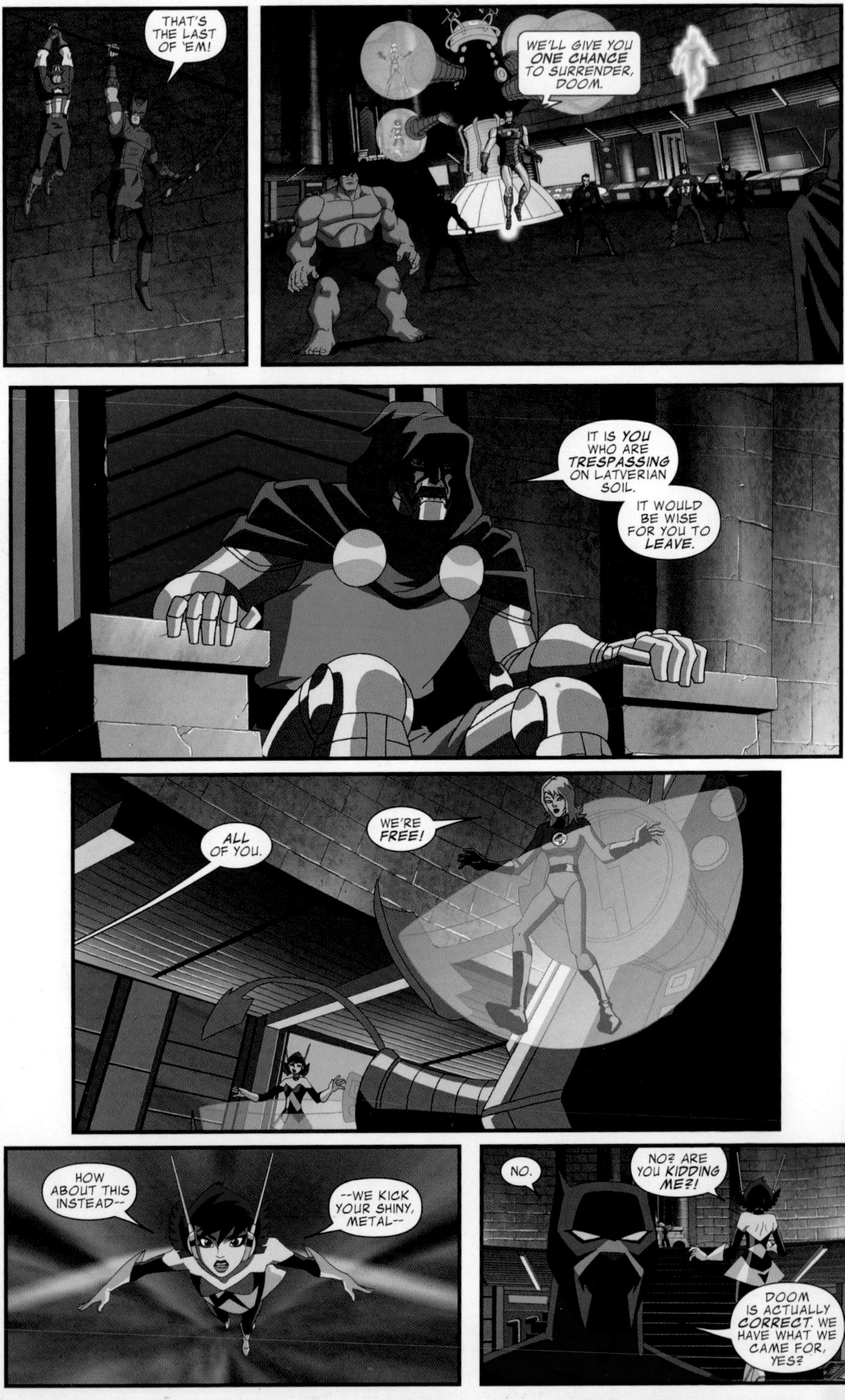
THAT'S THE LAST OF 'EM!
WE'LL GIVE YOU ONE CHANCE TO SURRENDER, DOOM.
IT IS YOU WHO ARE TRESPASSING ON LATVERIAN SOIL.
IT WOULD BE WISE FOR YOU TO LEAVE.
ALL OF YOU.
WE'RE FREE!
HOW ABOUT THIS INSTEAD--
--WE KICK YOUR SHINY, METAL--
NO.
NO? ARE YOU KIDDING ME?!
DOOM IS ACTUALLY CORRECT. WE HAVE WHAT WE CAME FOR, YES?

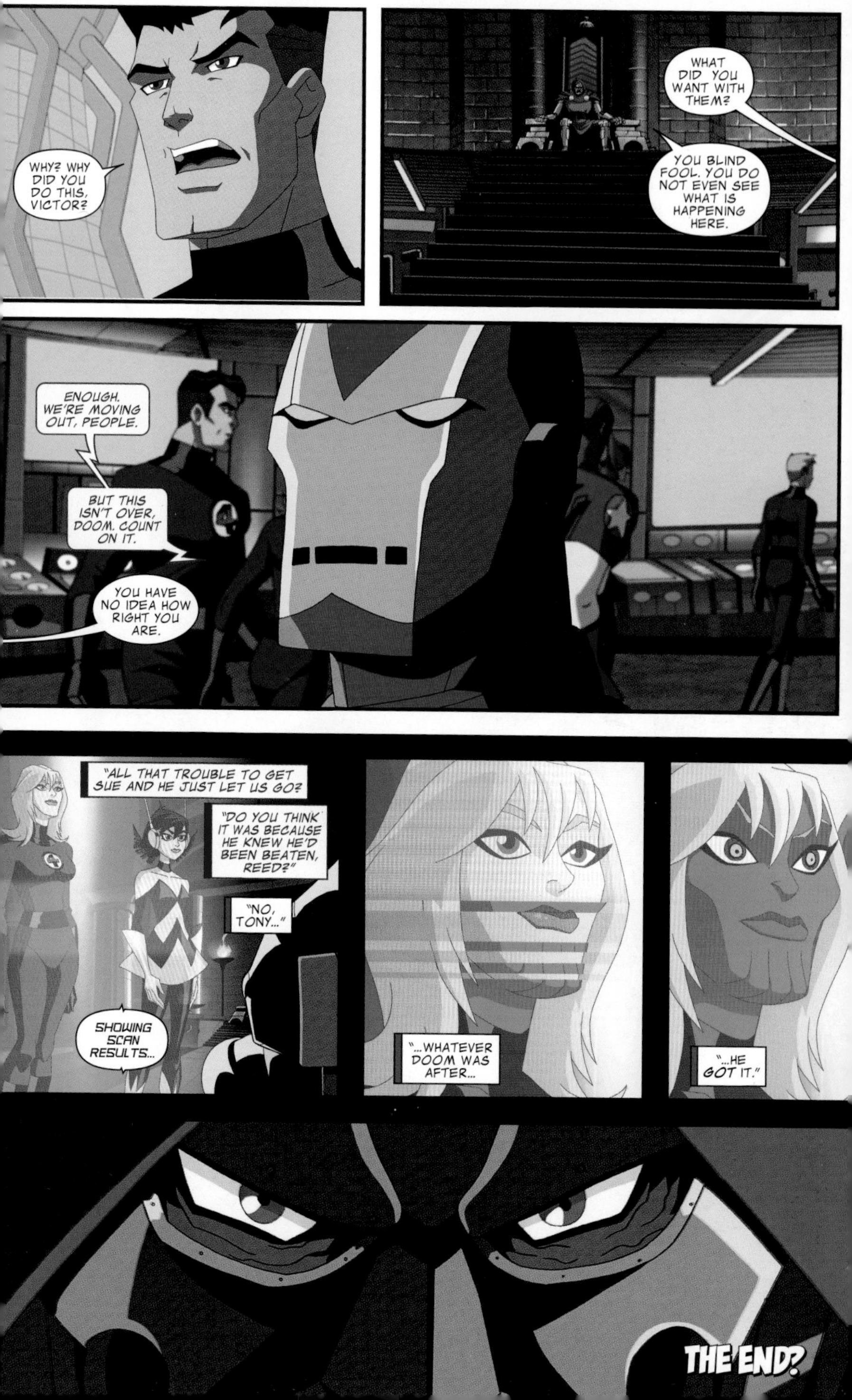
WHY? WHY DID YOU DO THIS, VICTOR?
WHAT DID YOU WANT WITH THEM?
YOU BLIND FOOL. YOU DO NOT EVEN SEE WHAT IS HAPPENING HERE.
ENOUGH. WE'RE MOVING OUT, PEOPLE.
BUT THIS ISN'T OVER, DOOM. COUNT ON IT.
YOU HAVE NO IDEA HOW RIGHT YOU ARE.
"ALL THAT TROUBLE TO GET SUE AND HE JUST LET US GO?
"DO YOU THINK IT WAS BECAUSE HE KNEW HE'D BEEN BEATEN, REED?"
"NO, TONY..."
SHOWING SCAN RESULTS...
"...WHATEVER DOOM WAS AFTER...
"...HE GOT IT."
THE END?

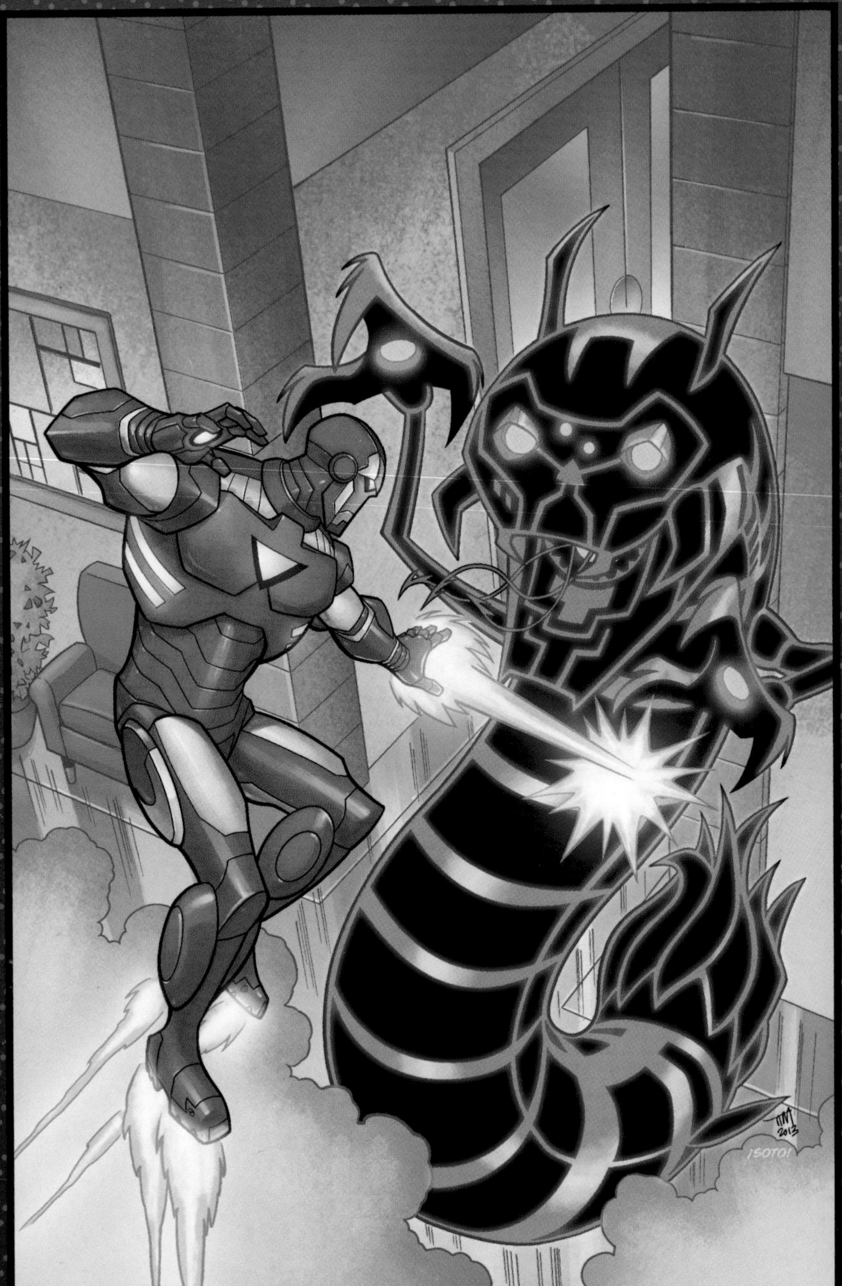
¡SOTO!

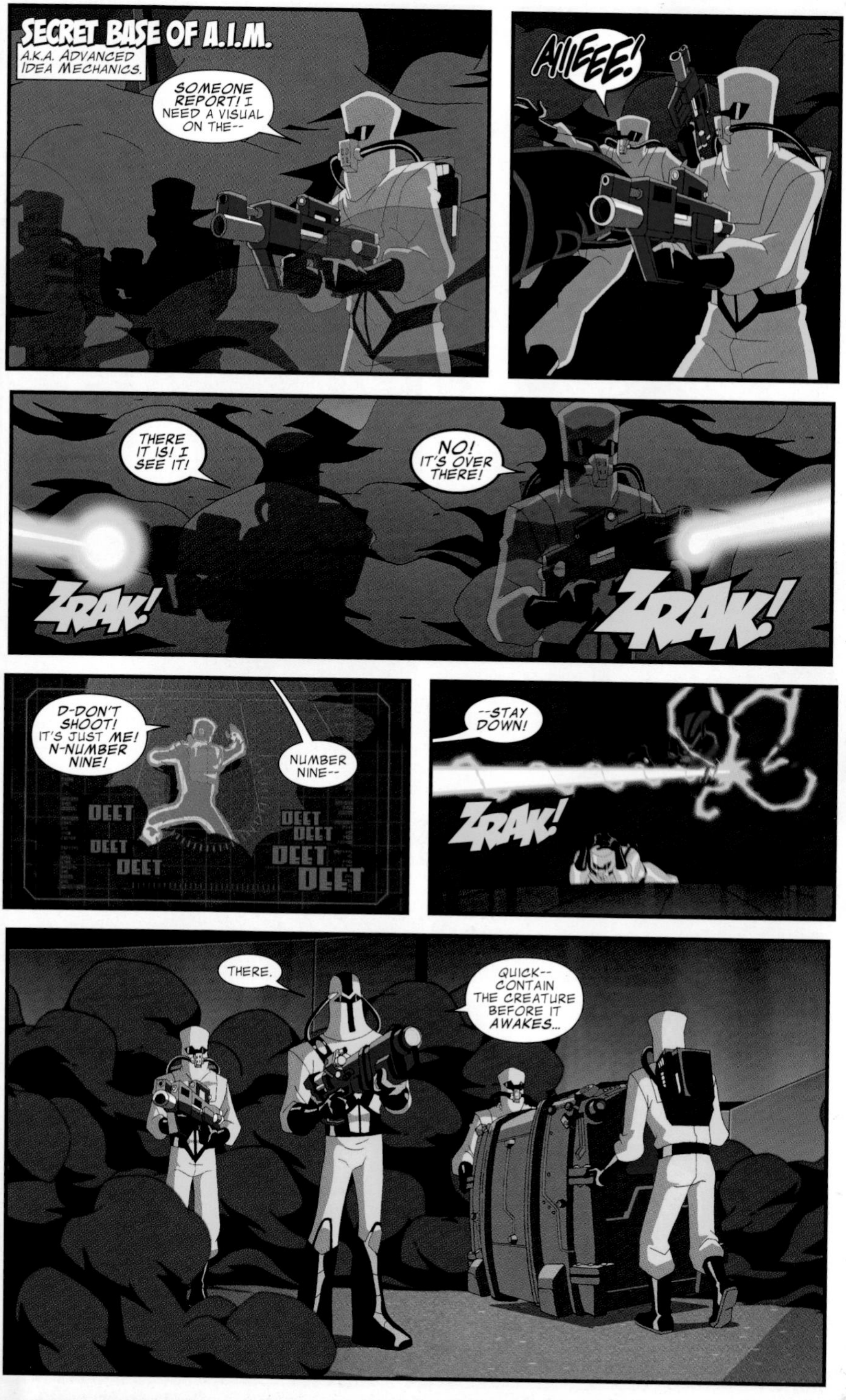
SECRET BASE OF A.I.M.
A.K.A. ADVANCED IDEA MECHANICS.
SOMEONE REPORT! I NEED A VISUAL ON THE--
AIIEEE!
THERE IT IS! I SEE IT!
NO! IT'S OVER THERE!
ZRAK!
ZRAK!
D-DON'T SHOOT! IT'S JUST ME! N-NUMBER NINE!
NUMBER NINE--
DEET
DEET
DEET
DEET
DEET
DEET
DEET
--STAY DOWN!
ZRAK!
THERE.
QUICK-- CONTAIN THE CREATURE BEFORE IT AWAKES...

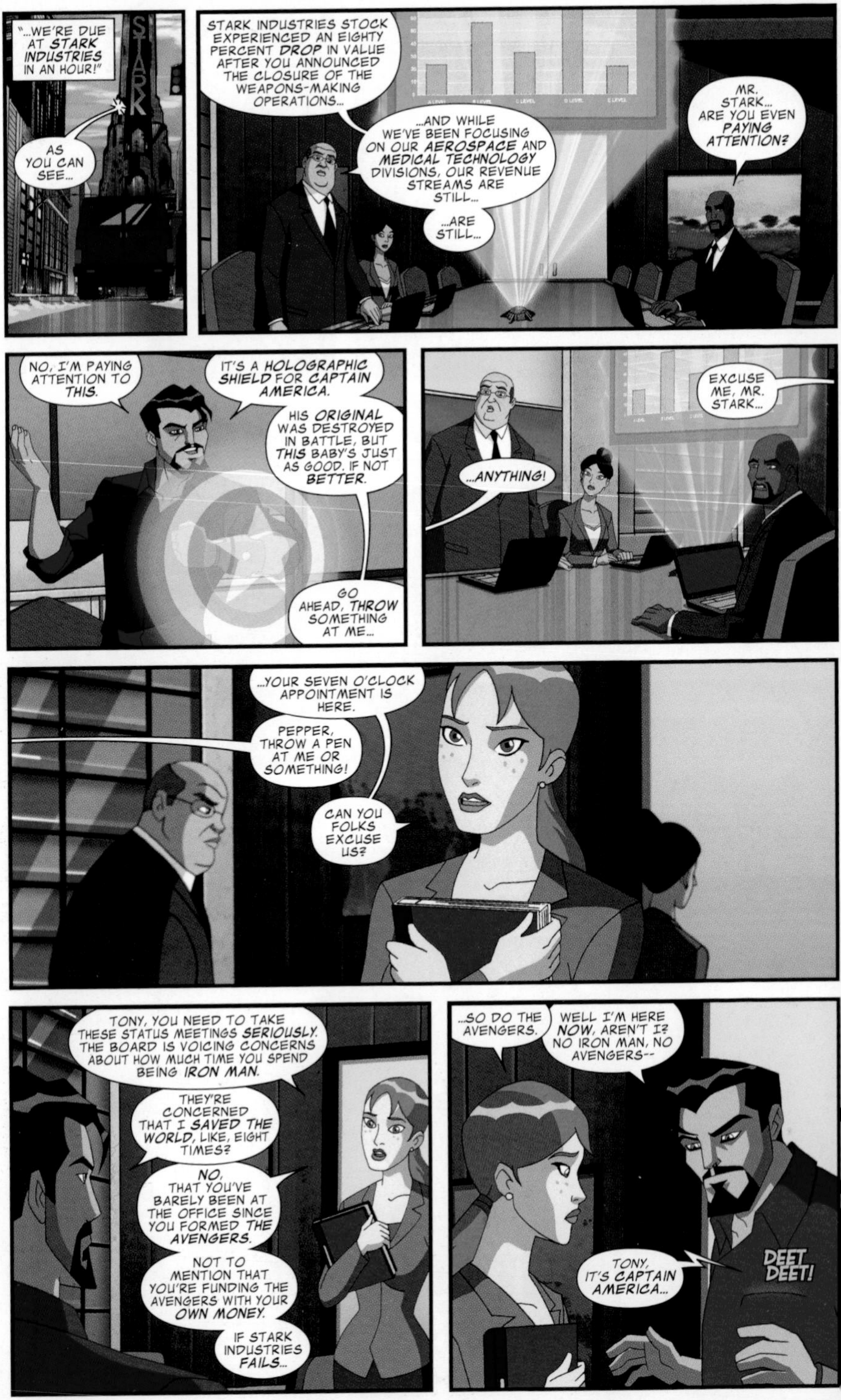
"...WE'RE DUE AT STARK INDUSTRIES IN AN HOUR!"
AS YOU CAN SEE...
STARK
STARK INDUSTRIES STOCK EXPERIENCED AN EIGHTY PERCENT DROP IN VALUE AFTER YOU ANNOUNCED THE CLOSURE OF THE WEAPONS-MAKING OPERATIONS...
...AND WHILE WE'VE BEEN FOCUSING ON OUR AEROSPACE AND MEDICAL TECHNOLOGY DIVISIONS, OUR REVENUE STREAMS ARE STILL...
...ARE STILL...
MR. STARK... ARE YOU EVEN PAYING ATTENTION?
NO, I'M PAYING ATTENTION TO THIS.
IT'S A HOLOGRAPHIC SHIELD FOR CAPTAIN AMERICA.
HIS ORIGINAL WAS DESTROYED IN BATTLE, BUT THIS BABY'S JUST AS GOOD. IF NOT BETTER.
GO AHEAD, THROW SOMETHING AT ME...
...ANYTHING!
EXCUSE ME, MR. STARK...
...YOUR SEVEN O'CLOCK APPOINTMENT IS HERE.
PEPPER, THROW A PEN AT ME OR SOMETHING!
CAN YOU FOLKS EXCUSE US?
TONY, YOU NEED TO TAKE THESE STATUS MEETINGS SERIOUSLY. THE BOARD IS VOICING CONCERNS ABOUT HOW MUCH TIME YOU SPEND BEING IRON MAN.
THEY'RE CONCERNED THAT I SAVED THE WORLD, LIKE, EIGHT TIMES?
NO, THAT YOU'VE BARELY BEEN AT THE OFFICE SINCE YOU FORMED THE AVENGERS.
NOT TO MENTION THAT YOU'RE FUNDING THE AVENGERS WITH YOUR OWN MONEY.
IF STARK INDUSTRIES FAILS...
...SO DO THE AVENGERS.
WELL I'M HERE NOW, AREN'T I? NO IRON MAN, NO AVENGERS--
DEET DEET!
TONY, IT'S CAPTAIN AMERICA...

...WE'RE READY TO MOVE THE REMAINING ARMOR FROM YOUR *ARMORY* TO AVENGERS MANSION.

I'LL, UH, BE RIGHT THERE, GUYS.

THERE ARE AVENGERS IN THE BUILDING RIGHT NOW?

THEY'RE MOVING ARMOR *OUT* OF HERE TO *PROTECT* STARK INDUSTRIES.

YOU'RE *RIGHT*, THE AVENGERS MAKE THIS PLACE A *TARGET*...

...AND I'M NOT GOING TO PUT MY PEOPLE AT RISK--

"--ESPECIALLY YOU."

MEANWHILE, OUTSIDE STARK INDUSTRIES.

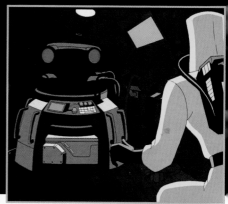

I'M ONLY DELIVERING THE CONCERNS OF THE *BOARD*, NOT MY *OWN* FEELINGS.

BUT YOUR SEVEN O'CLOCK APPOINTMENT'S OPINION HOLDS *MORE* WEIGHT THAN MINE.

WAIT... WHO'S THE APPOINTMENT?

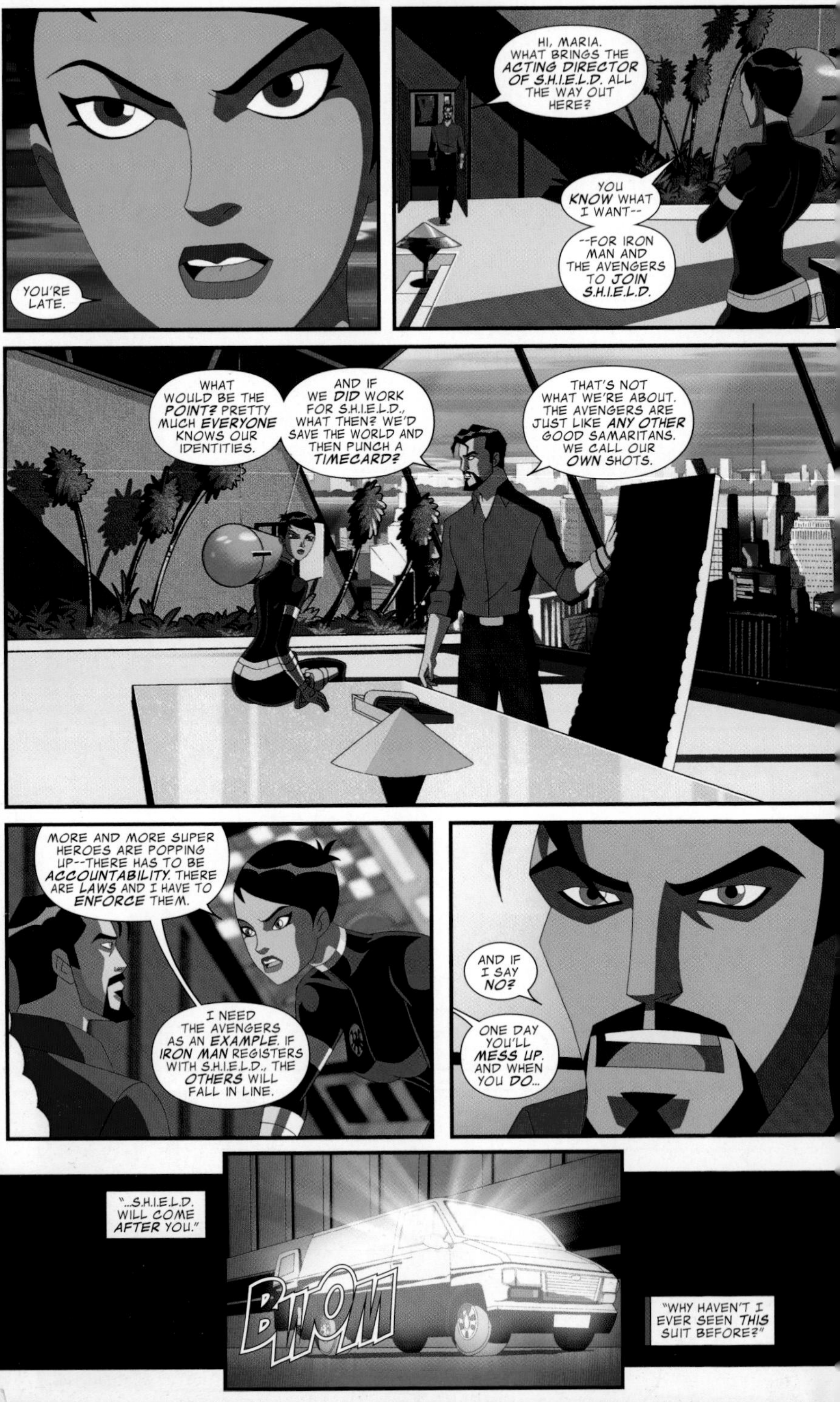
YOU'RE LATE.
HI, MARIA. WHAT BRINGS THE ACTING DIRECTOR OF S.H.I.E.L.D. ALL THE WAY OUT HERE?
YOU KNOW WHAT I WANT--
--FOR IRON MAN AND THE AVENGERS TO JOIN S.H.I.E.L.D.
WHAT WOULD BE THE POINT? PRETTY MUCH EVERYONE KNOWS OUR IDENTITIES.
AND IF WE DID WORK FOR S.H.I.E.L.D., WHAT THEN? WE'D SAVE THE WORLD AND THEN PUNCH A TIMECARD?
THAT'S NOT WHAT WE'RE ABOUT. THE AVENGERS ARE JUST LIKE ANY OTHER GOOD SAMARITANS. WE CALL OUR OWN SHOTS.
MORE AND MORE SUPER HEROES ARE POPPING UP--THERE HAS TO BE ACCOUNTABILITY. THERE ARE LAWS AND I HAVE TO ENFORCE THEM.
I NEED THE AVENGERS AS AN EXAMPLE. IF IRON MAN REGISTERS WITH S.H.I.E.L.D., THE OTHERS WILL FALL IN LINE.
AND IF I SAY NO?
ONE DAY YOU'LL MESS UP. AND WHEN YOU DO...
"...S.H.I.E.L.D. WILL COME AFTER YOU."
BDOOM
"WHY HAVEN'T I EVER SEEN THIS SUIT BEFORE?"

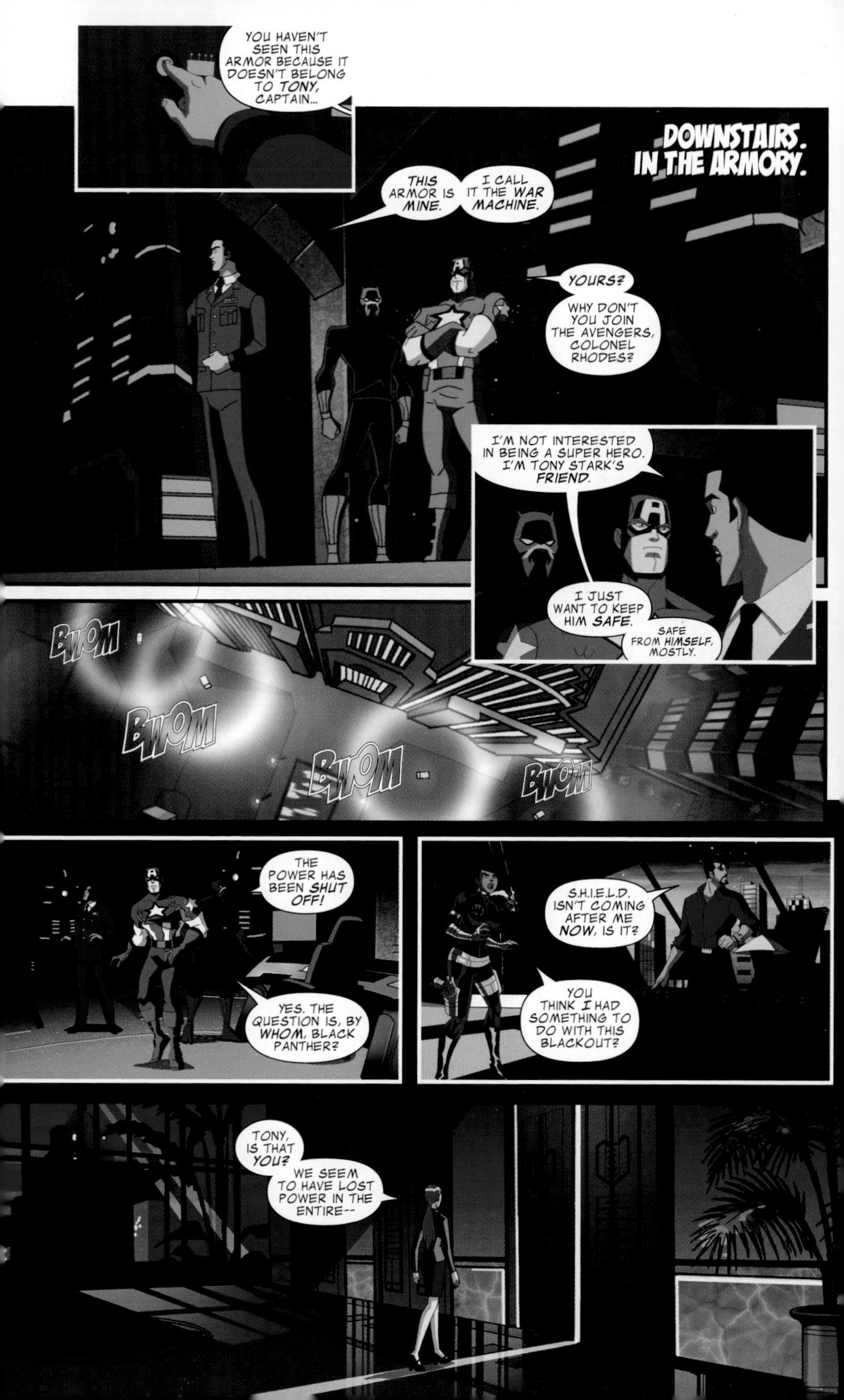
YOU HAVEN'T SEEN THIS ARMOR BECAUSE IT DOESN'T BELONG TO TONY, CAPTAIN...
DOWNSTAIRS. IN THE ARMORY.
THIS ARMOR IS MINE.
I CALL IT THE WAR MACHINE.
YOURS?
WHY DON'T YOU JOIN THE AVENGERS, COLONEL RHODES?
I'M NOT INTERESTED IN BEING A SUPER HERO. I'M TONY STARK'S FRIEND.
I JUST WANT TO KEEP HIM SAFE.
SAFE FROM HIMSELF, MOSTLY.
BWOM
BWOM
BWOM
BWOM
THE POWER HAS BEEN SHUT OFF!
YES. THE QUESTION IS, BY WHOM, BLACK PANTHER?
S.H.I.E.L.D. ISN'T COMING AFTER ME NOW, IS IT?
YOU THINK I HAD SOMETHING TO DO WITH THIS BLACKOUT?
TONY, IS THAT YOU?
WE SEEM TO HAVE LOST POWER IN THE ENTIRE--

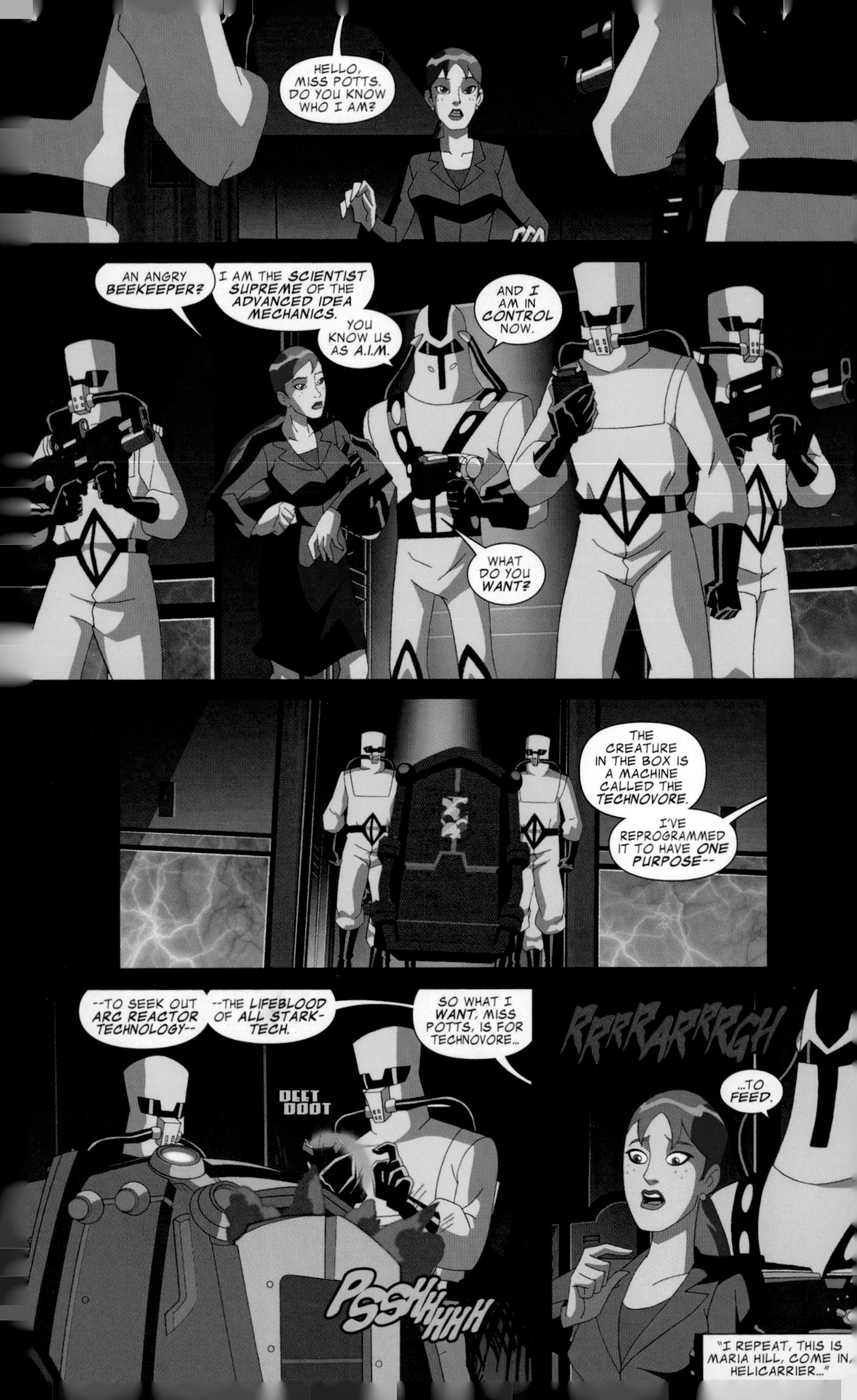
HELLO, MISS POTTS. DO YOU KNOW WHO I AM?
AN ANGRY BEEKEEPER?
I AM THE SCIENTIST SUPREME OF THE ADVANCED IDEA MECHANICS.
YOU KNOW US AS A.I.M.
AND I AM IN CONTROL NOW.
WHAT DO YOU WANT?
THE CREATURE IN THE BOX IS A MACHINE CALLED THE TECHNOVORE.
I'VE REPROGRAMMED IT TO HAVE ONE PURPOSE--
--TO SEEK OUT ARC REACTOR TECHNOLOGY--
--THE LIFEBLOOD OF ALL STARK-TECH.
SO WHAT I WANT, MISS POTTS, IS FOR TECHNOVORE...
RRRRARRRGH
BEET DOOT
...TO FEED.
PSSHHHHH
"I REPEAT, THIS IS MARIA HILL, COME IN, HELICARRIER..."

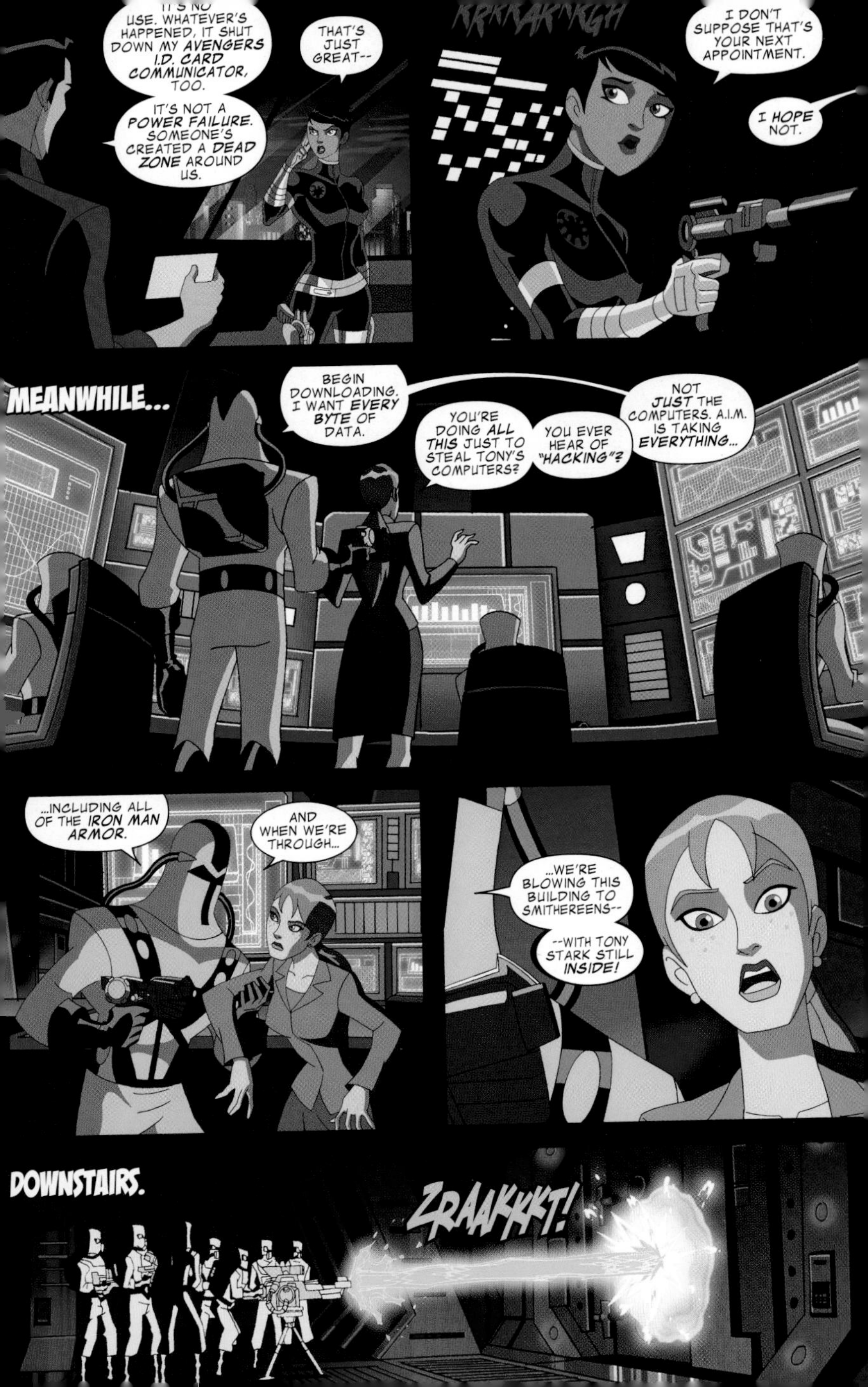
IT'S NO USE. WHATEVER'S HAPPENED, IT SHUT DOWN MY AVENGERS I.D. CARD COMMUNICATOR, TOO.
THAT'S JUST GREAT--
IT'S NOT A POWER FAILURE. SOMEONE'S CREATED A DEAD ZONE AROUND US.
KRKRAKNKGH
I DON'T SUPPOSE THAT'S YOUR NEXT APPOINTMENT.
I HOPE NOT.
MEANWHILE...
BEGIN DOWNLOADING. I WANT EVERY BYTE OF DATA.
YOU'RE DOING ALL THIS JUST TO STEAL TONY'S COMPUTERS?
YOU EVER HEAR OF "HACKING"?
NOT JUST THE COMPUTERS. A.I.M. IS TAKING EVERYTHING...
...INCLUDING ALL OF THE IRON MAN ARMOR.
AND WHEN WE'RE THROUGH...
...WE'RE BLOWING THIS BUILDING TO SMITHEREENS--
--WITH TONY STARK STILL INSIDE!
DOWNSTAIRS.
ZRAAKKKT!

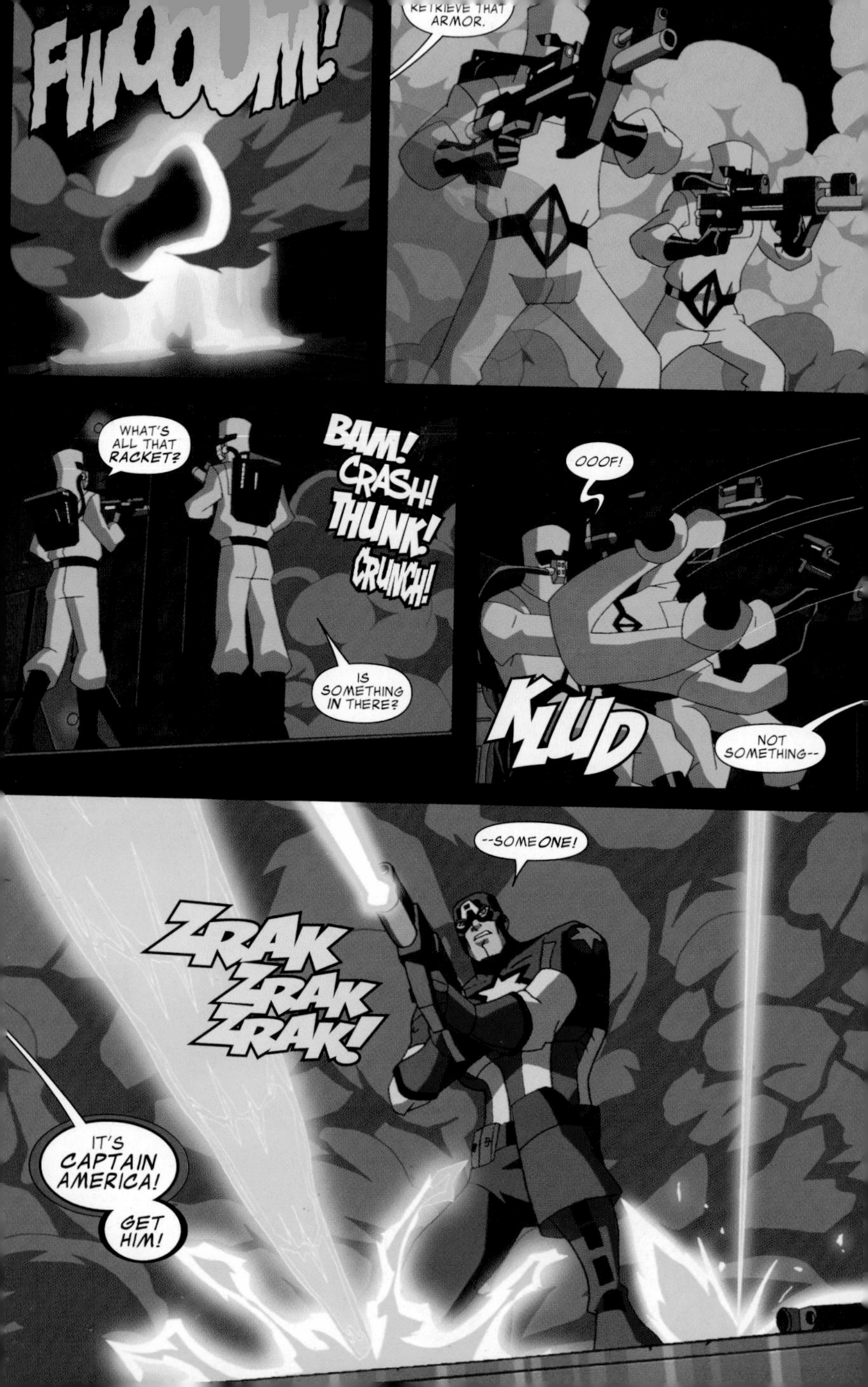
FWOOOM!
RETRIEVE THAT ARMOR.
WHAT'S ALL THAT RACKET?
BAM! CRASH! THUNK! CRUNCH!
IS SOMETHING IN THERE?
OOOF!
KLUD
NOT SOMETHING--
--SOMEONE!
ZRAK ZRAK ZRAK!
IT'S CAPTAIN AMERICA!
GET HIM!

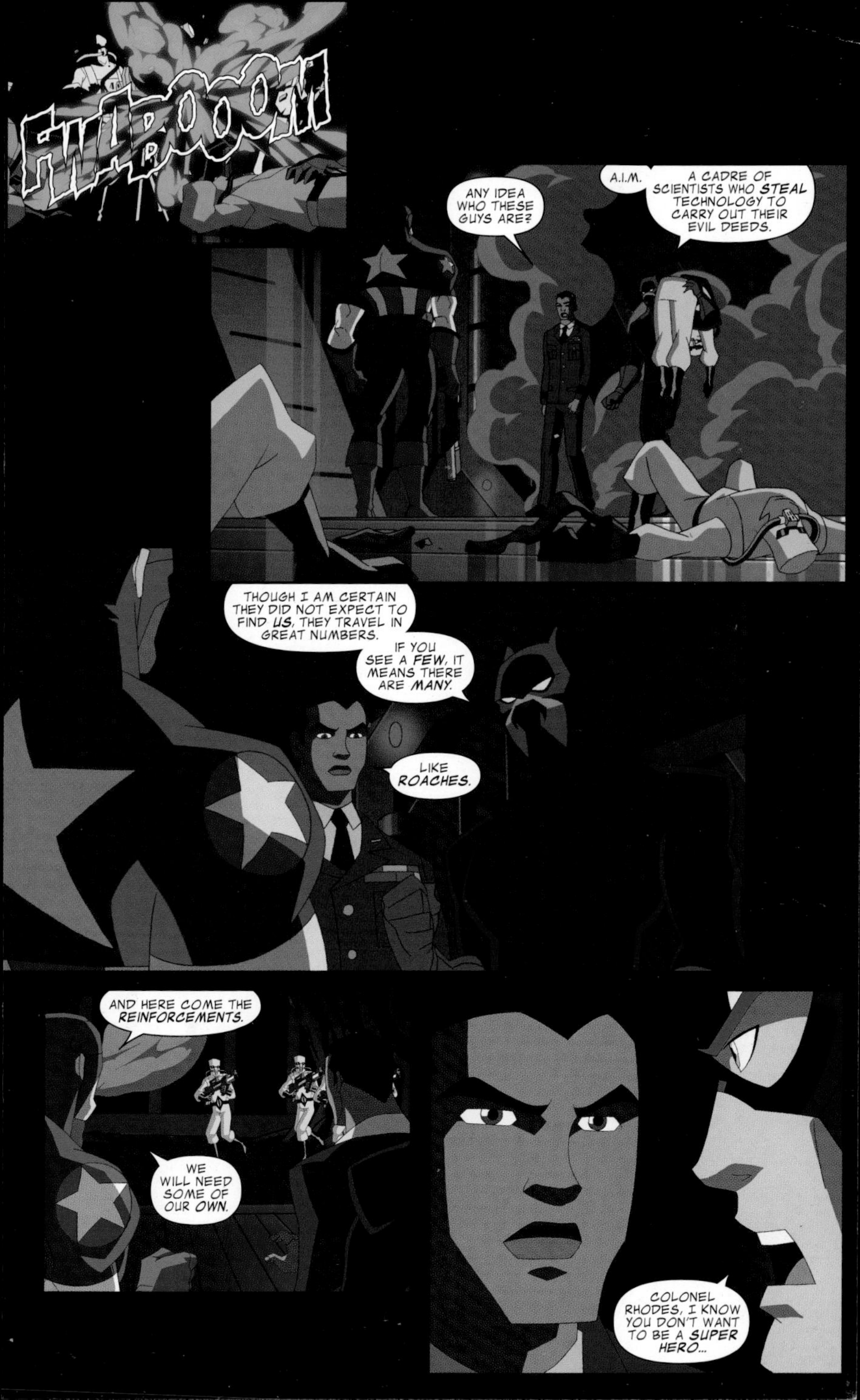
KWABOOOM
ANY IDEA WHO THESE GUYS ARE?
A.I.M.
A CADRE OF SCIENTISTS WHO STEAL TECHNOLOGY TO CARRY OUT THEIR EVIL DEEDS.
THOUGH I AM CERTAIN THEY DID NOT EXPECT TO FIND US, THEY TRAVEL IN GREAT NUMBERS.
IF YOU SEE A FEW, IT MEANS THERE ARE MANY.
LIKE ROACHES.
AND HERE COME THE REINFORCEMENTS.
WE WILL NEED SOME OF OUR OWN.
COLONEL RHODES, I KNOW YOU DON'T WANT TO BE A SUPER HERO...

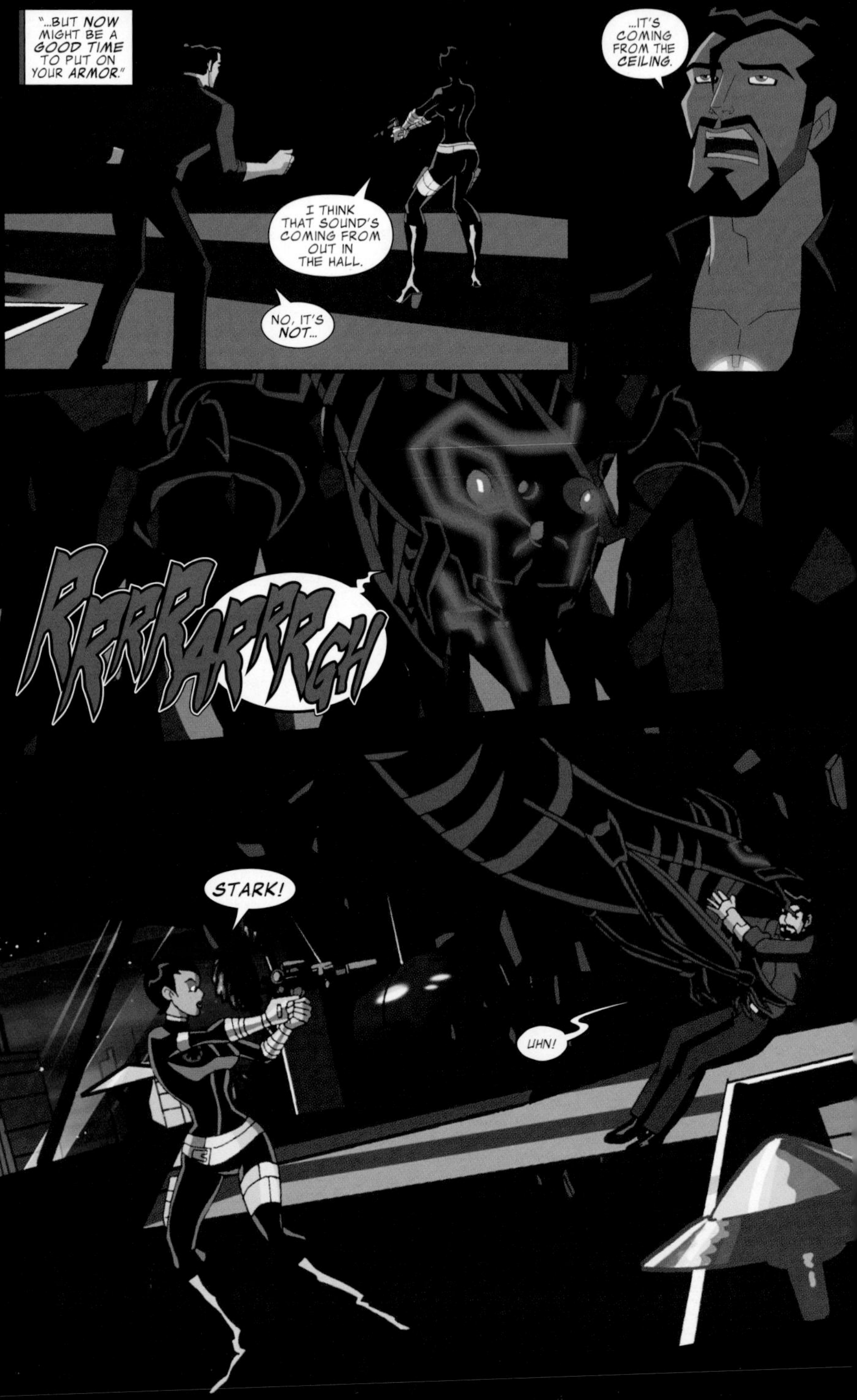
"...BUT NOW MIGHT BE A GOOD TIME TO PUT ON YOUR ARMOR."
I THINK THAT SOUND'S COMING FROM OUT IN THE HALL.
NO, IT'S NOT...
...IT'S COMING FROM THE CEILING.
RRRRARRRGH
STARK!
UHN!

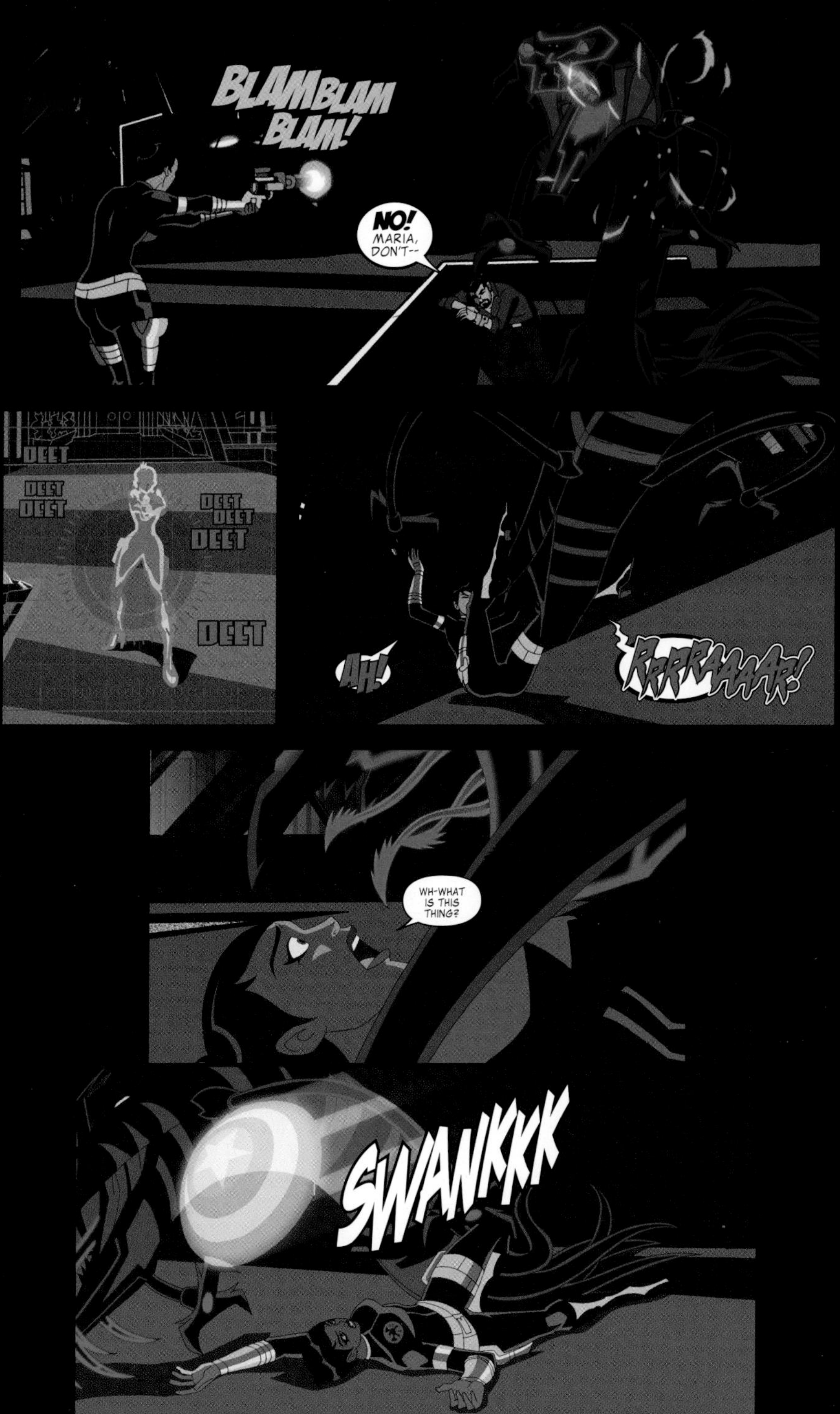
BLAMBLAM BLAM!
NO! MARIA, DON'T--
DEET
DEET DEET
DEET DEET DEET
DEET
AH!
RRRRAAAAR!
WH-WHAT IS THIS THING?
SWANKKK

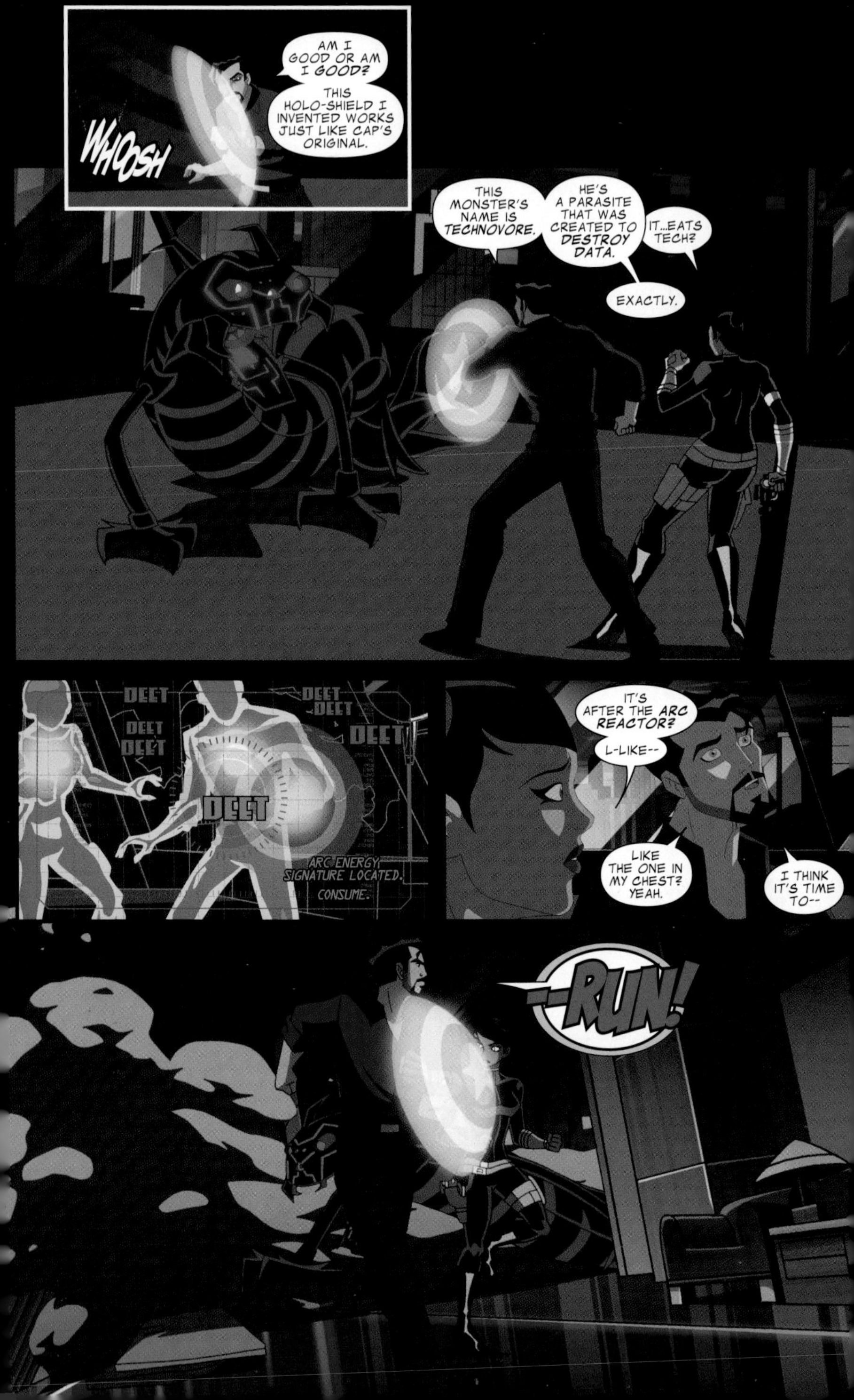
AM I GOOD OR AM I GOOD?
THIS HOLO-SHIELD I INVENTED WORKS JUST LIKE CAP'S ORIGINAL.
WHOOSH
THIS MONSTER'S NAME IS TECHNOVORE.
HE'S A PARASITE THAT WAS CREATED TO DESTROY DATA.
IT...EATS TECH?
EXACTLY.
DEET
DEET DEET
DEET DEET
DEET
DEET
ARC ENERGY SIGNATURE LOCATED.
CONSUME.
IT'S AFTER THE ARC REACTOR?
L-LIKE--
LIKE THE ONE IN MY CHEST? YEAH.
I THINK IT'S TIME TO--
--RUN!

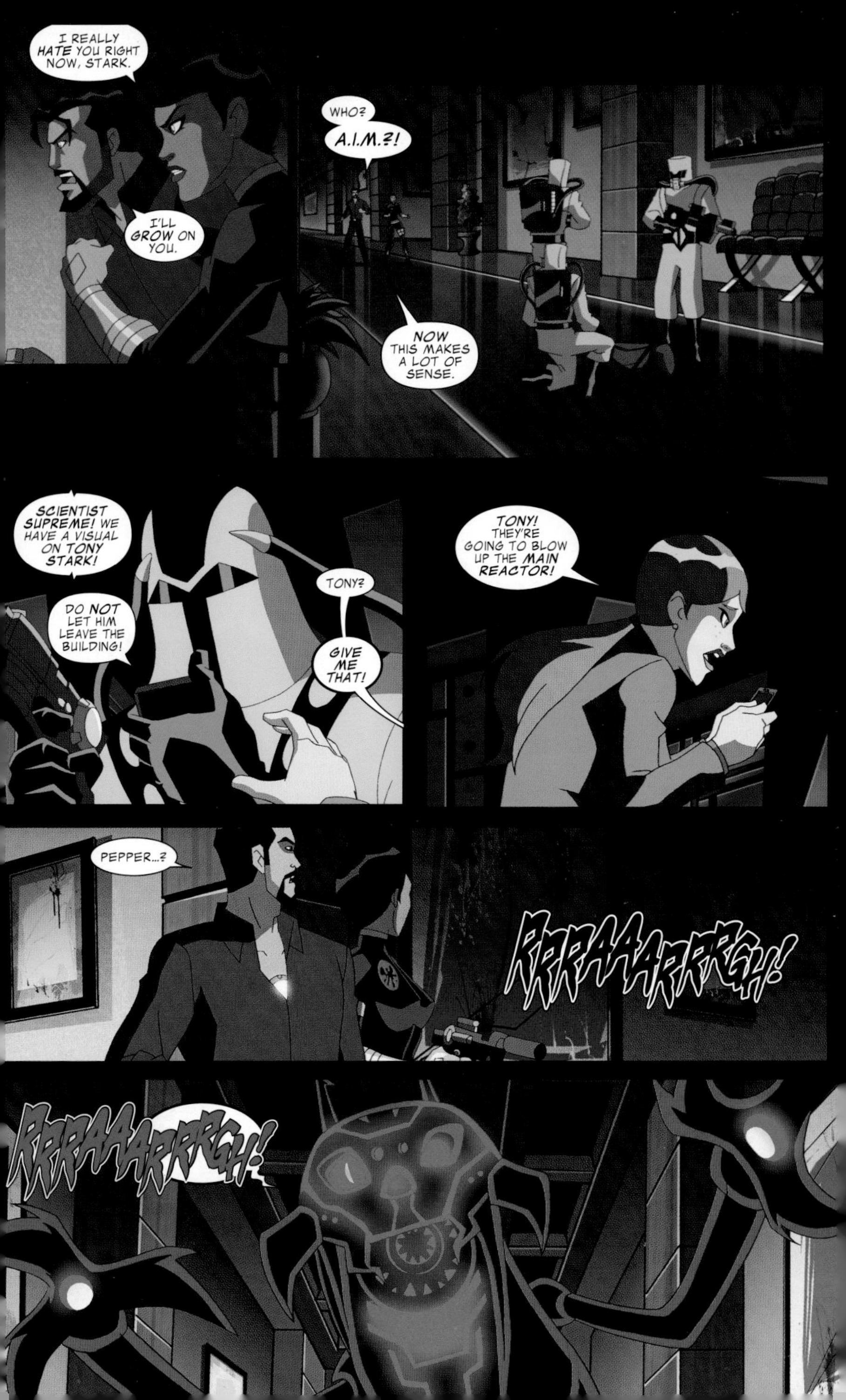
I REALLY HATE YOU RIGHT NOW, STARK.
I'LL GROW ON YOU.
WHO? A.I.M.?!
NOW THIS MAKES A LOT OF SENSE.
SCIENTIST SUPREME! WE HAVE A VISUAL ON TONY STARK!
DO NOT LET HIM LEAVE THE BUILDING!
TONY?
GIVE ME THAT!
TONY! THEY'RE GOING TO BLOW UP THE MAIN REACTOR!
PEPPER...?
RRRAAAARRRGH!
RRRAAAARRRGH!

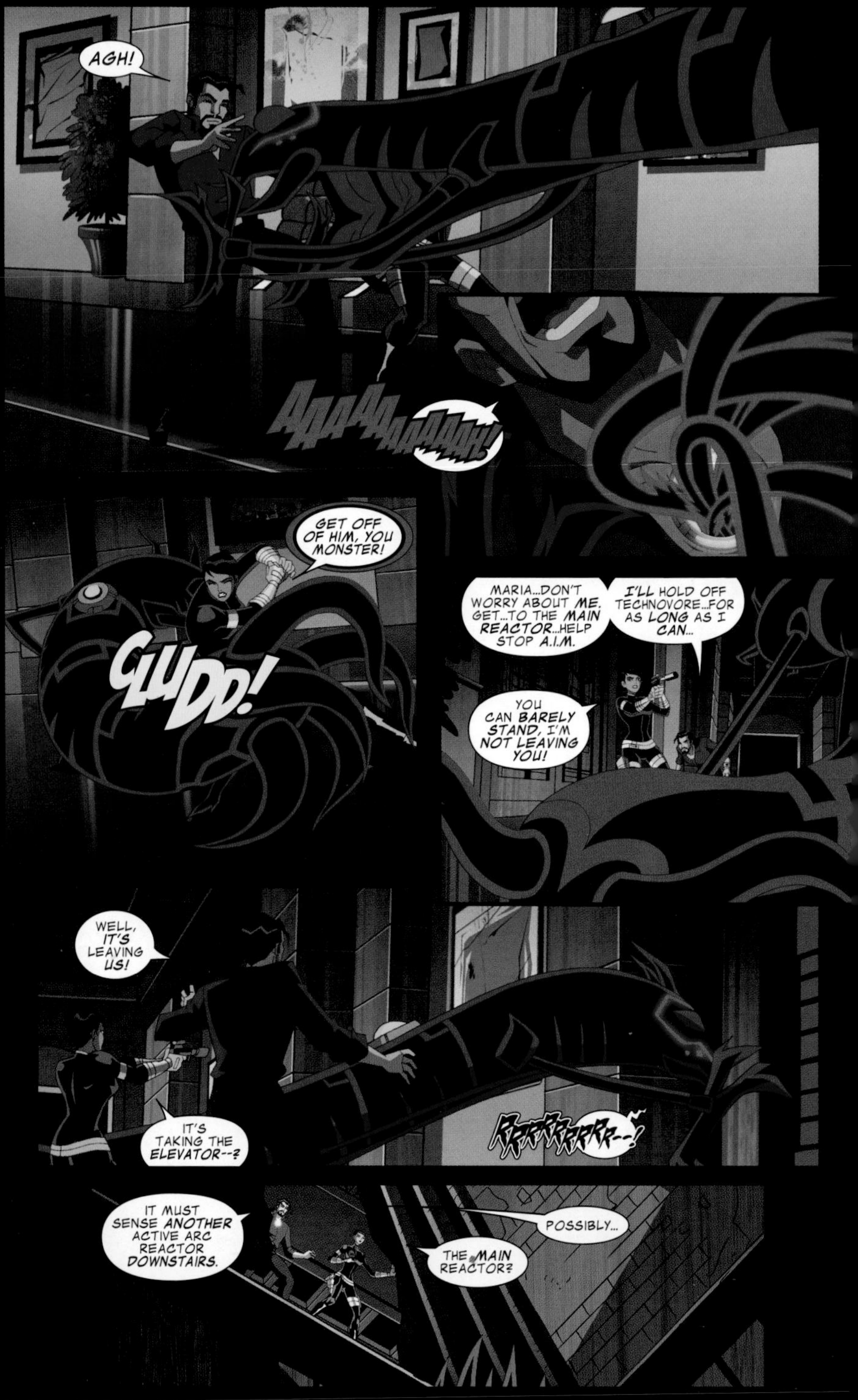
AGH!
AAAAAAAAAAH!
GET OFF OF HIM, YOU MONSTER!
GLUDD!
MARIA...DON'T WORRY ABOUT ME. GET...TO THE MAIN REACTOR...HELP STOP A.I.M.
I'LL HOLD OFF TECHNOVORE...FOR AS LONG AS I CAN...
YOU CAN BARELY STAND, I'M NOT LEAVING YOU!
WELL, IT'S LEAVING US!
IT'S TAKING THE ELEVATOR--?
RRRRRRRRR--!
IT MUST SENSE ANOTHER ACTIVE ARC REACTOR DOWNSTAIRS.
POSSIBLY...
THE MAIN REACTOR?

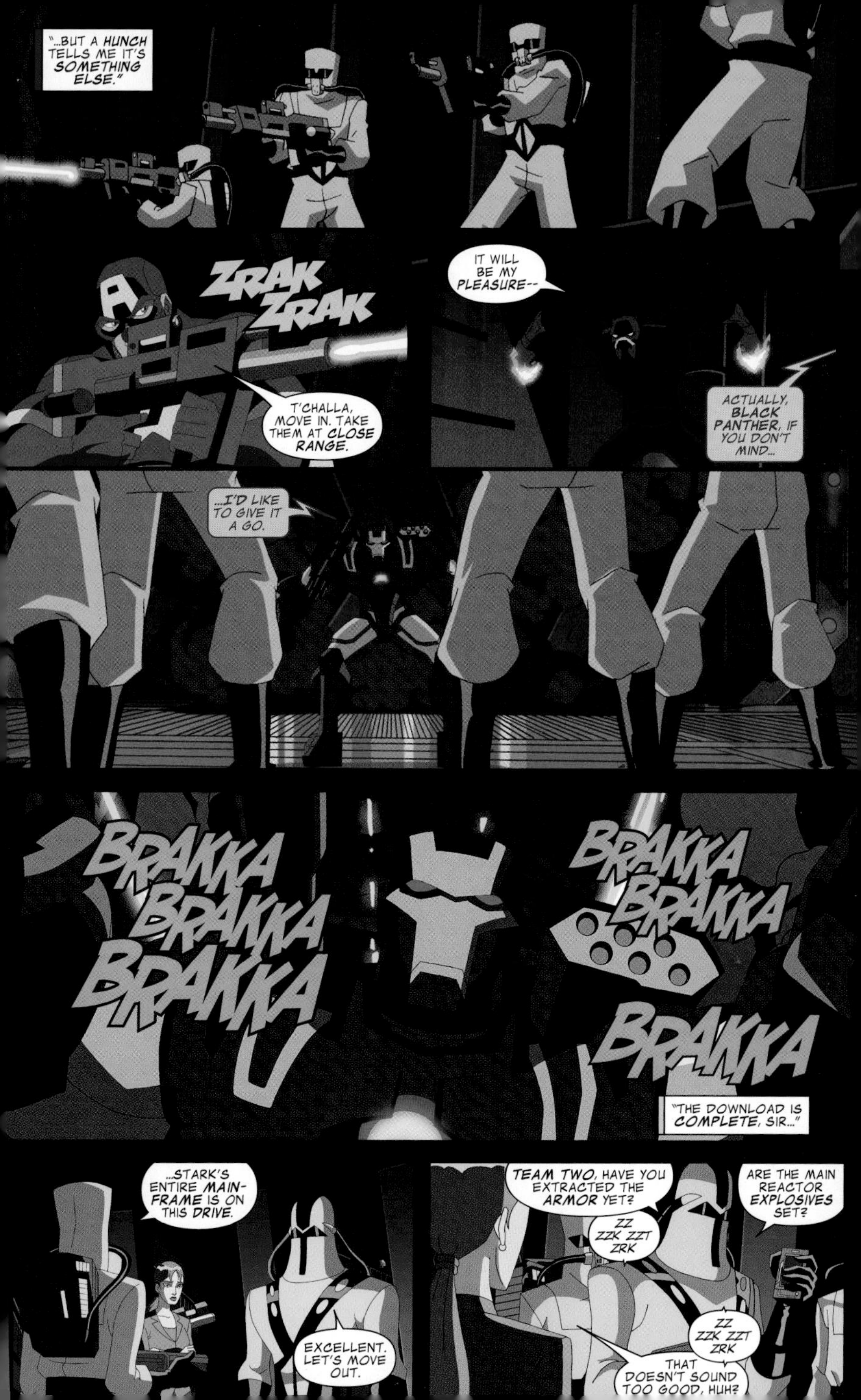
"...BUT A HUNCH TELLS ME IT'S SOMETHING ELSE."
ZRAK ZRAK
T'CHALLA, MOVE IN. TAKE THEM AT CLOSE RANGE.
IT WILL BE MY PLEASURE--
ACTUALLY, BLACK PANTHER, IF YOU DON'T MIND...
...I'D LIKE TO GIVE IT A GO.
BRAKKA BRAKKA BRAKKA
BRAKKA BRAKKA
BRAKKA
"THE DOWNLOAD IS COMPLETE, SIR..."
...STARK'S ENTIRE MAIN-FRAME IS ON THIS DRIVE.
EXCELLENT. LET'S MOVE OUT.
TEAM TWO, HAVE YOU EXTRACTED THE ARMOR YET?
ZZ ZZK ZZT ZRK
ARE THE MAIN REACTOR EXPLOSIVES SET?
ZZ ZZK ZZT ZRK
THAT DOESN'T SOUND TOO GOOD, HUH?

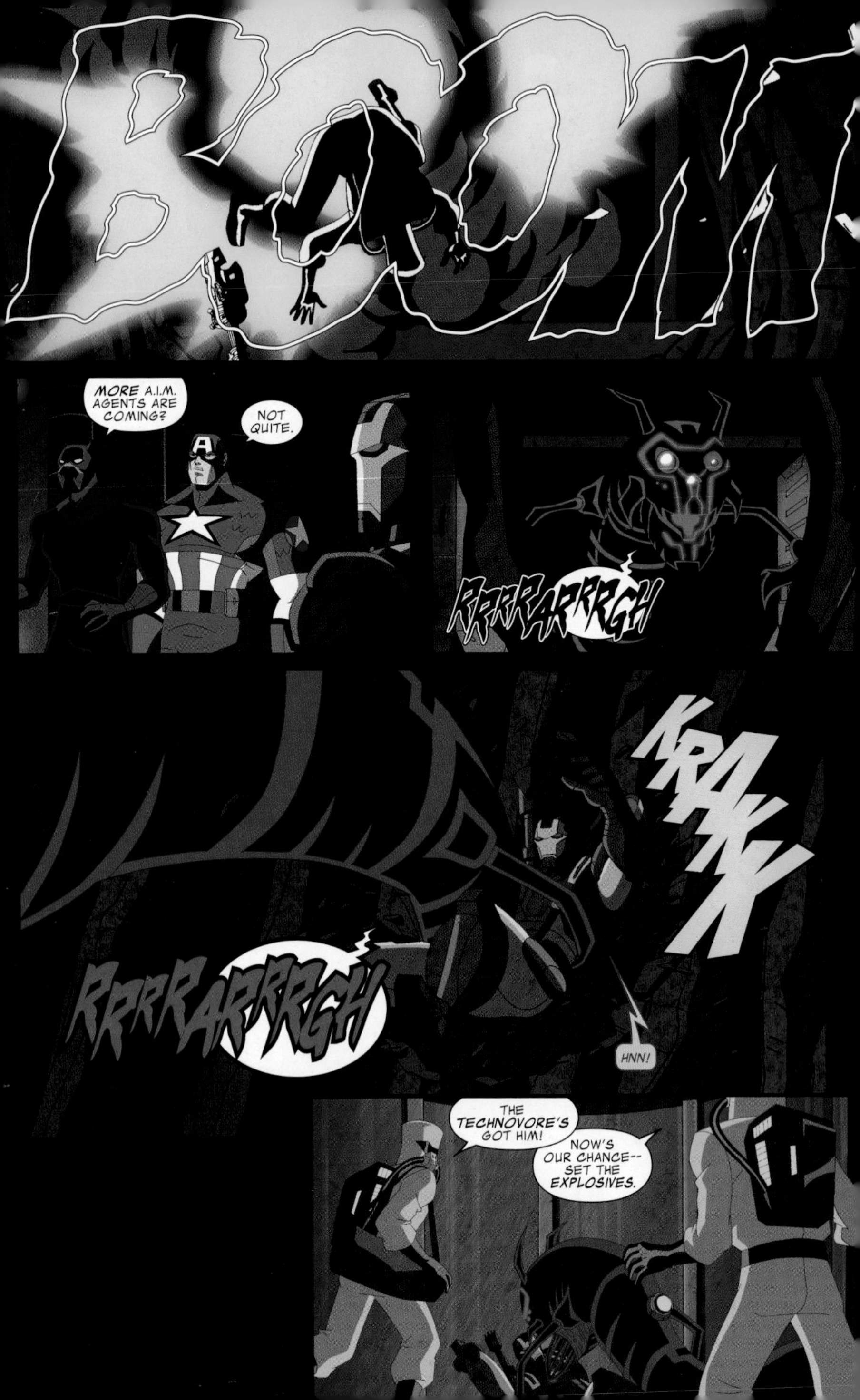
BOOM
MORE A.I.M. AGENTS ARE COMING?
NOT QUITE.
RRRRARRRGH
KRAK
RRRRARRRGH
HNN!
THE TECHNOVORE'S GOT HIM!
NOW'S OUR CHANCE-- SET THE EXPLOSIVES.

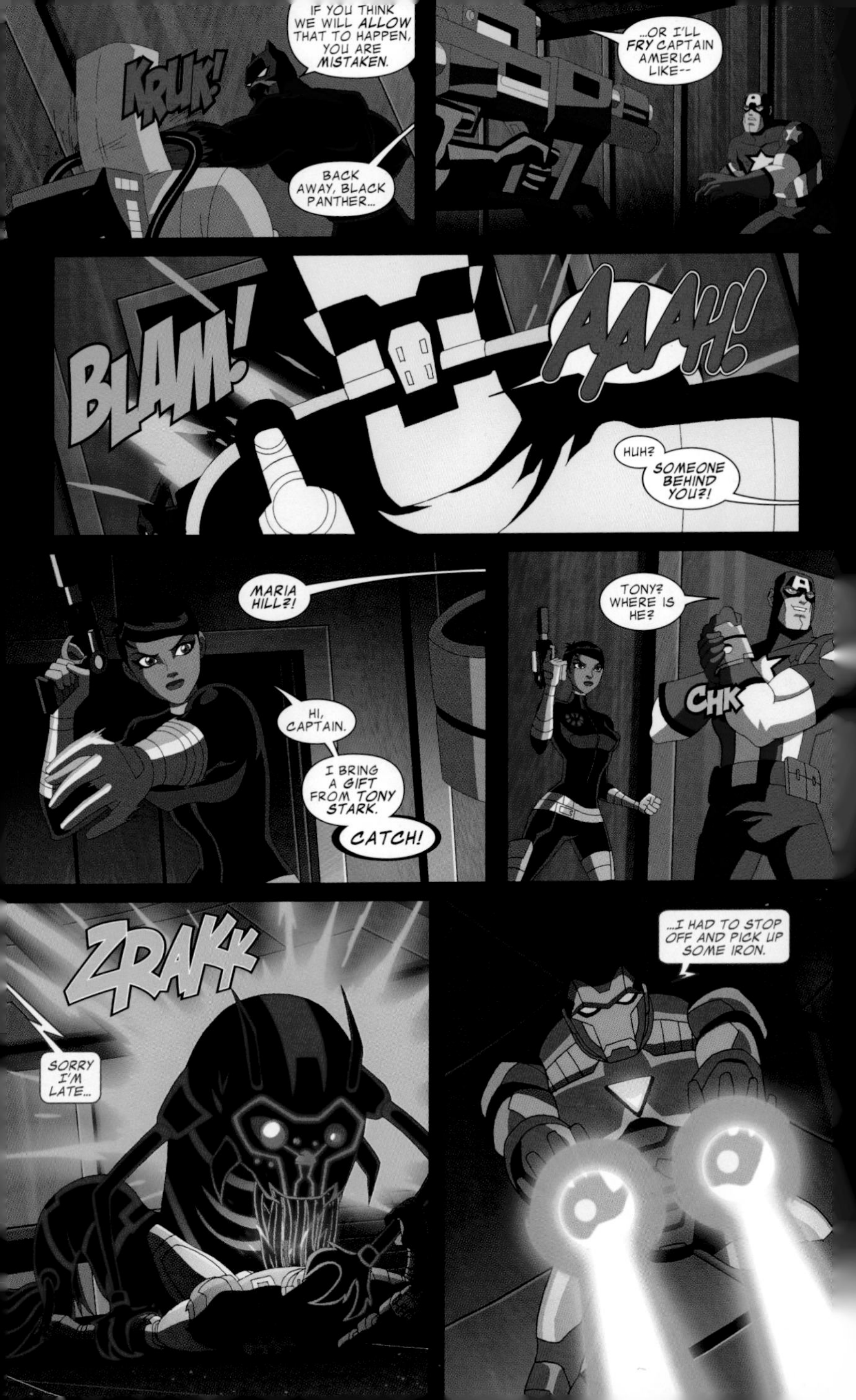
IF YOU THINK WE WILL ALLOW THAT TO HAPPEN, YOU ARE MISTAKEN.
KRUK!
BACK AWAY, BLACK PANTHER...
...OR I'LL FRY CAPTAIN AMERICA LIKE--
BLAM!
AAAH!
HUH? SOMEONE BEHIND YOU?!
MARIA HILL?!
HI, CAPTAIN.
I BRING A GIFT FROM TONY STARK.
CATCH!
TONY? WHERE IS HE?
CHK
ZRAKK
SORRY I'M LATE...
...I HAD TO STOP OFF AND PICK UP SOME IRON.

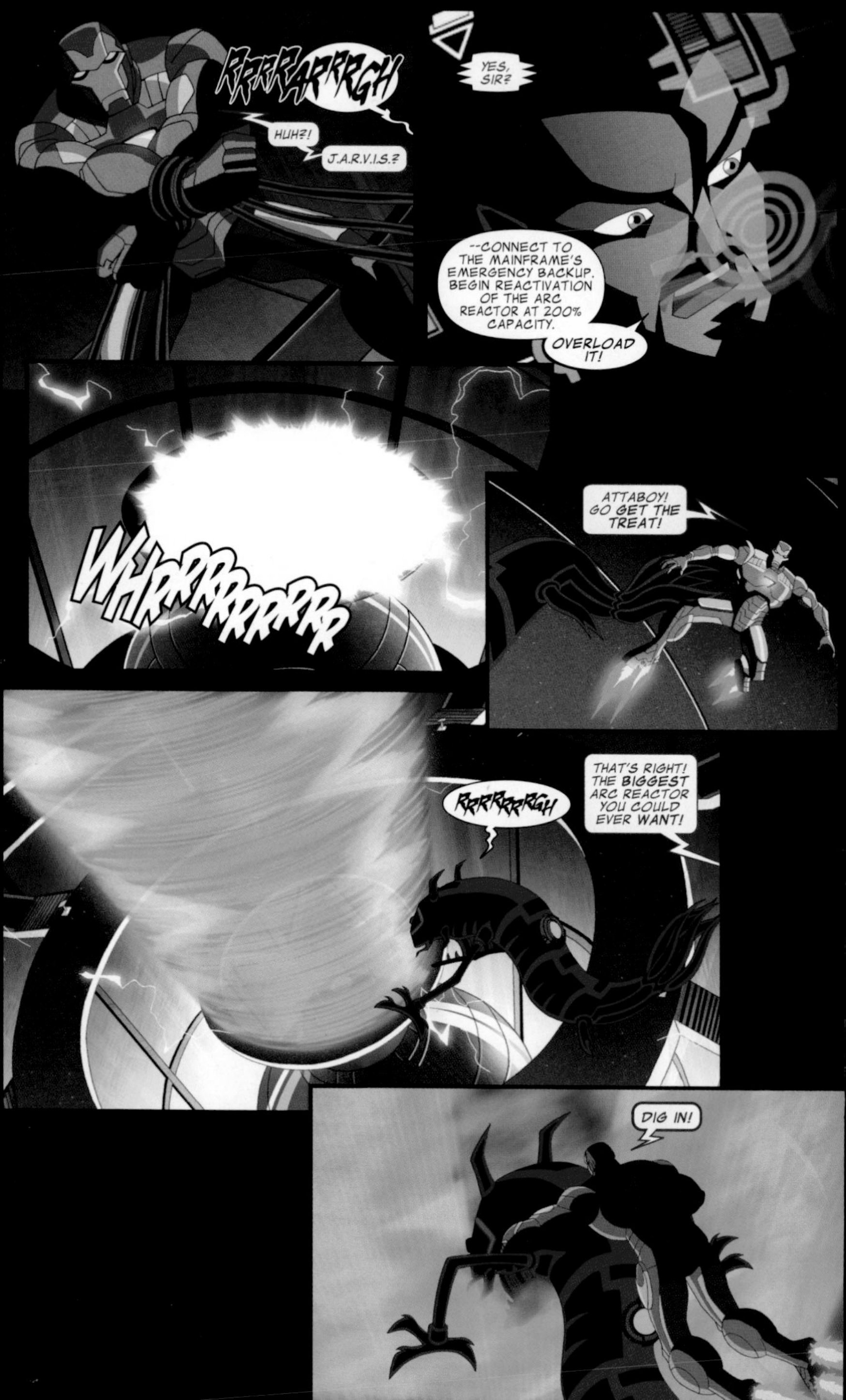
RRRRARRRGH
HUH?!
J.A.R.V.I.S.?
YES, SIR?
--CONNECT TO THE MAINFRAME'S EMERGENCY BACKUP. BEGIN REACTIVATION OF THE ARC REACTOR AT 200% CAPACITY.
OVERLOAD IT!
WHRRRRRRRRRRR
ATTABOY! GO GET THE TREAT!
RRRRRRRGH
THAT'S RIGHT! THE BIGGEST ARC REACTOR YOU COULD EVER WANT!
DIG IN!

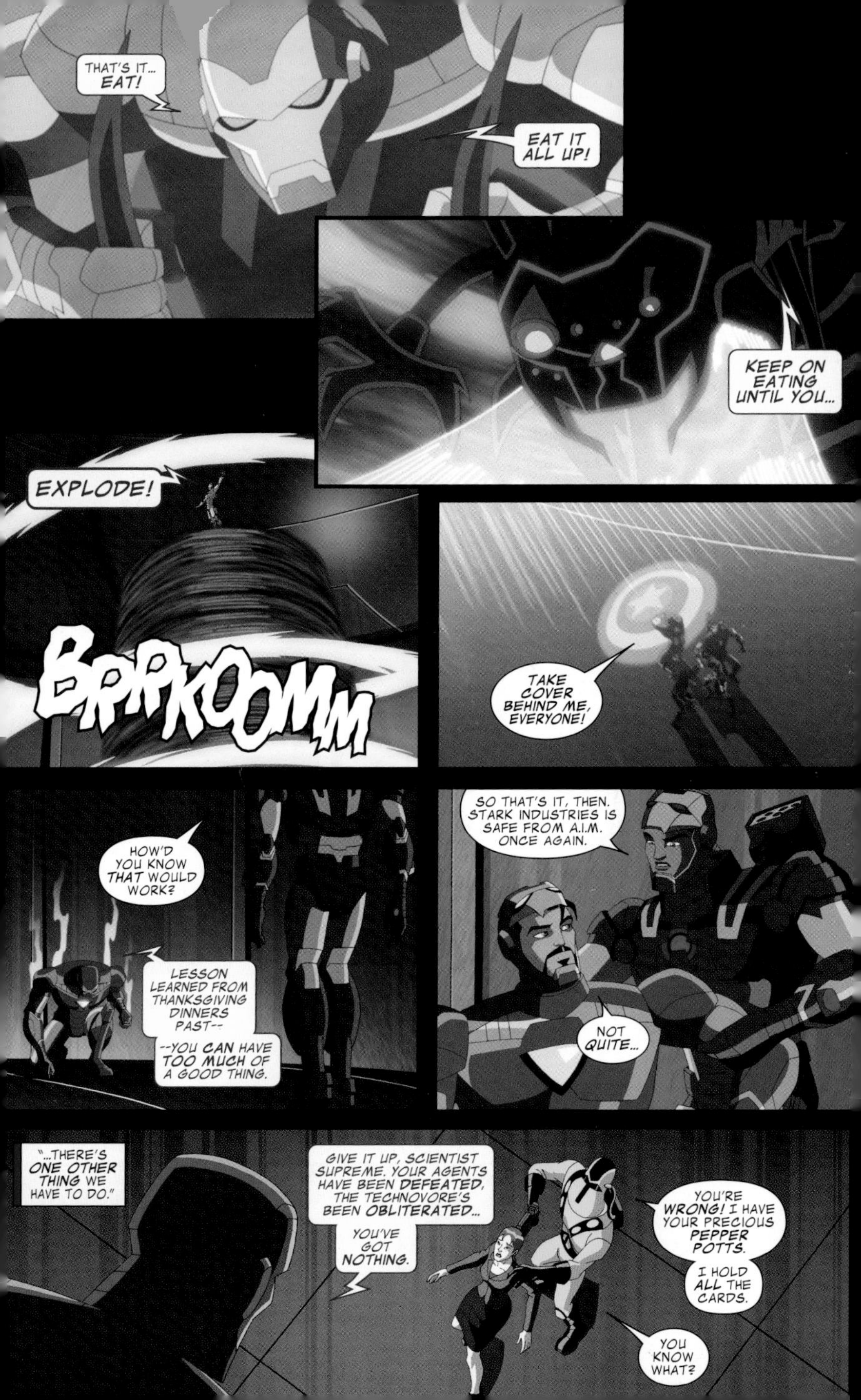
THAT'S IT... EAT!
EAT IT ALL UP!
KEEP ON EATING UNTIL YOU...
EXPLODE!
BRRKOOMM
TAKE COVER BEHIND ME, EVERYONE!
HOW'D YOU KNOW THAT WOULD WORK?
LESSON LEARNED FROM THANKSGIVING DINNERS PAST--
--YOU CAN HAVE TOO MUCH OF A GOOD THING.
SO THAT'S IT, THEN. STARK INDUSTRIES IS SAFE FROM A.I.M. ONCE AGAIN.
NOT QUITE...
"...THERE'S ONE OTHER THING WE HAVE TO DO."
GIVE IT UP, SCIENTIST SUPREME. YOUR AGENTS HAVE BEEN DEFEATED, THE TECHNOVORE'S BEEN OBLITERATED...
YOU'VE GOT NOTHING.
YOU'RE WRONG! I HAVE YOUR PRECIOUS PEPPER POTTS.
I HOLD ALL THE CARDS.
YOU KNOW WHAT?

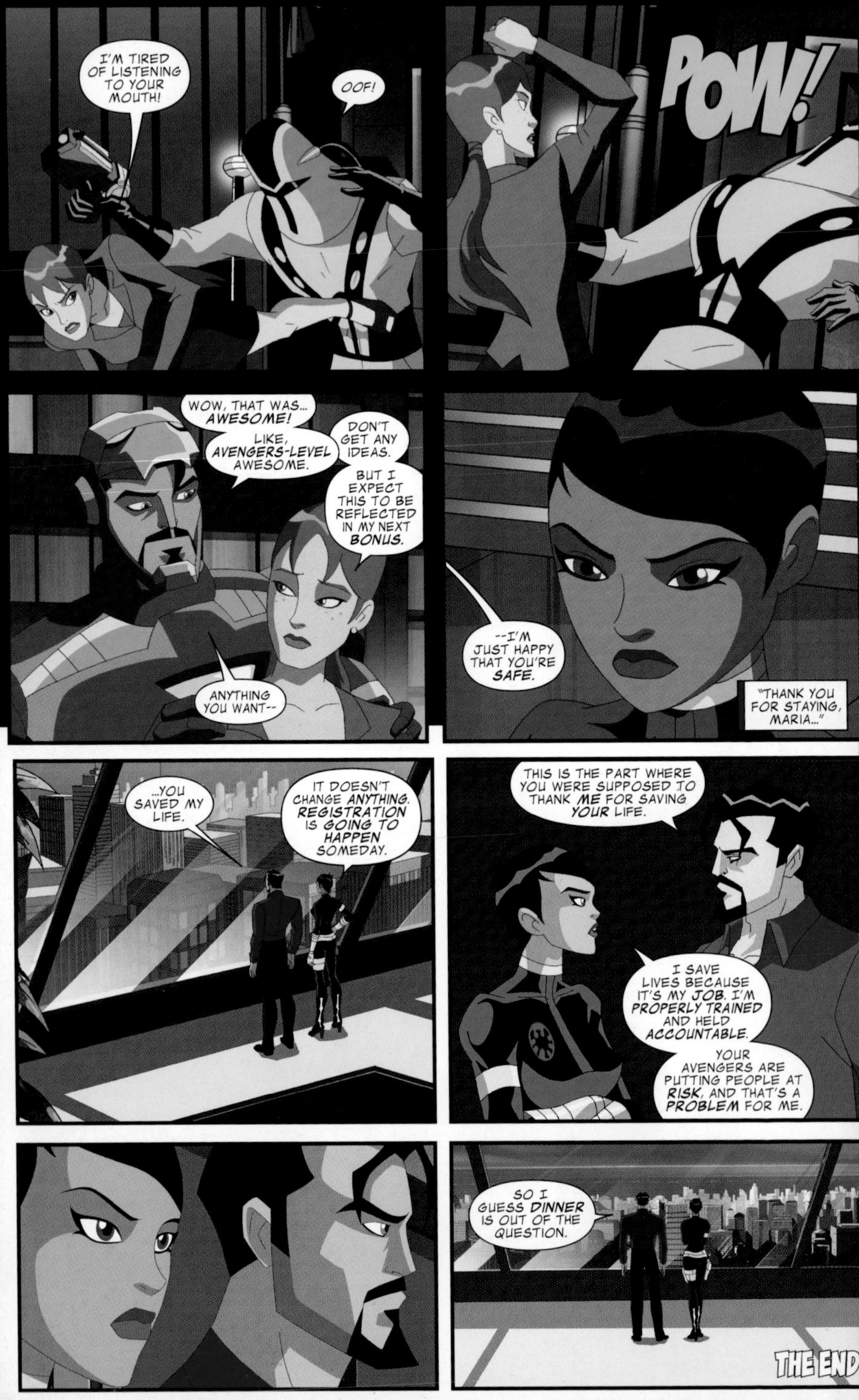

I'M TIRED OF LISTENING TO YOUR MOUTH!
OOF!
POW!
WOW, THAT WAS... AWESOME!
LIKE, AVENGERS-LEVEL AWESOME.
DON'T GET ANY IDEAS.
BUT I EXPECT THIS TO BE REFLECTED IN MY NEXT BONUS.
ANYTHING YOU WANT--
--I'M JUST HAPPY THAT YOU'RE SAFE.
"THANK YOU FOR STAYING, MARIA..."
...YOU SAVED MY LIFE.
IT DOESN'T CHANGE ANYTHING. REGISTRATION IS GOING TO HAPPEN SOMEDAY.
THIS IS THE PART WHERE YOU WERE SUPPOSED TO THANK ME FOR SAVING YOUR LIFE.
I SAVE LIVES BECAUSE IT'S MY JOB. I'M PROPERLY TRAINED AND HELD ACCOUNTABLE.
YOUR AVENGERS ARE PUTTING PEOPLE AT RISK, AND THAT'S A PROBLEM FOR ME.
SO I GUESS DINNER IS OUT OF THE QUESTION.
THE END

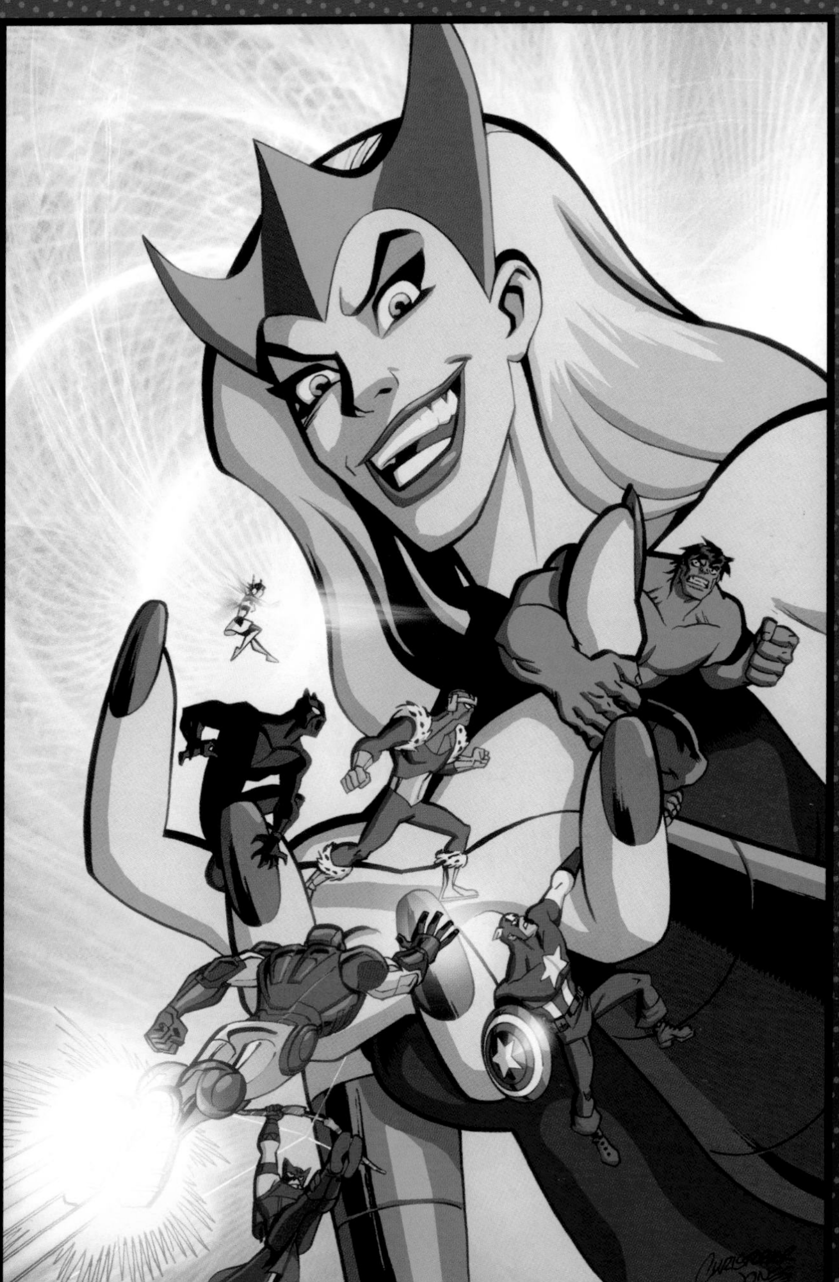

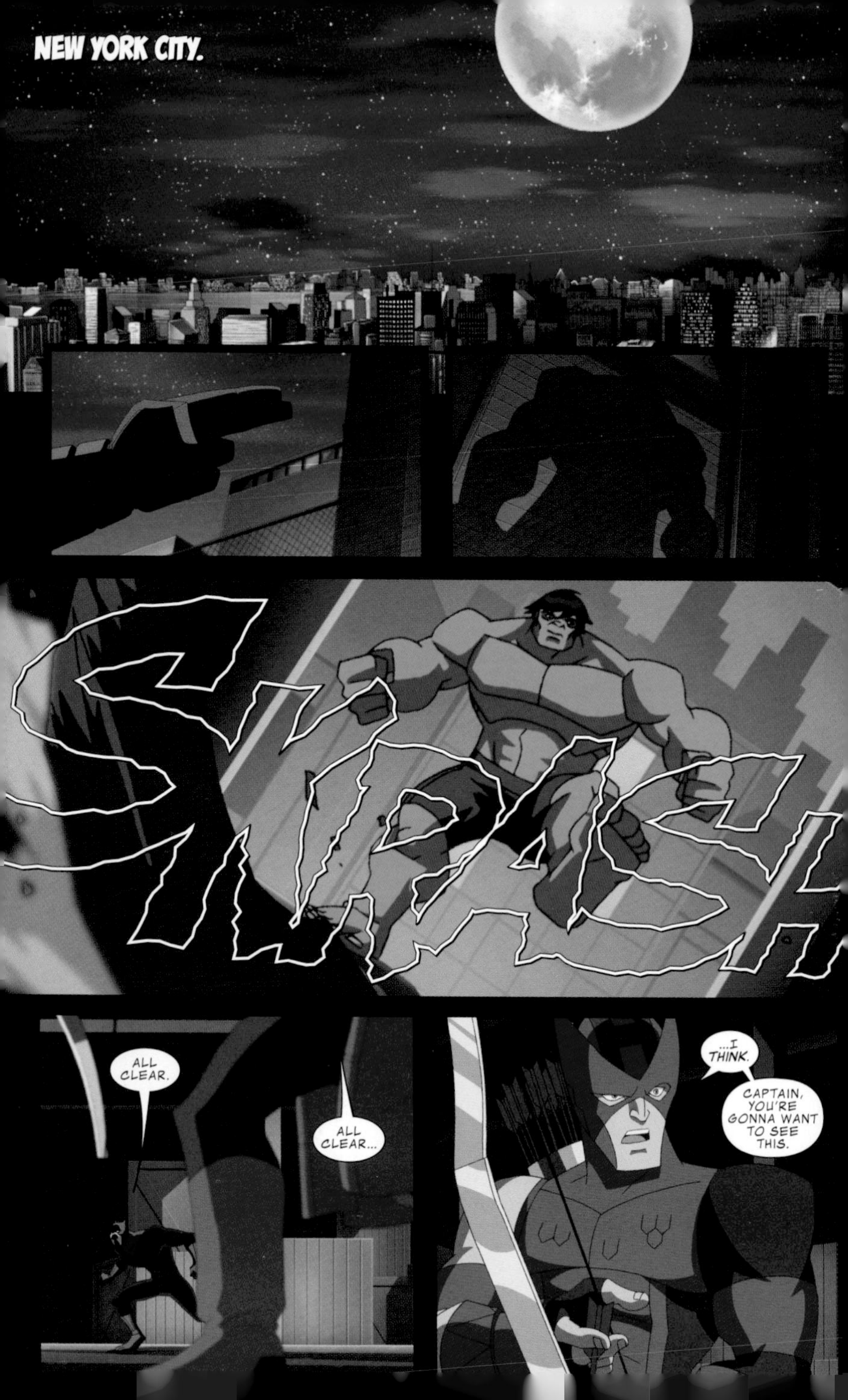
NEW YORK CITY.
SMASH!
ALL CLEAR.
ALL CLEAR...
...I THINK.
CAPTAIN, YOU'RE GONNA WANT TO SEE THIS.

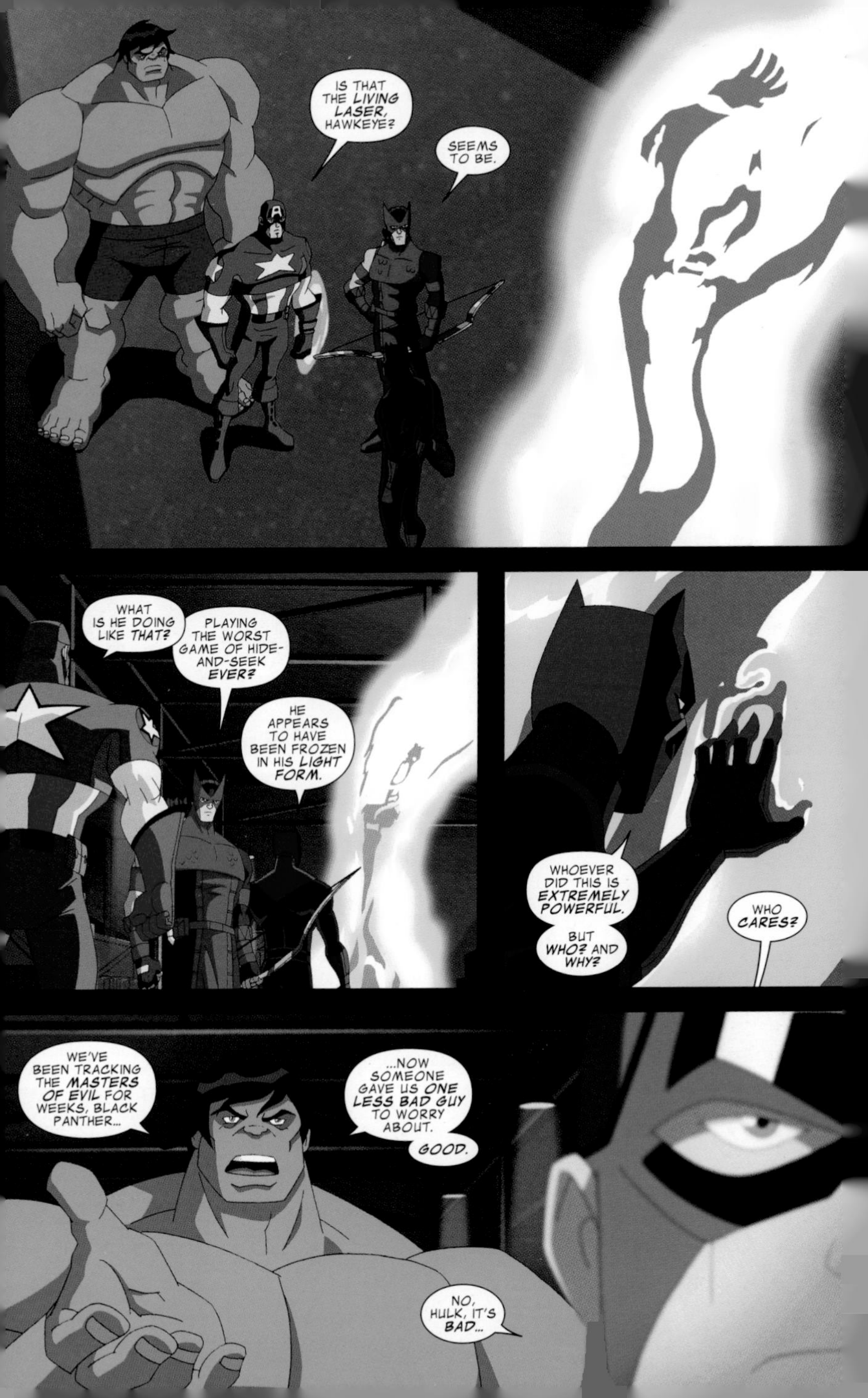
IS THAT THE LIVING LASER, HAWKEYE?
SEEMS TO BE.
WHAT IS HE DOING LIKE THAT?
PLAYING THE WORST GAME OF HIDE-AND-SEEK EVER?
HE APPEARS TO HAVE BEEN FROZEN IN HIS LIGHT FORM.
WHOEVER DID THIS IS EXTREMELY POWERFUL.
BUT WHO? AND WHY?
WHO CARES?
WE'VE BEEN TRACKING THE MASTERS OF EVIL FOR WEEKS, BLACK PANTHER...
...NOW SOMEONE GAVE US ONE LESS BAD GUY TO WORRY ABOUT.
GOOD.
NO, HULK, IT'S BAD...

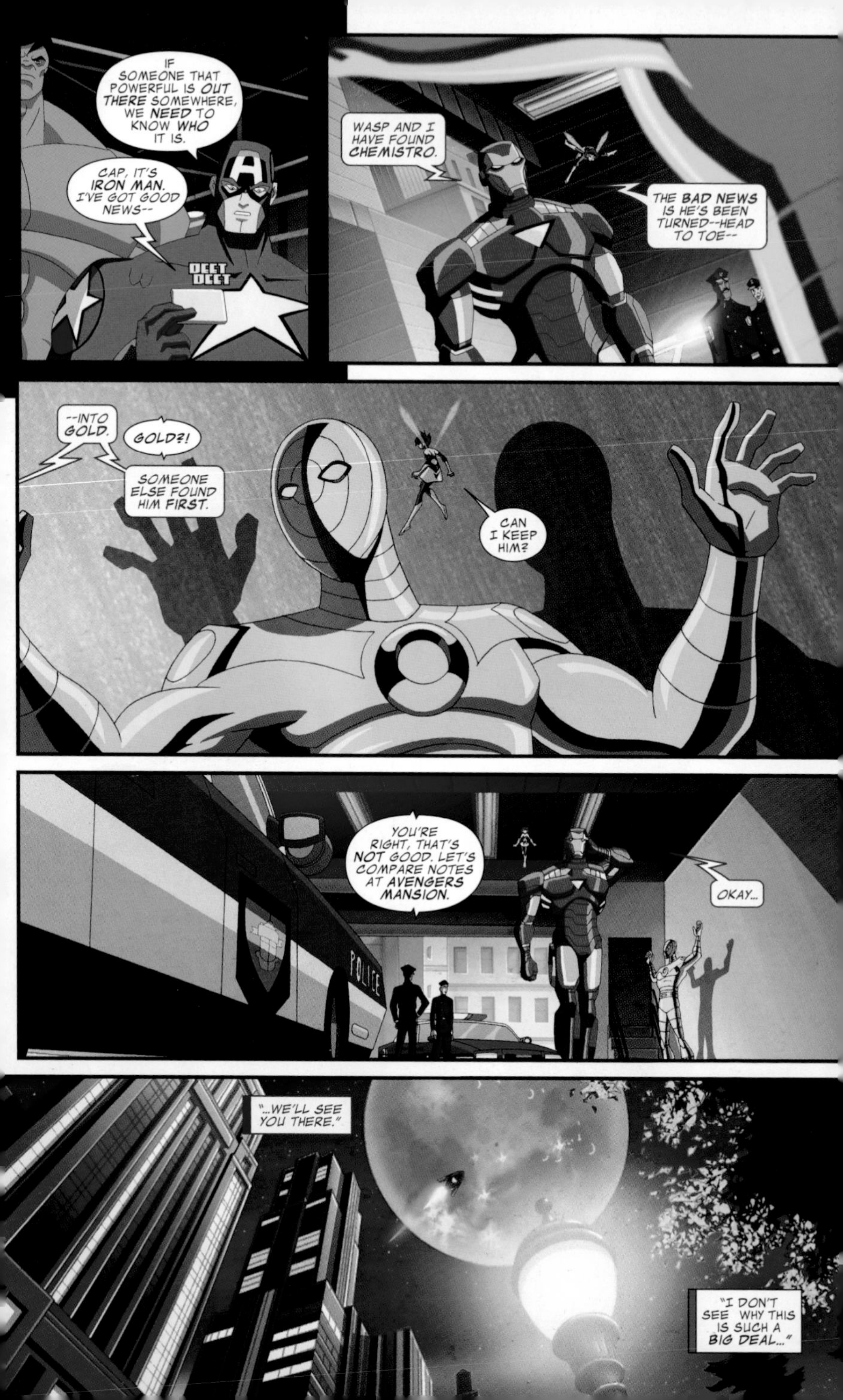

IF SOMEONE THAT POWERFUL IS OUT THERE SOMEWHERE, WE NEED TO KNOW WHO IT IS.
CAP, IT'S IRON MAN. I'VE GOT GOOD NEWS--
DEET DEET
WASP AND I HAVE FOUND CHEMISTRO.
THE BAD NEWS IS HE'S BEEN TURNED--HEAD TO TOE--
--INTO GOLD.
GOLD?!
SOMEONE ELSE FOUND HIM FIRST.
CAN I KEEP HIM?
YOU'RE RIGHT, THAT'S NOT GOOD. LET'S COMPARE NOTES AT AVENGERS MANSION.
OKAY...
POLICE
"...WE'LL SEE YOU THERE."
"I DON'T SEE WHY THIS IS SUCH A BIG DEAL..."

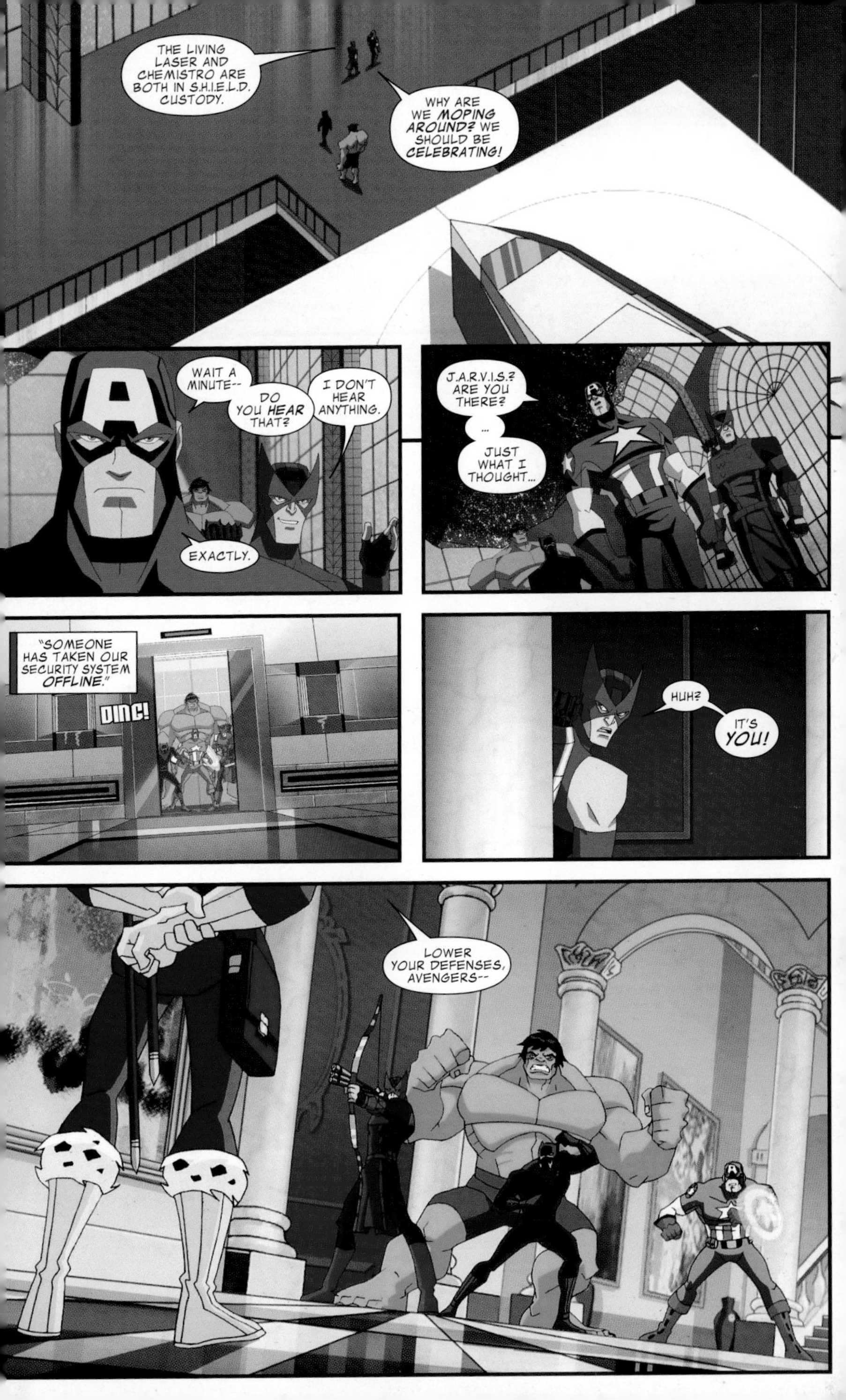
THE LIVING LASER AND CHEMISTRO ARE BOTH IN S.H.I.E.L.D. CUSTODY.
WHY ARE WE MOPING AROUND? WE SHOULD BE CELEBRATING!
WAIT A MINUTE--
DO YOU HEAR THAT?
I DON'T HEAR ANYTHING.
EXACTLY.
J.A.R.V.I.S.? ARE YOU THERE?
...
JUST WHAT I THOUGHT...
"SOMEONE HAS TAKEN OUR SECURITY SYSTEM OFFLINE."
DING!
HUH?
IT'S YOU!
LOWER YOUR DEFENSES, AVENGERS--

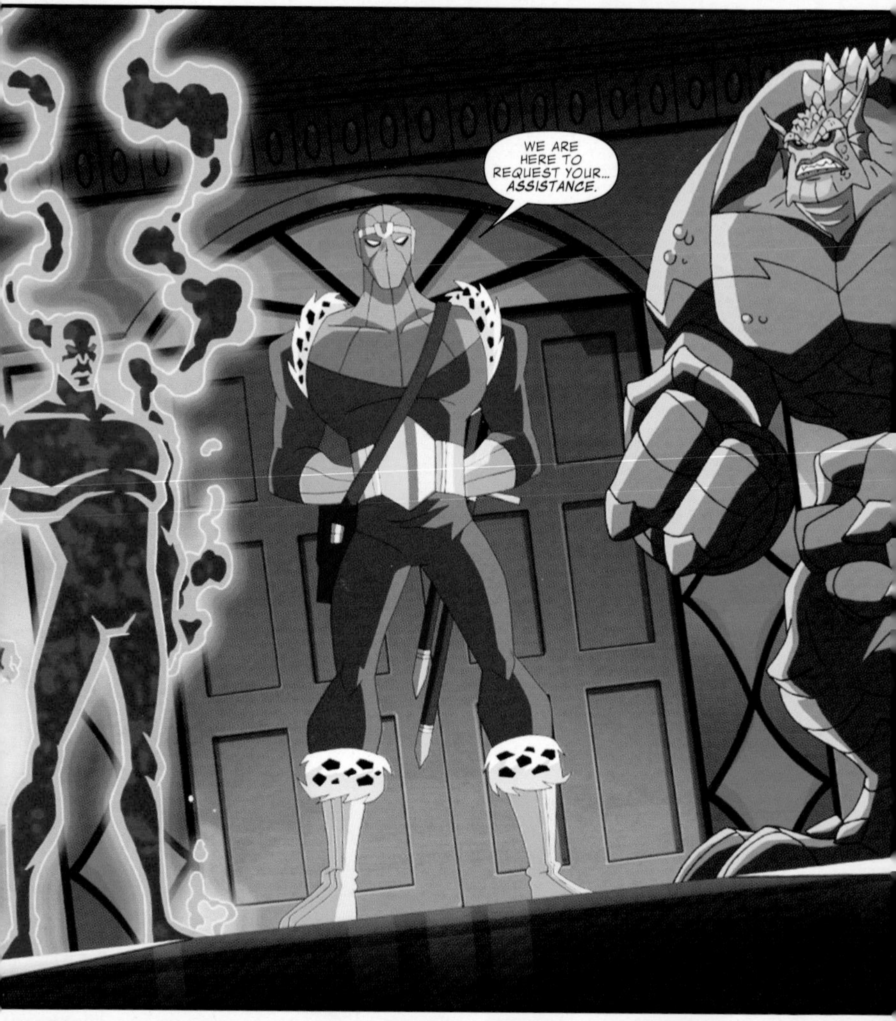
WE ARE HERE TO REQUEST YOUR... ASSISTANCE.

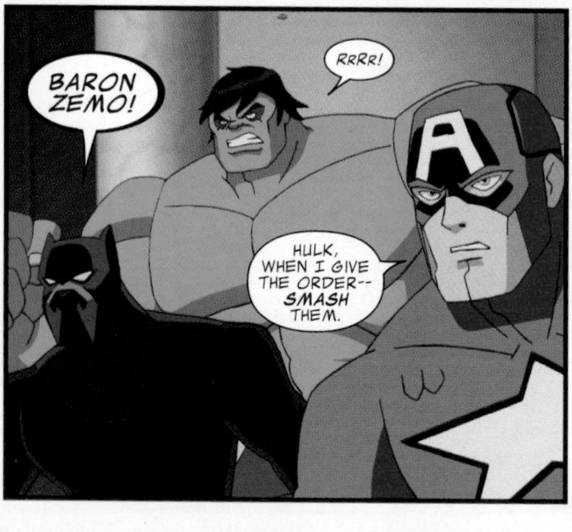
BARON ZEMO!
RRRR!
HULK, WHEN I GIVE THE ORDER-- SMASH THEM.

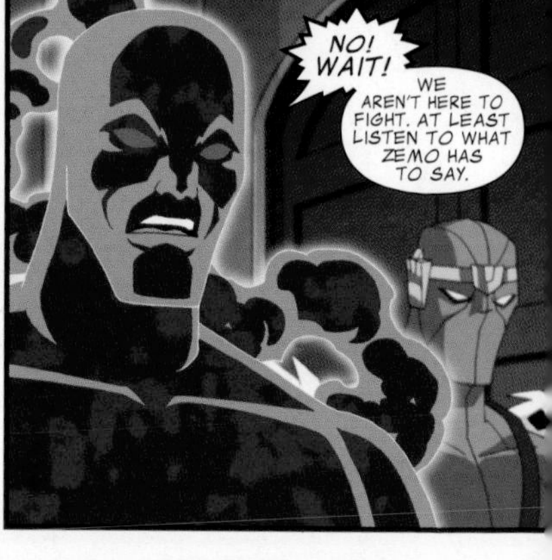
NO! WAIT!
WE AREN'T HERE TO FIGHT. AT LEAST LISTEN TO WHAT ZEMO HAS TO SAY.

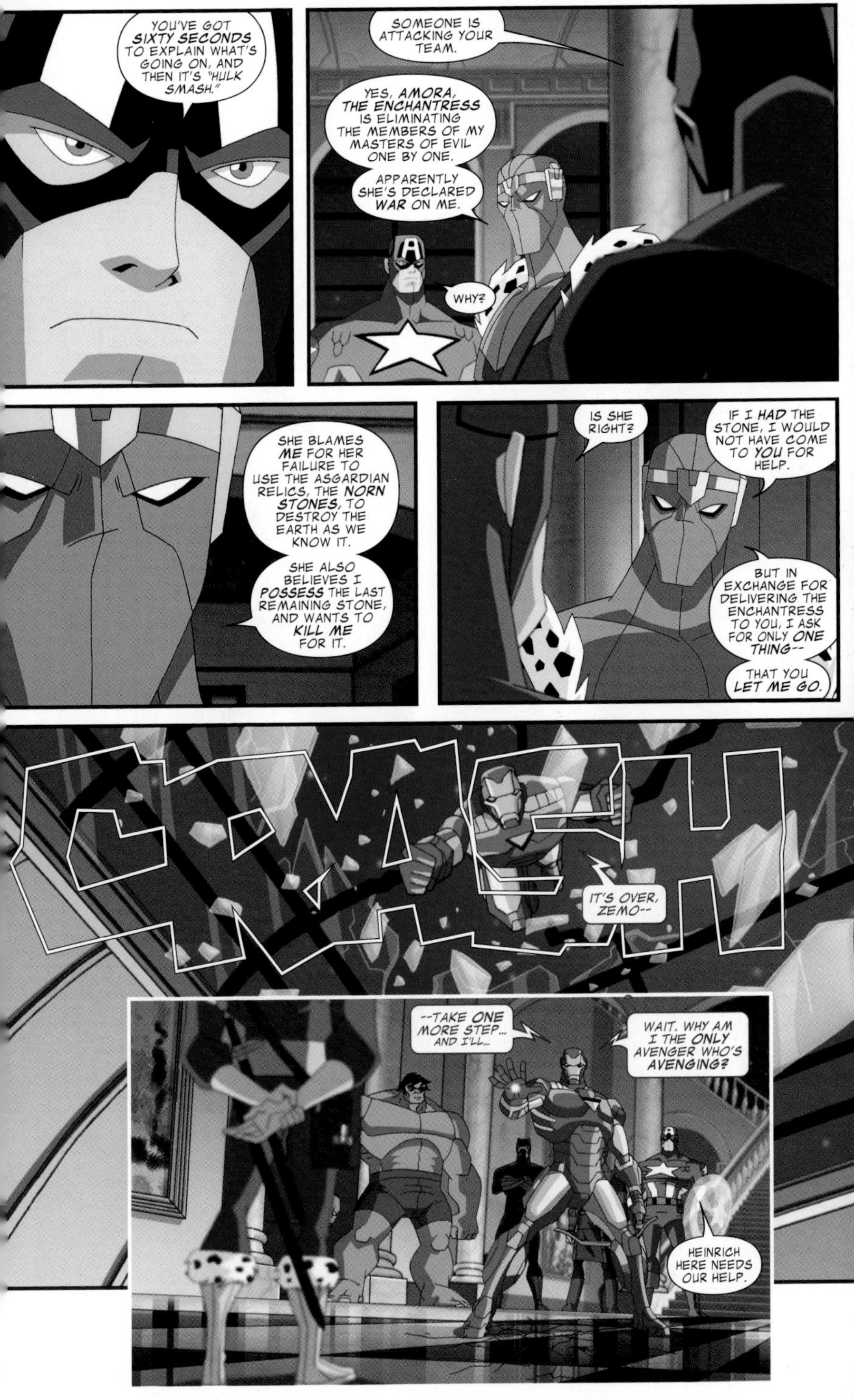

YOU'VE GOT SIXTY SECONDS TO EXPLAIN WHAT'S GOING ON, AND THEN IT'S "HULK SMASH."
SOMEONE IS ATTACKING YOUR TEAM.
YES, AMORA, THE ENCHANTRESS IS ELIMINATING THE MEMBERS OF MY MASTERS OF EVIL ONE BY ONE.
APPARENTLY SHE'S DECLARED WAR ON ME.
WHY?
SHE BLAMES ME FOR HER FAILURE TO USE THE ASGARDIAN RELICS, THE NORN STONES, TO DESTROY THE EARTH AS WE KNOW IT.
SHE ALSO BELIEVES I POSSESS THE LAST REMAINING STONE, AND WANTS TO KILL ME FOR IT.
IS SHE RIGHT?
IF I HAD THE STONE, I WOULD NOT HAVE COME TO YOU FOR HELP.
BUT IN EXCHANGE FOR DELIVERING THE ENCHANTRESS TO YOU, I ASK FOR ONLY ONE THING--
THAT YOU LET ME GO.
SMASH
IT'S OVER, ZEMO--
--TAKE ONE MORE STEP... AND I'LL...
WAIT. WHY AM I THE ONLY AVENGER WHO'S AVENGING?
HEINRICH HERE NEEDS OUR HELP.

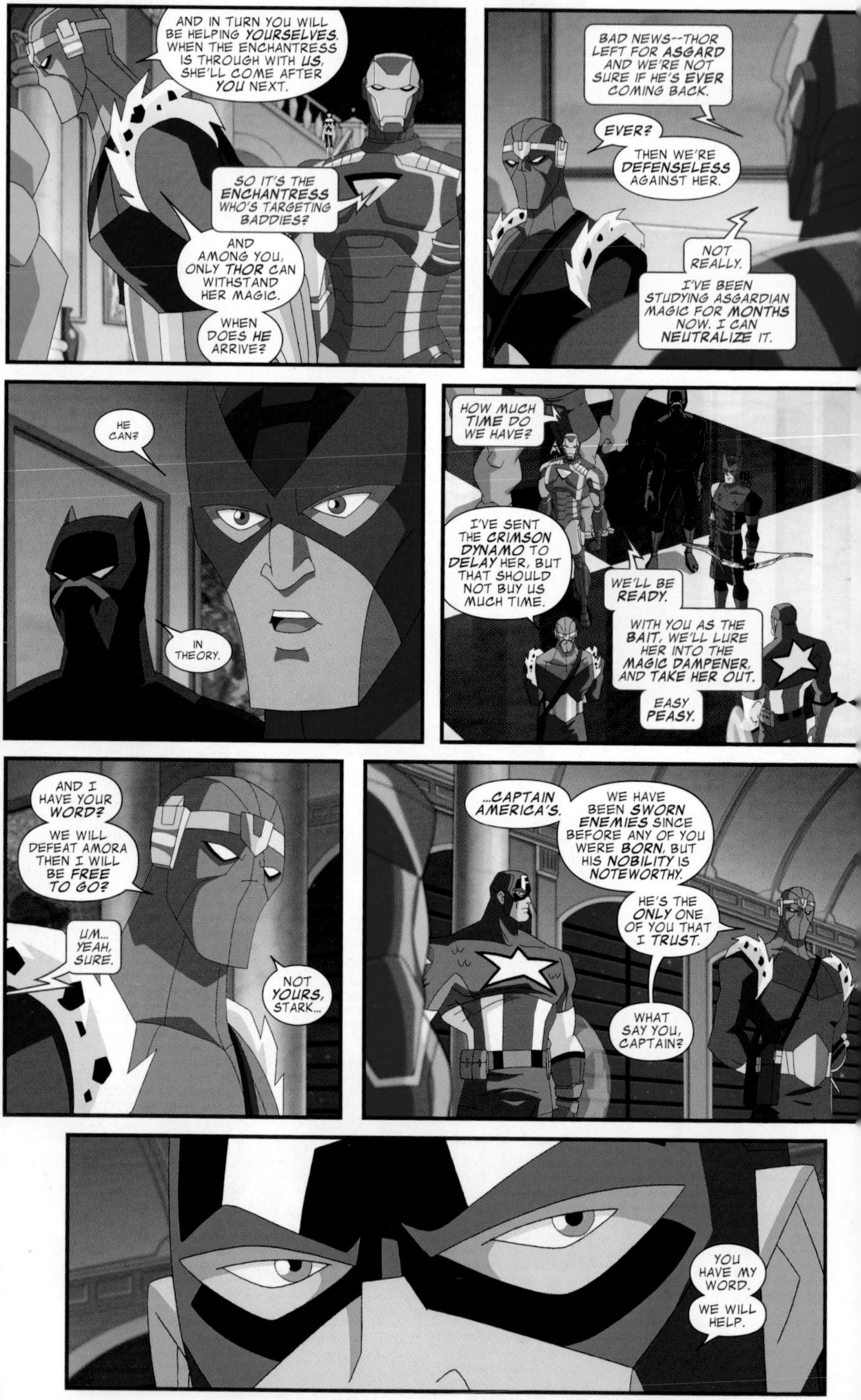
AND IN TURN YOU WILL BE HELPING YOURSELVES. WHEN THE ENCHANTRESS IS THROUGH WITH US, SHE'LL COME AFTER YOU NEXT.
SO IT'S THE ENCHANTRESS WHO'S TARGETING BADDIES?
AND AMONG YOU, ONLY THOR CAN WITHSTAND HER MAGIC.
WHEN DOES HE ARRIVE?
BAD NEWS--THOR LEFT FOR ASGARD AND WE'RE NOT SURE IF HE'S EVER COMING BACK.
EVER?
THEN WE'RE DEFENSELESS AGAINST HER.
NOT REALLY.
I'VE BEEN STUDYING ASGARDIAN MAGIC FOR MONTHS NOW. I CAN NEUTRALIZE IT.
HE CAN?
IN THEORY.
HOW MUCH TIME DO WE HAVE?
I'VE SENT THE CRIMSON DYNAMO TO DELAY HER, BUT THAT SHOULD NOT BUY US MUCH TIME.
WE'LL BE READY.
WITH YOU AS THE BAIT, WE'LL LURE HER INTO THE MAGIC DAMPENER, AND TAKE HER OUT.
EASY PEASY.
AND I HAVE YOUR WORD?
WE WILL DEFEAT AMORA THEN I WILL BE FREE TO GO?
UM... YEAH, SURE.
NOT YOURS, STARK...
...CAPTAIN AMERICA'S.
WE HAVE BEEN SWORN ENEMIES SINCE BEFORE ANY OF YOU WERE BORN, BUT HIS NOBILITY IS NOTEWORTHY.
HE'S THE ONLY ONE OF YOU THAT I TRUST.
WHAT SAY YOU, CAPTAIN?
YOU HAVE MY WORD.
WE WILL HELP.

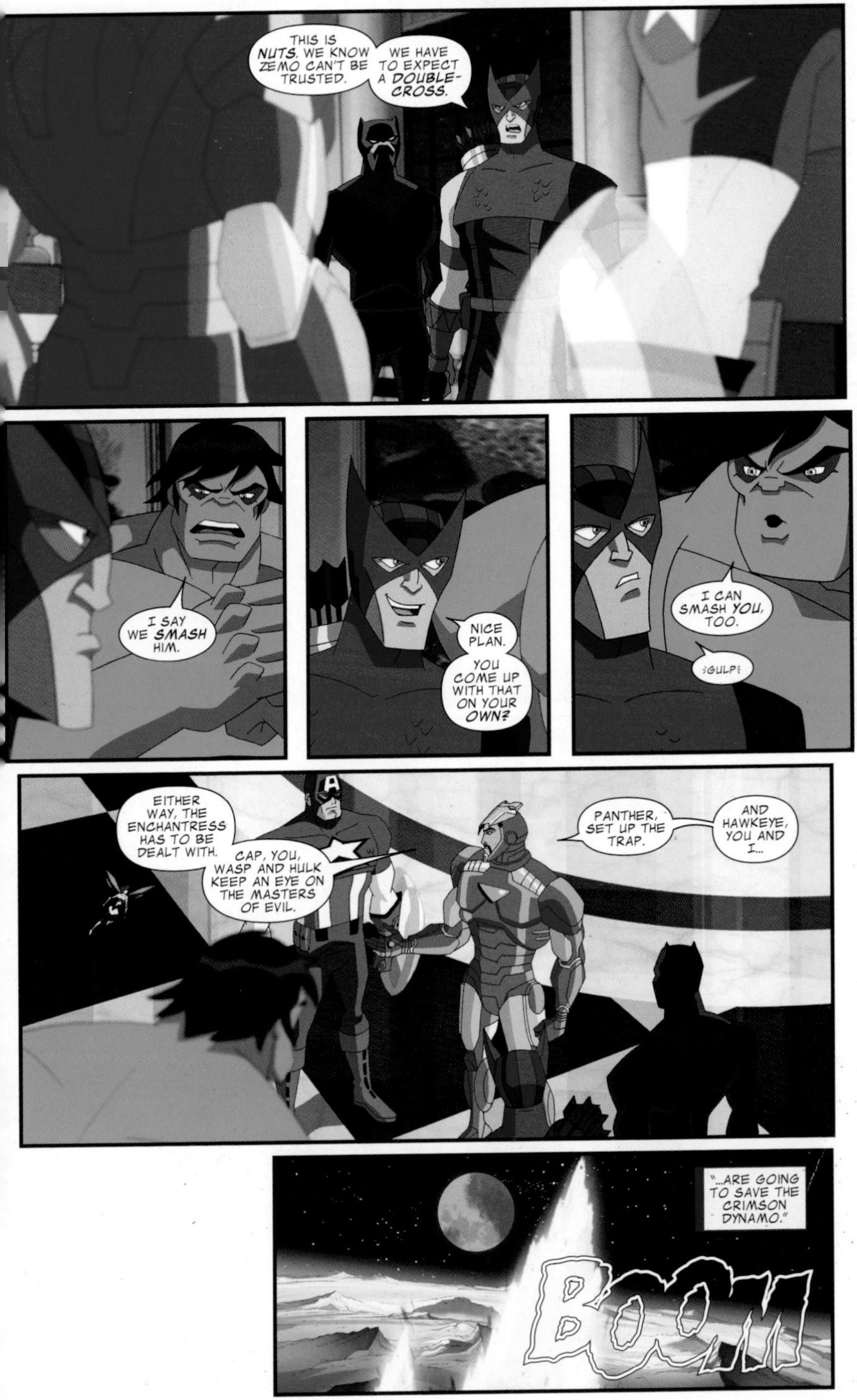
THIS IS NUTS. WE KNOW ZEMO CAN'T BE TRUSTED.
WE HAVE TO EXPECT A DOUBLE-CROSS.
I SAY WE SMASH HIM.
NICE PLAN.
YOU COME UP WITH THAT ON YOUR OWN?
I CAN SMASH YOU, TOO.
GULP
EITHER WAY, THE ENCHANTRESS HAS TO BE DEALT WITH.
CAP, YOU, WASP AND HULK KEEP AN EYE ON THE MASTERS OF EVIL.
PANTHER, SET UP THE TRAP.
AND HAWKEYE, YOU AND I...
"...ARE GOING TO SAVE THE CRIMSON DYNAMO."
BOOM

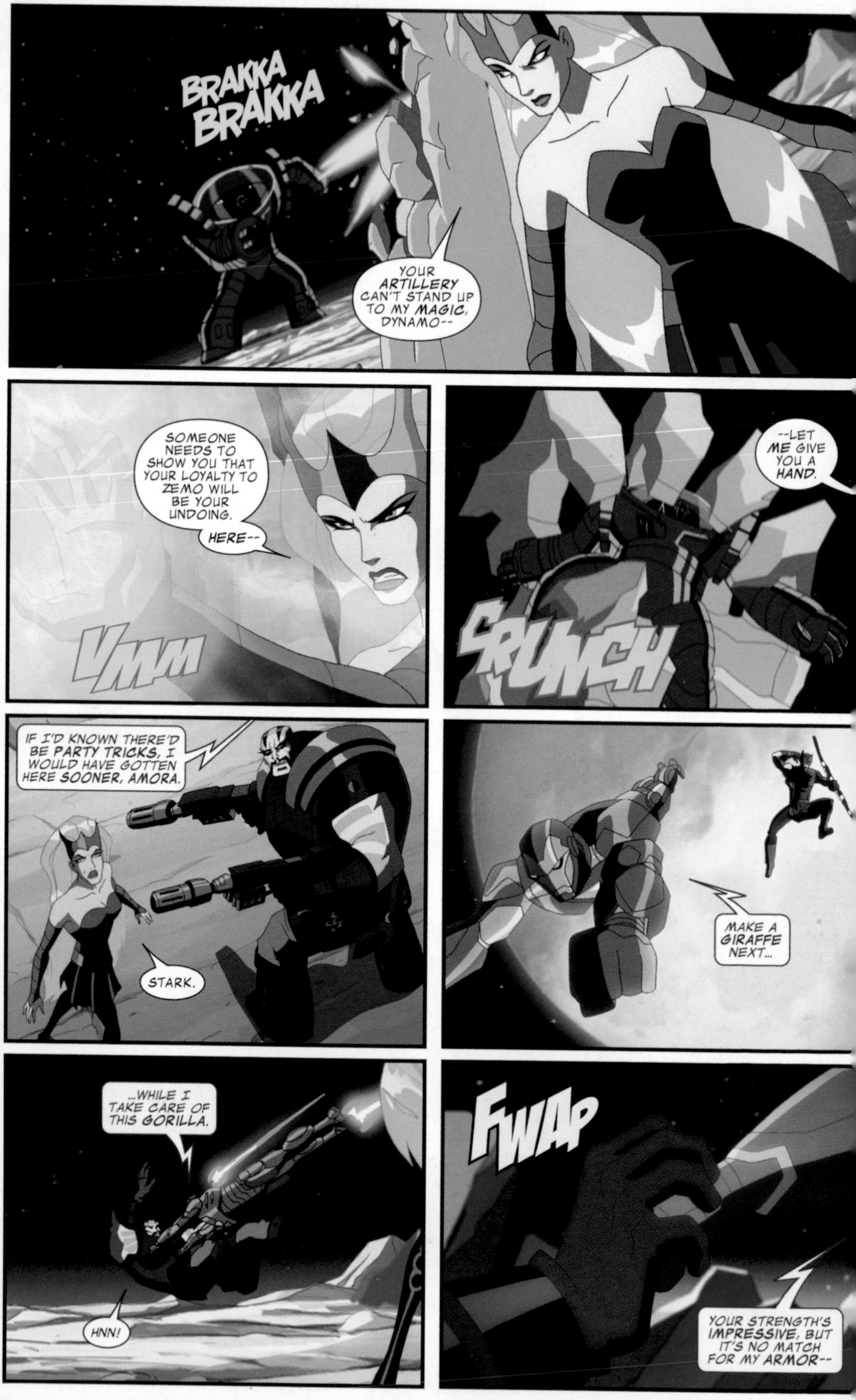
BRAKKA BRAKKA
YOUR ARTILLERY CAN'T STAND UP TO MY MAGIC, DYNAMO--
SOMEONE NEEDS TO SHOW YOU THAT YOUR LOYALTY TO ZEMO WILL BE YOUR UNDOING.
HERE--
VMM
--LET ME GIVE YOU A HAND.
CRUNCH
IF I'D KNOWN THERE'D BE PARTY TRICKS, I WOULD HAVE GOTTEN HERE SOONER, AMORA.
STARK.
MAKE A GIRAFFE NEXT...
...WHILE I TAKE CARE OF THIS GORILLA.
HNN!
FWAP
YOUR STRENGTH'S IMPRESSIVE, BUT IT'S NO MATCH FOR MY ARMOR--

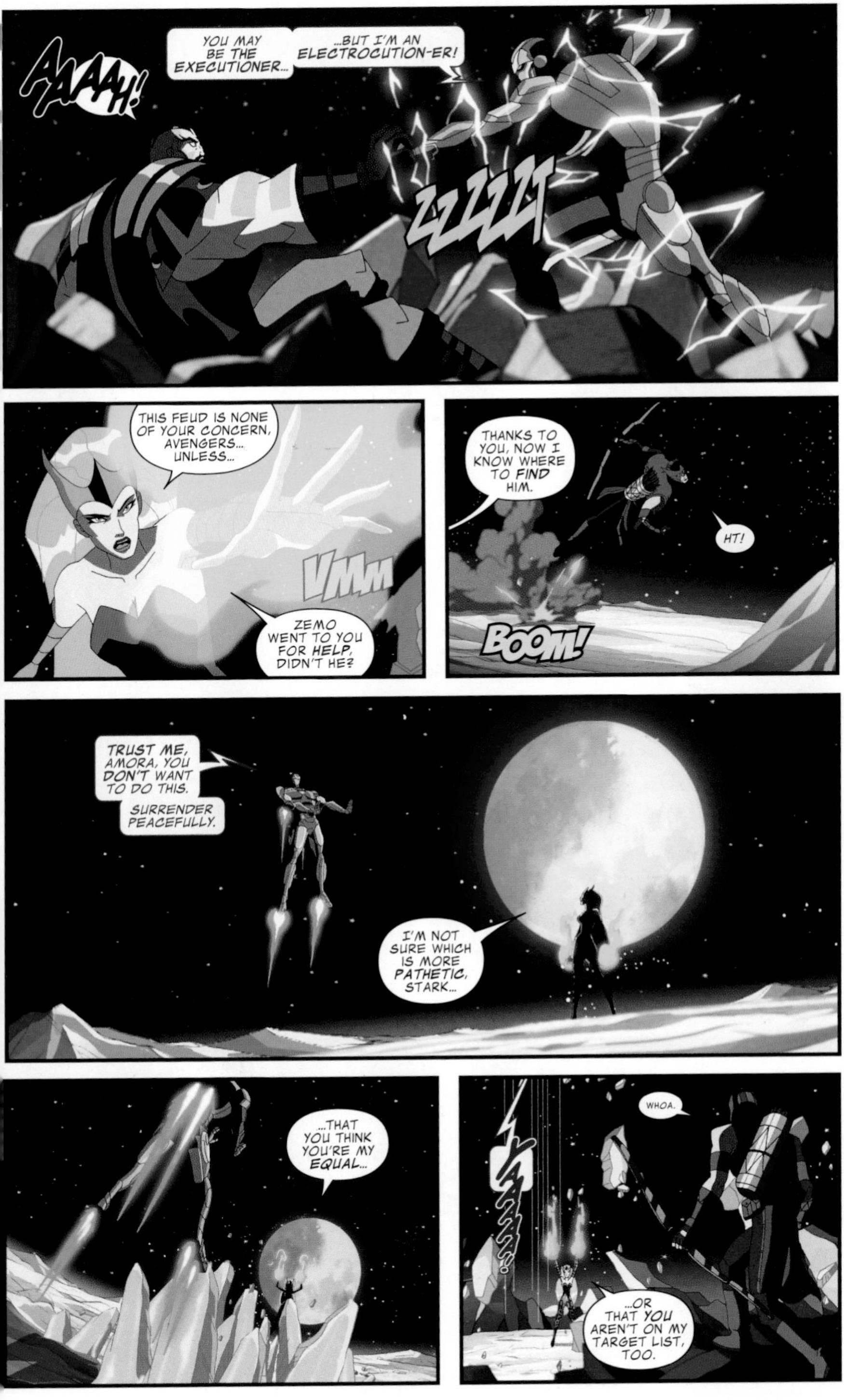
AAAAH!
YOU MAY BE THE EXECUTIONER...
...BUT I'M AN ELECTROCUTION-ER!
ZZZZZT
THIS FEUD IS NONE OF YOUR CONCERN, AVENGERS... UNLESS...
VMMM
ZEMO WENT TO YOU FOR HELP, DIDN'T HE?
THANKS TO YOU, NOW I KNOW WHERE TO FIND HIM.
HT!
BOOM!
TRUST ME, AMORA, YOU DON'T WANT TO DO THIS.
SURRENDER PEACEFULLY.
I'M NOT SURE WHICH IS MORE PATHETIC, STARK...
...THAT YOU THINK YOU'RE MY EQUAL...
WHOA.
...OR THAT YOU AREN'T ON MY TARGET LIST, TOO.

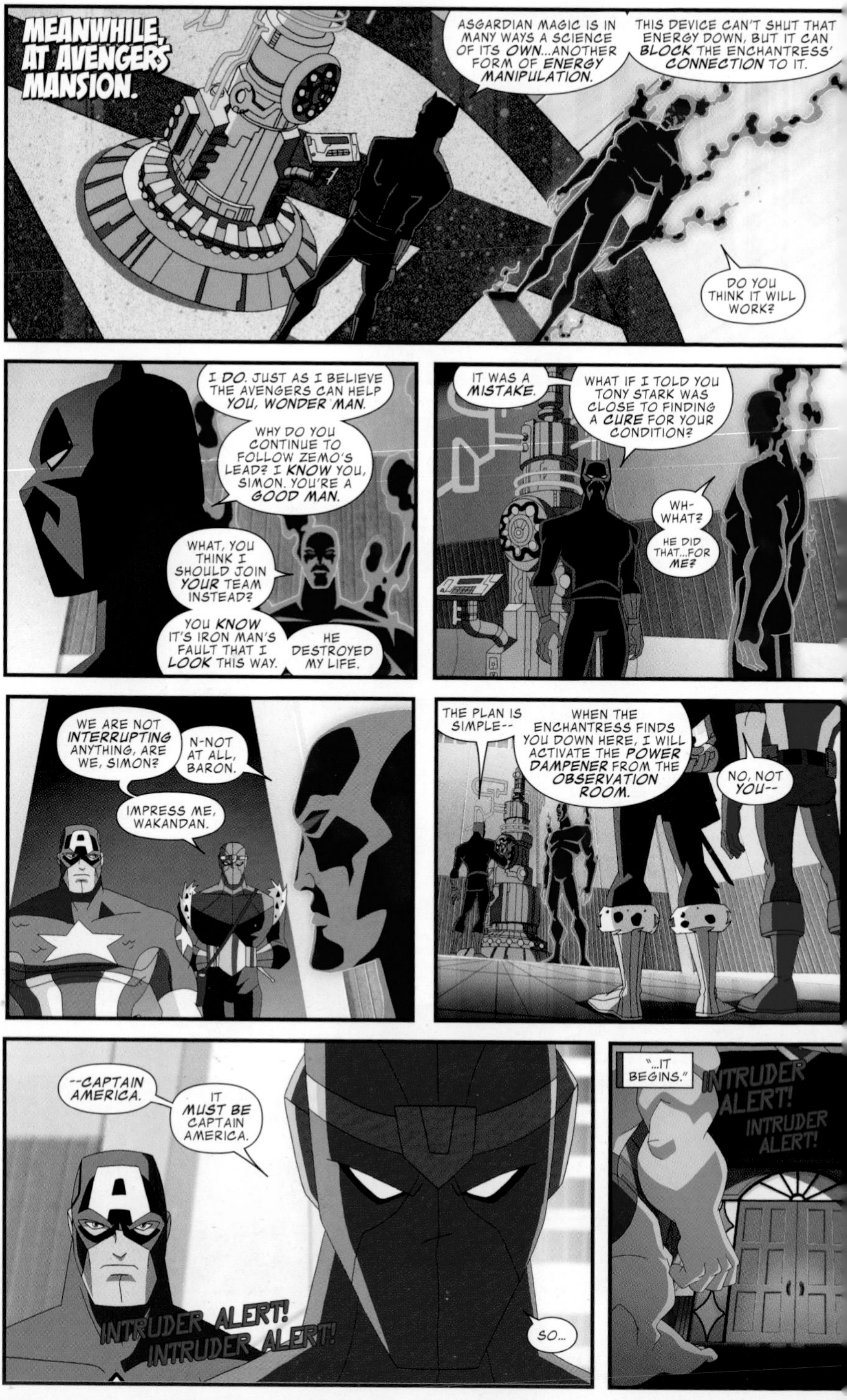
MEANWHILE, AT AVENGERS MANSION.
ASGARDIAN MAGIC IS IN MANY WAYS A SCIENCE OF ITS OWN...ANOTHER FORM OF ENERGY MANIPULATION.
THIS DEVICE CAN'T SHUT THAT ENERGY DOWN, BUT IT CAN BLOCK THE ENCHANTRESS' CONNECTION TO IT.
DO YOU THINK IT WILL WORK?
I DO. JUST AS I BELIEVE THE AVENGERS CAN HELP YOU, WONDER MAN.
WHY DO YOU CONTINUE TO FOLLOW ZEMO'S LEAD? I KNOW YOU, SIMON. YOU'RE A GOOD MAN.
WHAT, YOU THINK I SHOULD JOIN YOUR TEAM INSTEAD?
YOU KNOW IT'S IRON MAN'S FAULT THAT I LOOK THIS WAY.
HE DESTROYED MY LIFE.
IT WAS A MISTAKE.
WHAT IF I TOLD YOU TONY STARK WAS CLOSE TO FINDING A CURE FOR YOUR CONDITION?
WH-WHAT?
HE DID THAT...FOR ME?
WE ARE NOT INTERRUPTING ANYTHING, ARE WE, SIMON?
N-NOT AT ALL, BARON.
IMPRESS ME, WAKANDAN.
THE PLAN IS SIMPLE--
WHEN THE ENCHANTRESS FINDS YOU DOWN HERE, I WILL ACTIVATE THE POWER DAMPENER FROM THE OBSERVATION ROOM.
NO, NOT YOU--
--CAPTAIN AMERICA.
IT MUST BE CAPTAIN AMERICA.
INTRUDER ALERT! INTRUDER ALERT!
SO...
"...IT BEGINS."
INTRUDER ALERT! INTRUDER ALERT!

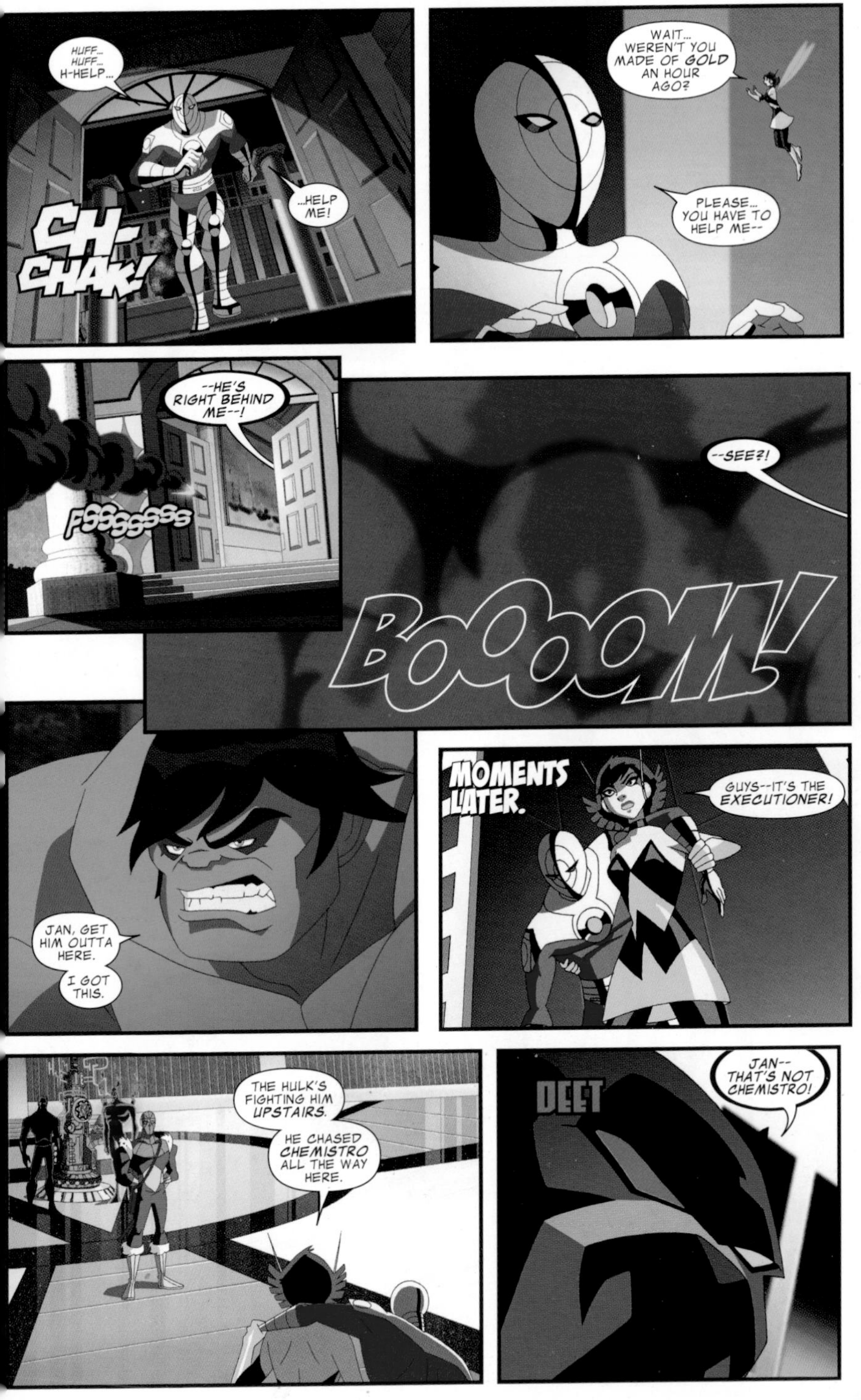
HUFF... HUFF... H-HELP...
...HELP ME!
CH-CHAK!
WAIT... WEREN'T YOU MADE OF GOLD AN HOUR AGO?
PLEASE... YOU HAVE TO HELP ME--
--HE'S RIGHT BEHIND ME--!
FSSSSSSS
--SEE?!
BOOOOM!
JAN, GET HIM OUTTA HERE.
I GOT THIS.
MOMENTS LATER.
GUYS--IT'S THE EXECUTIONER!
THE HULK'S FIGHTING HIM UPSTAIRS.
HE CHASED CHEMISTRO ALL THE WAY HERE.
DEET
JAN-- THAT'S NOT CHEMISTRO!

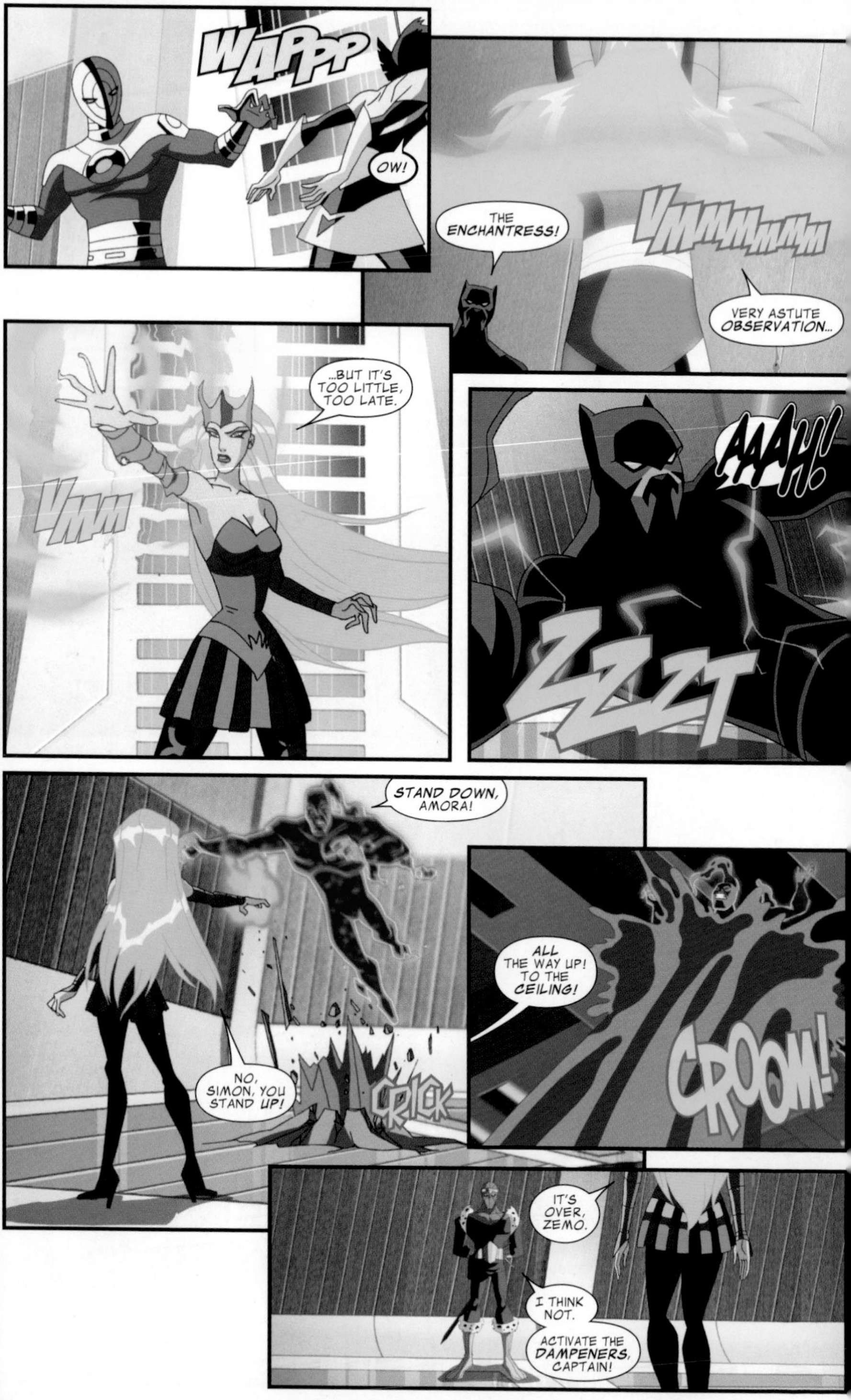
WAPPP
OW!
THE ENCHANTRESS!
VMMMMMMM
VERY ASTUTE OBSERVATION...
...BUT IT'S TOO LITTLE, TOO LATE.
VMM
AAAH!
ZZZT
STAND DOWN, AMORA!
NO, SIMON, YOU STAND UP!
CRICK
ALL THE WAY UP! TO THE CEILING!
CROOM!
IT'S OVER, ZEMO.
I THINK NOT.
ACTIVATE THE DAMPENERS, CAPTAIN!

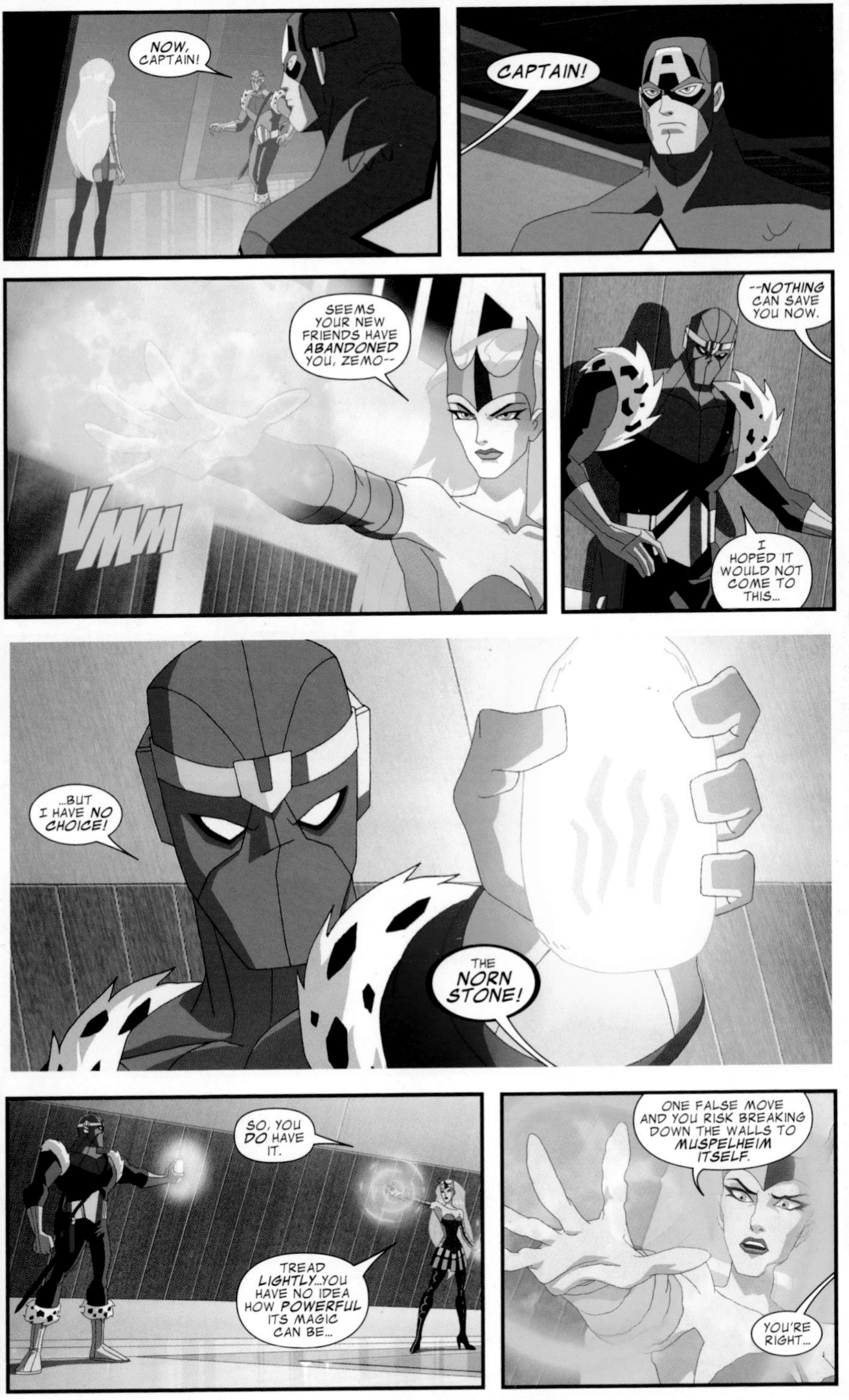
NOW, CAPTAIN!
CAPTAIN!
SEEMS YOUR NEW FRIENDS HAVE ABANDONED YOU, ZEMO--
--NOTHING CAN SAVE YOU NOW.
VMM
I HOPED IT WOULD NOT COME TO THIS...
...BUT I HAVE NO CHOICE!
THE NORN STONE!
SO, YOU DO HAVE IT.
TREAD LIGHTLY...YOU HAVE NO IDEA HOW POWERFUL ITS MAGIC CAN BE...
ONE FALSE MOVE AND YOU RISK BREAKING DOWN THE WALLS TO MUSPELHEIM ITSELF.
YOU'RE RIGHT...

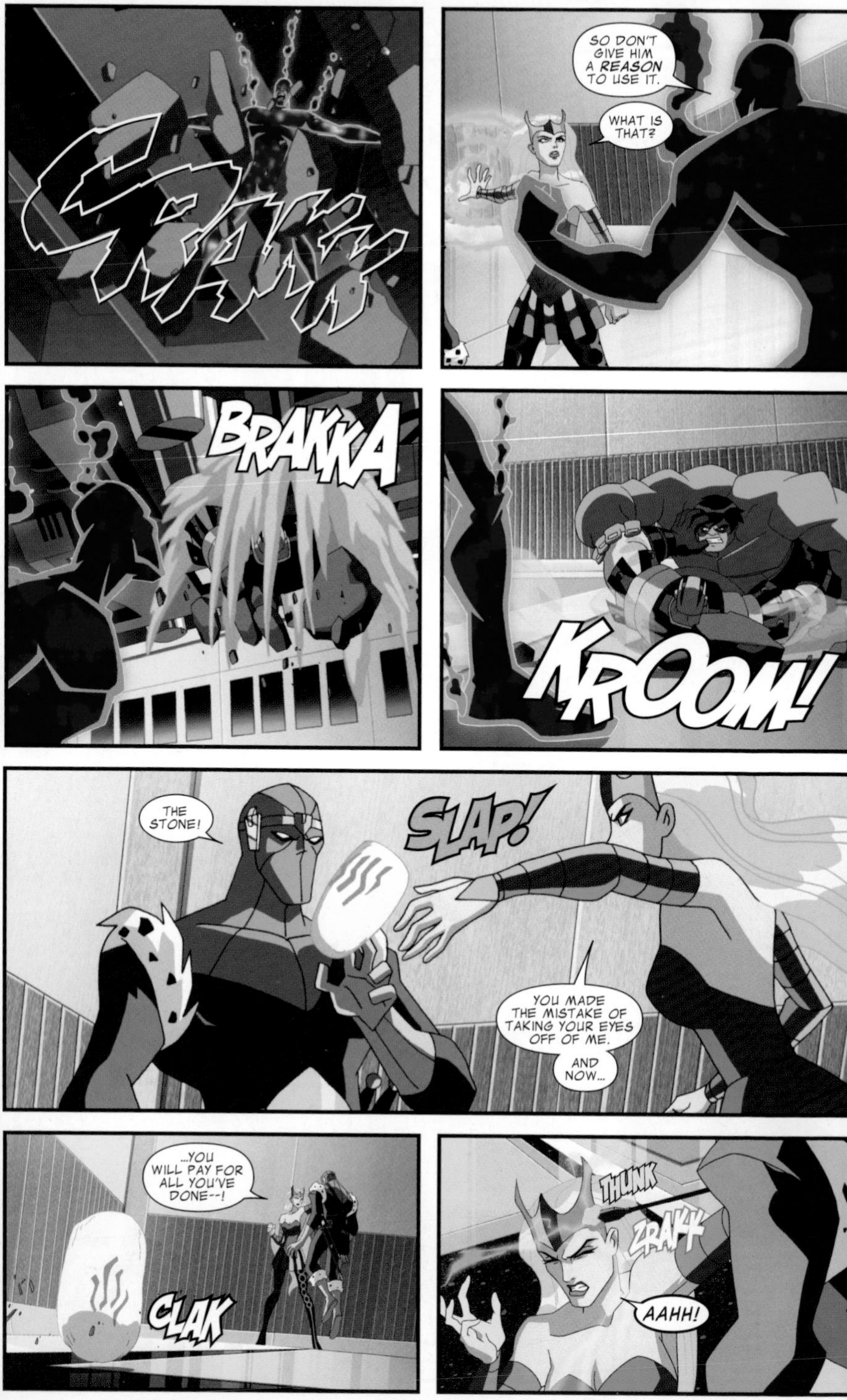
SO DON'T GIVE HIM A REASON TO USE IT.
WHAT IS THAT?
BRAKKA
KROOOM!
THE STONE!
SLAP!
YOU MADE THE MISTAKE OF TAKING YOUR EYES OFF OF ME.
AND NOW...
...YOU WILL PAY FOR ALL YOU'VE DONE--!
CLAK
THUNK
ZRAKK
AAHH!

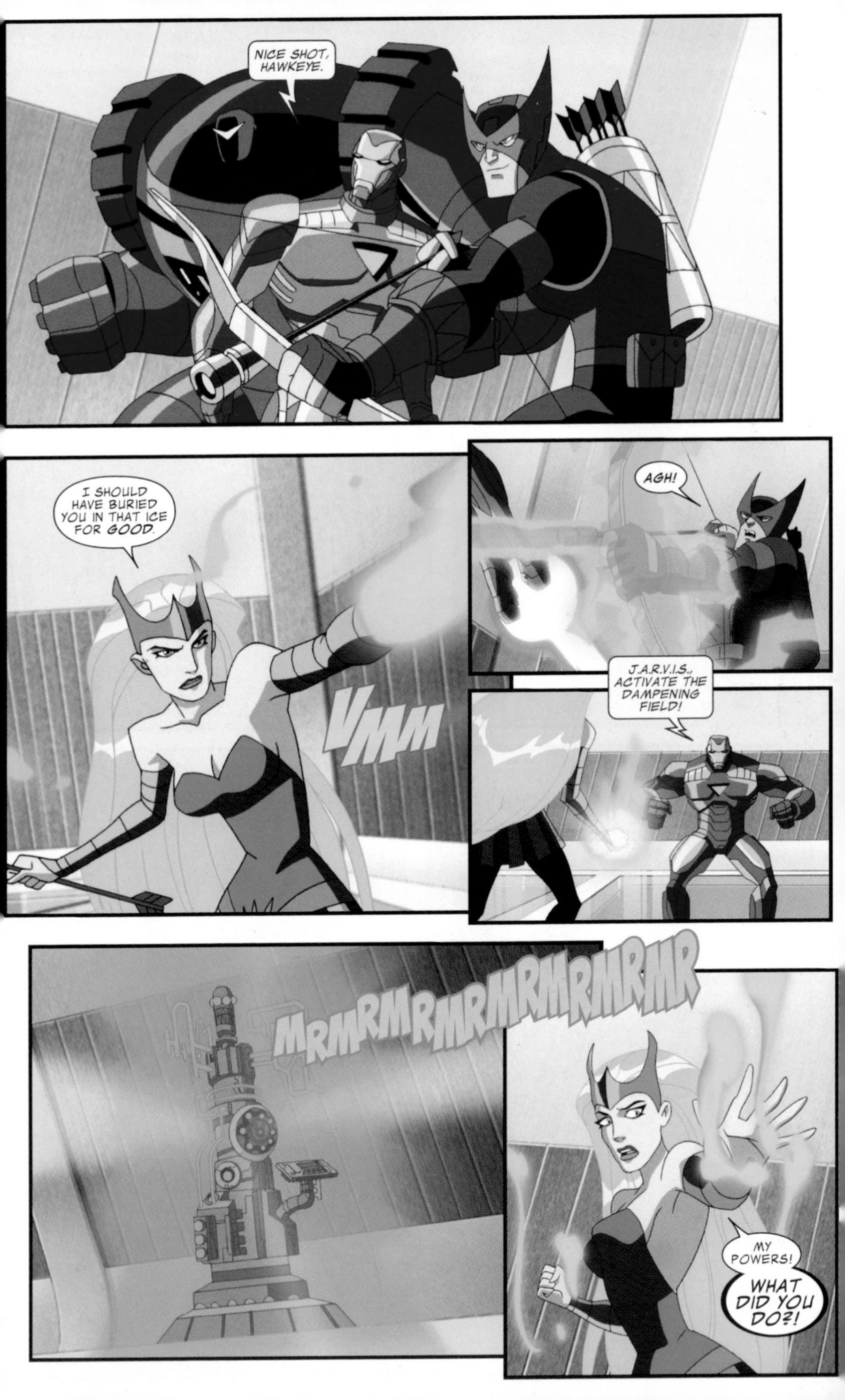
NICE SHOT, HAWKEYE.
I SHOULD HAVE BURIED YOU IN THAT ICE FOR GOOD.
VMM
AGH!
J.A.R.V.I.S., ACTIVATE THE DAMPENING FIELD!
MRMRMRMRMRMRMRMRMR
MY POWERS!
WHAT DID YOU DO?!

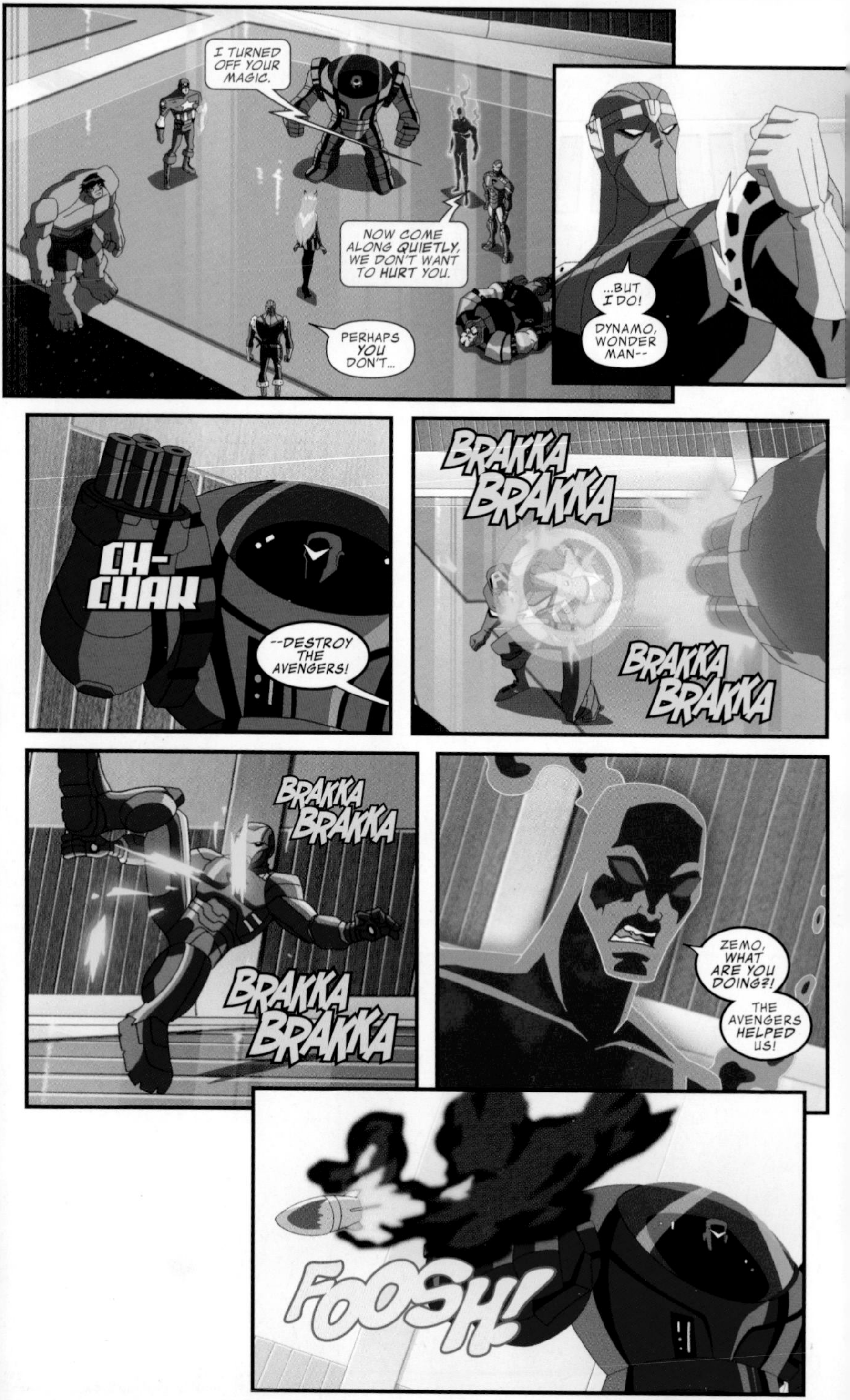
I TURNED OFF YOUR MAGIC.
NOW COME ALONG QUIETLY, WE DON'T WANT TO HURT YOU.
PERHAPS YOU DON'T...
...BUT I DO!
DYNAMO, WONDER MAN--
CH-CHAK
--DESTROY THE AVENGERS!
BRAKKA BRAKKA
BRAKKA BRAKKA
BRAKKA BRAKKA
BRAKKA BRAKKA
ZEMO, WHAT ARE YOU DOING?!
THE AVENGERS HELPED US!
FOOSH!

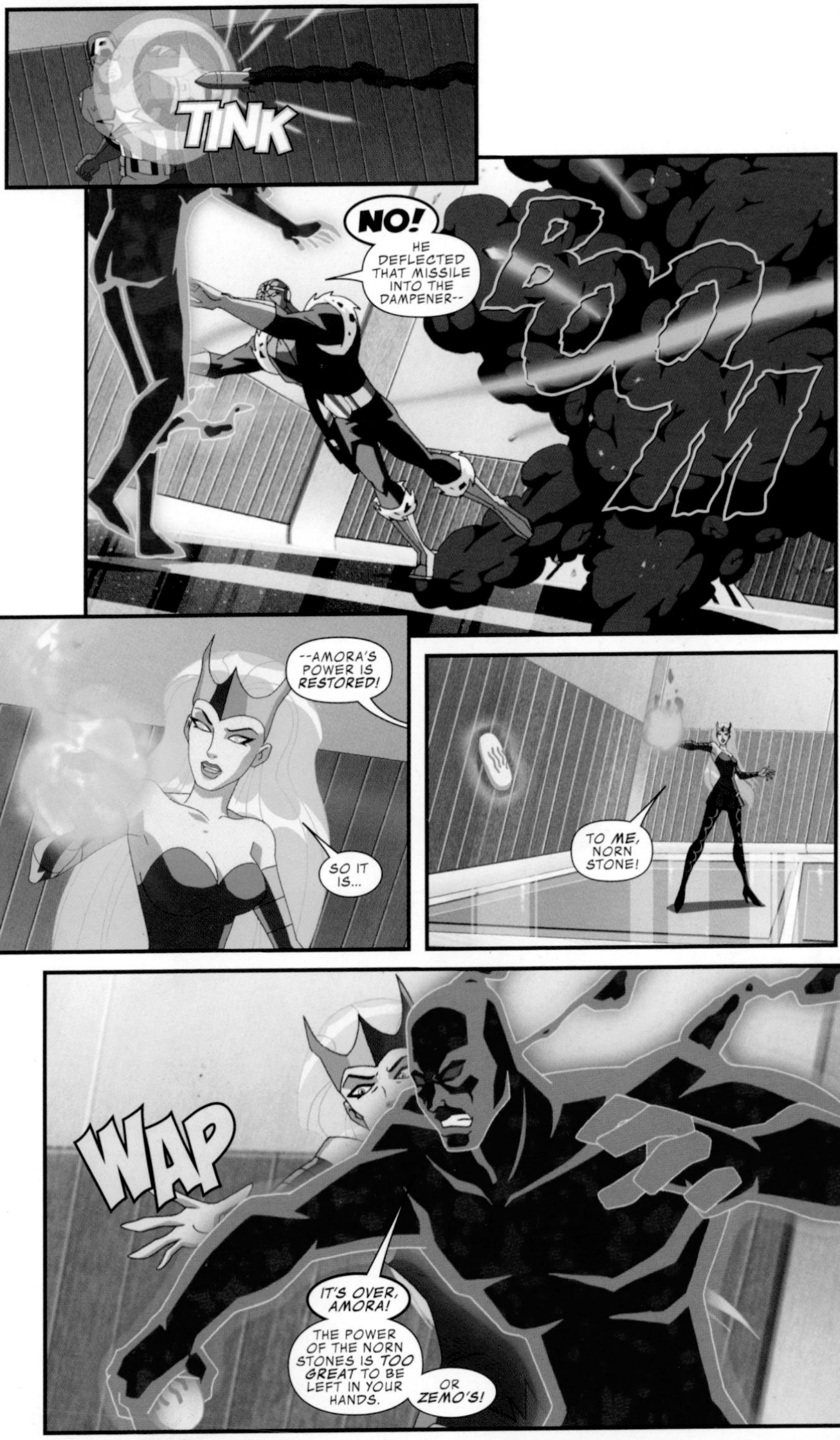
TINK
NO!
HE DEFLECTED THAT MISSILE INTO THE DAMPENER--
BOOM
--AMORA'S POWER IS RESTORED!
SO IT IS...
TO ME, NORN STONE!
WAP
IT'S OVER, AMORA!
THE POWER OF THE NORN STONES IS TOO GREAT TO BE LEFT IN YOUR HANDS.
OR ZEMO'S!

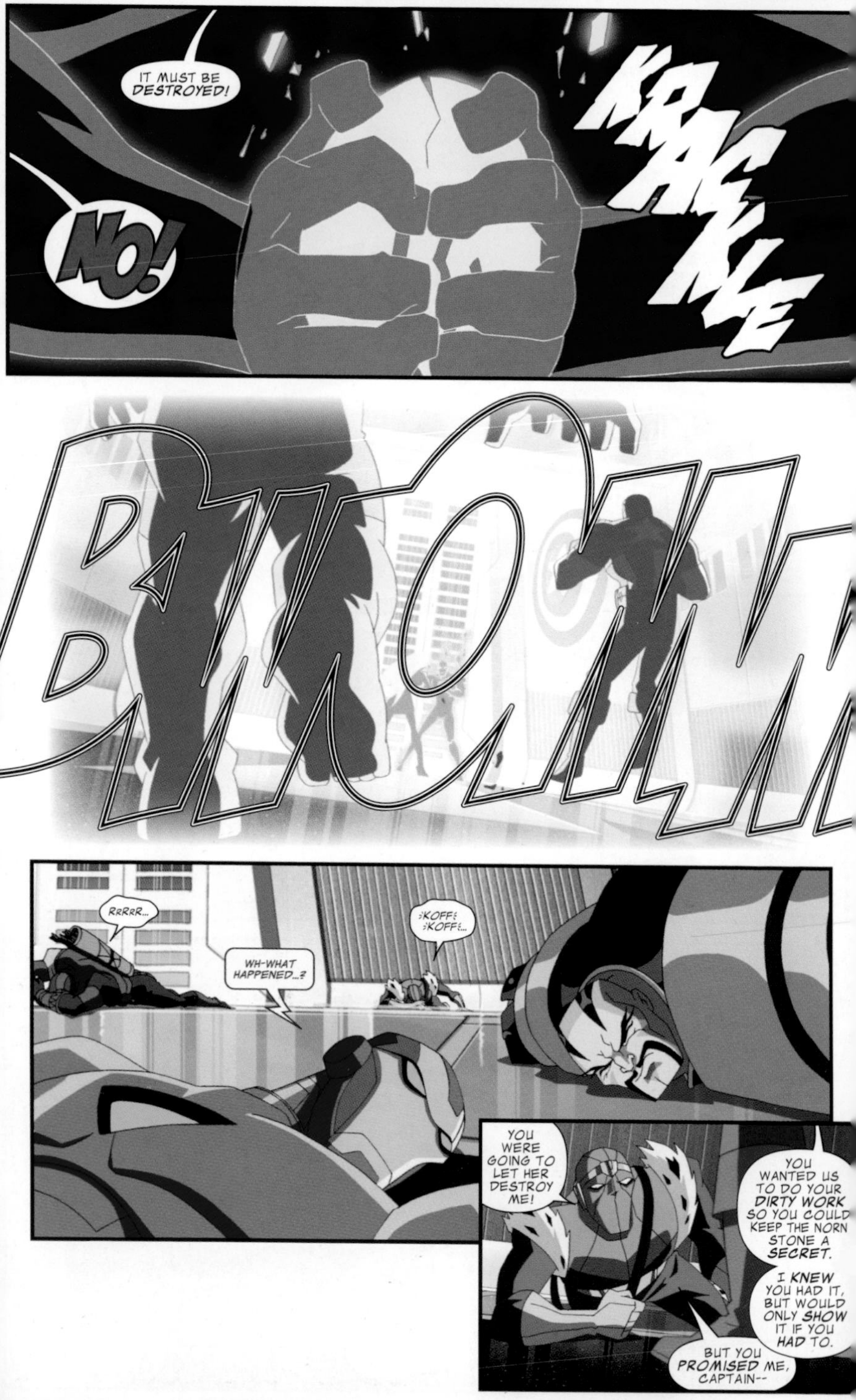
IT MUST BE DESTROYED!
NO!
KRACKLE
BLOOM
RRRRR...
WH-WHAT HAPPENED...?
KOFF KOFF...
YOU WERE GOING TO LET HER DESTROY ME!
YOU WANTED US TO DO YOUR DIRTY WORK SO YOU COULD KEEP THE NORN STONE A SECRET.
I KNEW YOU HAD IT, BUT WOULD ONLY SHOW IT IF YOU HAD TO.
BUT YOU PROMISED ME, CAPTAIN--

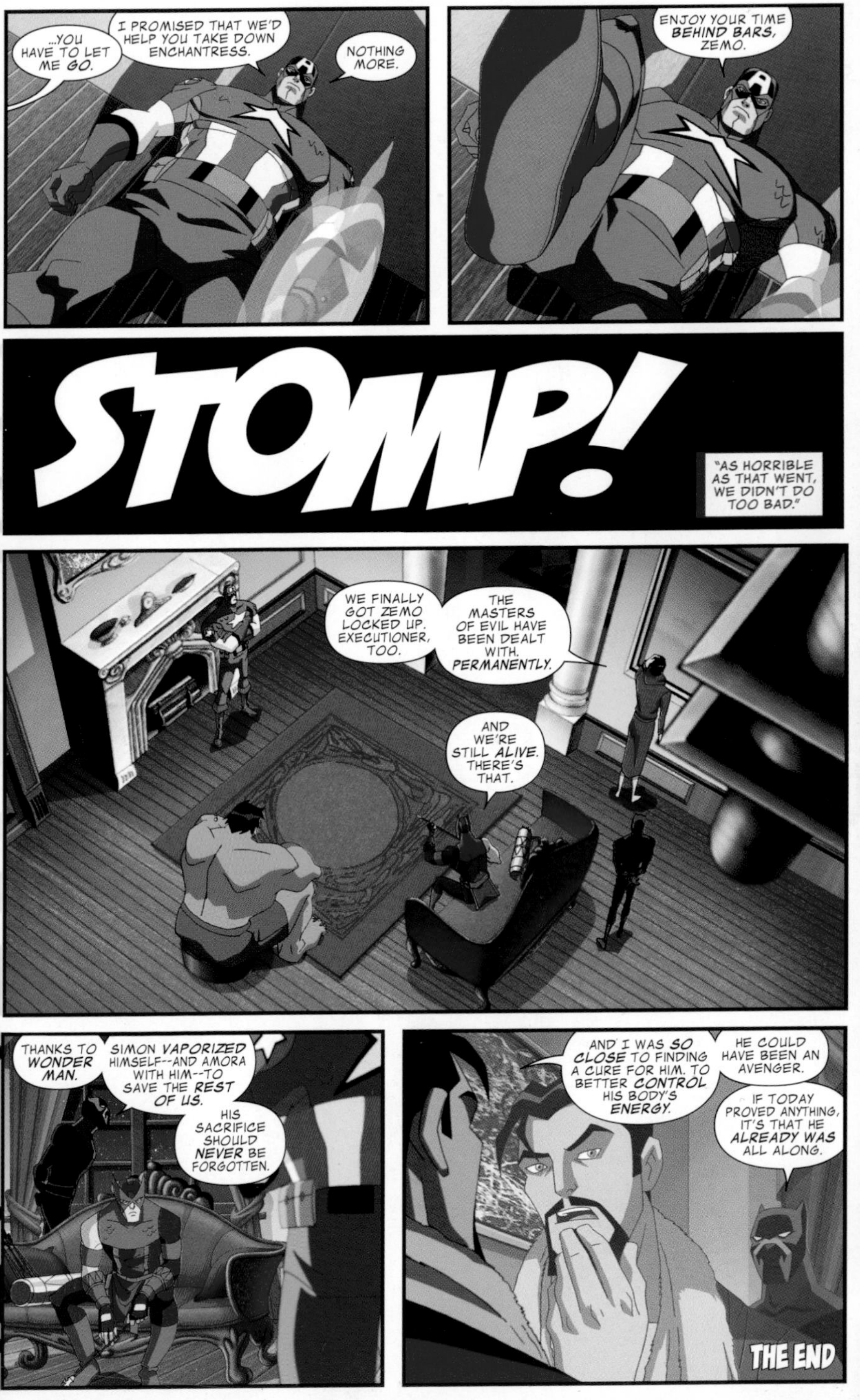
...YOU HAVE TO LET ME GO.
I PROMISED THAT WE'D HELP YOU TAKE DOWN ENCHANTRESS.
NOTHING MORE.
ENJOY YOUR TIME BEHIND BARS, ZEMO.
STOMP!
"AS HORRIBLE AS THAT WENT, WE DIDN'T DO TOO BAD."
WE FINALLY GOT ZEMO LOCKED UP. EXECUTIONER, TOO.
THE MASTERS OF EVIL HAVE BEEN DEALT WITH. PERMANENTLY.
AND WE'RE STILL ALIVE. THERE'S THAT.
THANKS TO WONDER MAN.
SIMON VAPORIZED HIMSELF--AND AMORA WITH HIM--TO SAVE THE REST OF US.
HIS SACRIFICE SHOULD NEVER BE FORGOTTEN.
AND I WAS SO CLOSE TO FINDING A CURE FOR HIM. TO BETTER CONTROL HIS BODY'S ENERGY.
HE COULD HAVE BEEN AN AVENGER.
IF TODAY PROVED ANYTHING, IT'S THAT HE ALREADY WAS ALL ALONG.
THE END

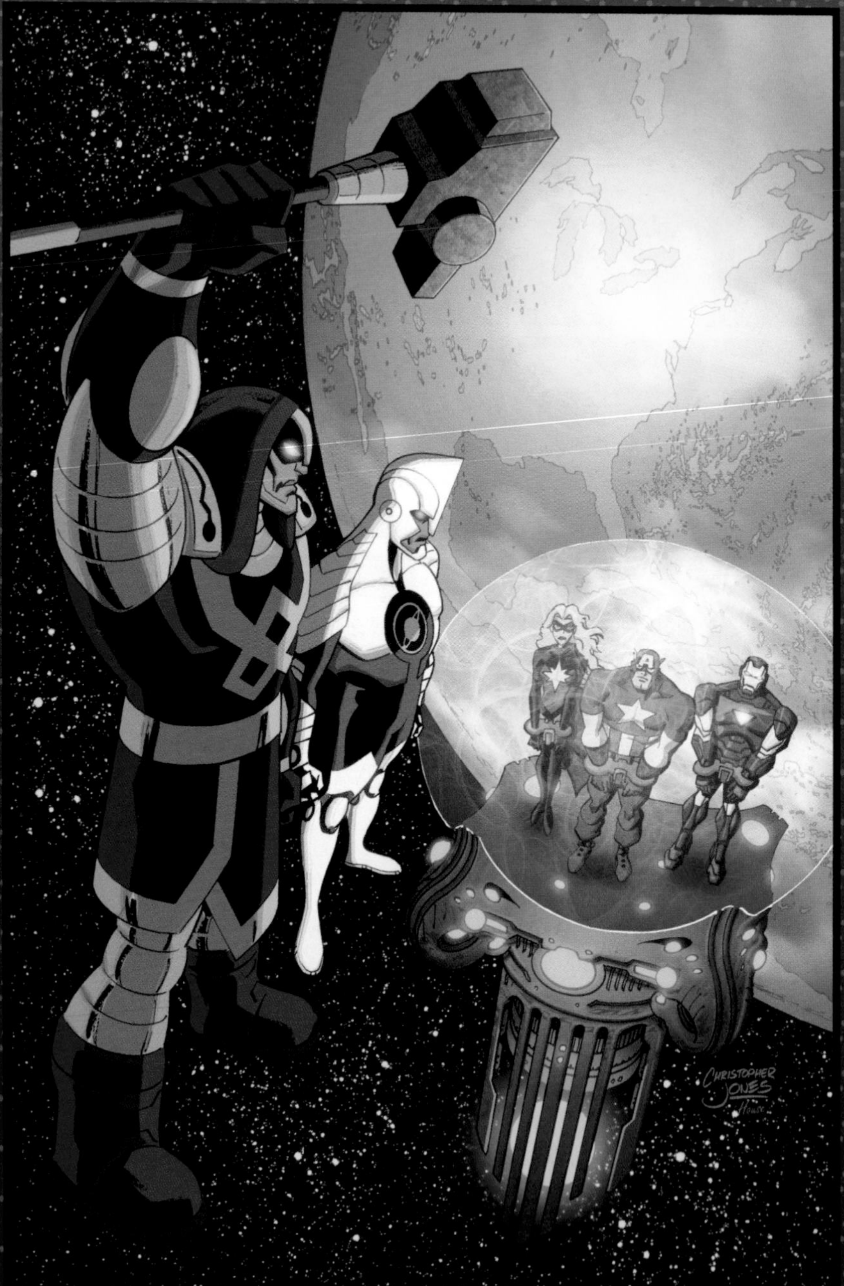
CHRISTOPHER JONES
House

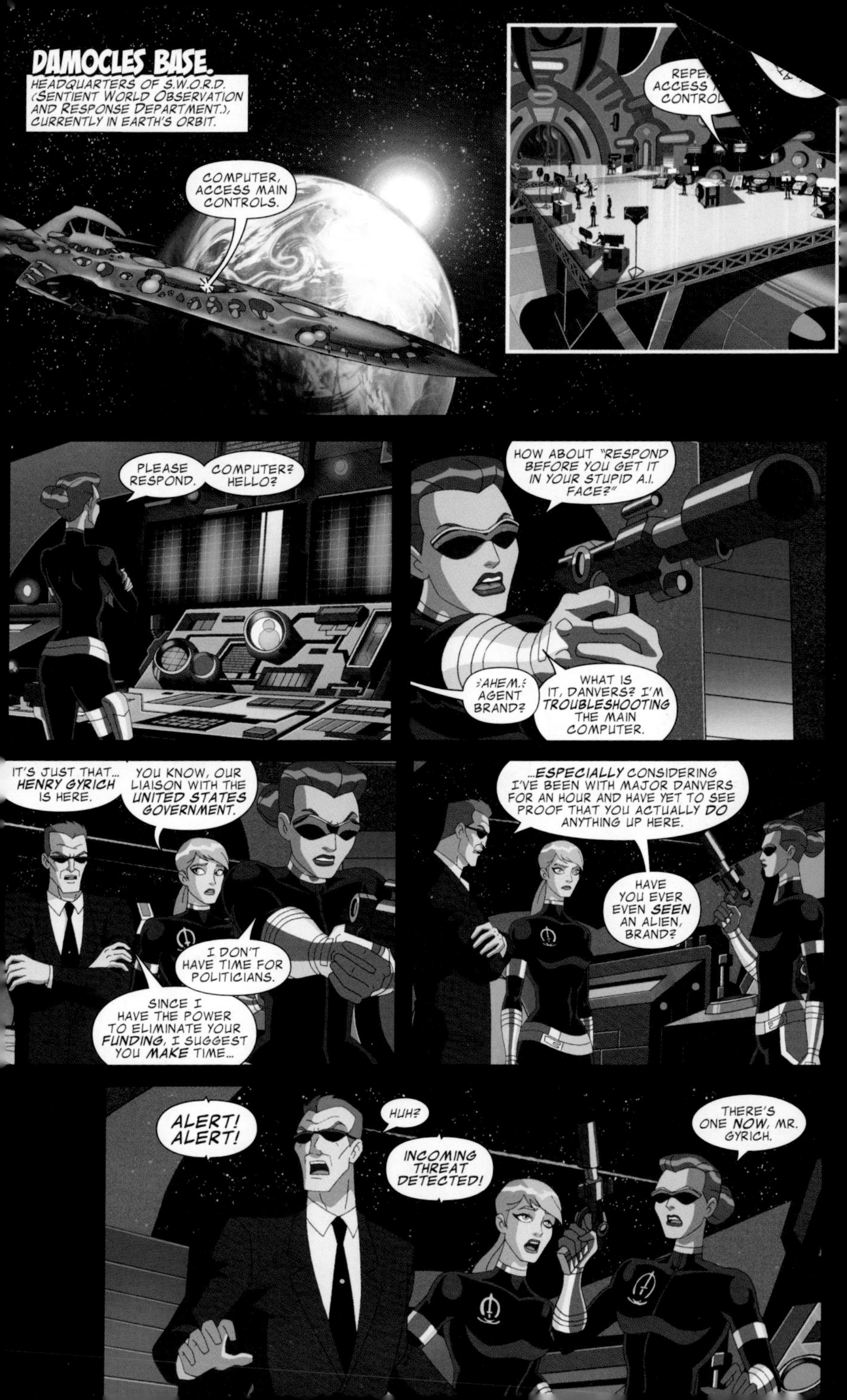
DAMOCLES BASE.
HEADQUARTERS OF S.W.O.R.D. (SENTIENT WORLD OBSERVATION AND RESPONSE DEPARTMENT.), CURRENTLY IN EARTH'S ORBIT.
COMPUTER, ACCESS MAIN CONTROLS.
ACCESS
PLEASE RESPOND.
COMPUTER? HELLO?
HOW ABOUT "RESPOND BEFORE YOU GET IT IN YOUR STUPID A.I. FACE?"
:AHEM.: AGENT BRAND?
WHAT IS IT, DANVERS? I'M TROUBLESHOOTING THE MAIN COMPUTER.
IT'S JUST THAT... HENRY GYRICH IS HERE.
YOU KNOW, OUR LIAISON WITH THE UNITED STATES GOVERNMENT.
I DON'T HAVE TIME FOR POLITICIANS.
SINCE I HAVE THE POWER TO ELIMINATE YOUR FUNDING, I SUGGEST YOU MAKE TIME...
...ESPECIALLY CONSIDERING I'VE BEEN WITH MAJOR DANVERS FOR AN HOUR AND HAVE YET TO SEE PROOF THAT YOU ACTUALLY DO ANYTHING UP HERE.
HAVE YOU EVER EVEN SEEN AN ALIEN, BRAND?
ALERT! ALERT!
HUH?
INCOMING THREAT DETECTED!
THERE'S ONE NOW, MR. GYRICH.

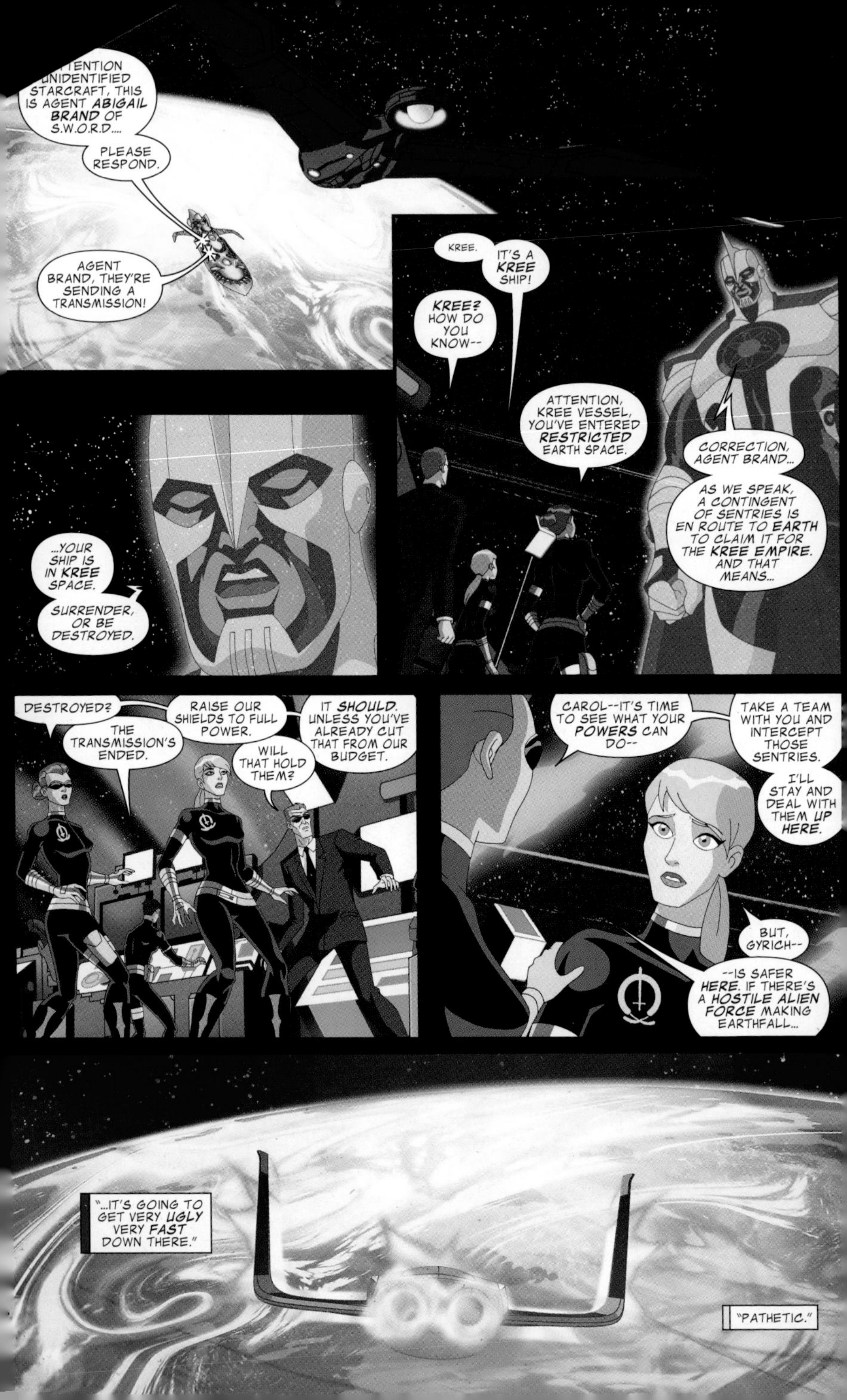

...TENTION UNIDENTIFIED STARCRAFT, THIS IS AGENT ABIGAIL BRAND OF S.W.O.R.D....
PLEASE RESPOND.
AGENT BRAND, THEY'RE SENDING A TRANSMISSION!
KREE.
IT'S A KREE SHIP!
KREE? HOW DO YOU KNOW--
ATTENTION, KREE VESSEL, YOU'VE ENTERED RESTRICTED EARTH SPACE.
CORRECTION, AGENT BRAND...
AS WE SPEAK, A CONTINGENT OF SENTRIES IS EN ROUTE TO EARTH TO CLAIM IT FOR THE KREE EMPIRE. AND THAT MEANS...
...YOUR SHIP IS IN KREE SPACE.
SURRENDER, OR BE DESTROYED.
DESTROYED?
THE TRANSMISSION'S ENDED.
RAISE OUR SHIELDS TO FULL POWER.
WILL THAT HOLD THEM?
IT SHOULD. UNLESS YOU'VE ALREADY CUT THAT FROM OUR BUDGET.
CAROL--IT'S TIME TO SEE WHAT YOUR POWERS CAN DO--
TAKE A TEAM WITH YOU AND INTERCEPT THOSE SENTRIES.
I'LL STAY AND DEAL WITH THEM UP HERE.
BUT, GYRICH--
--IS SAFER HERE. IF THERE'S A HOSTILE ALIEN FORCE MAKING EARTHFALL...
"...IT'S GOING TO GET VERY UGLY VERY FAST DOWN THERE."
"PATHETIC."

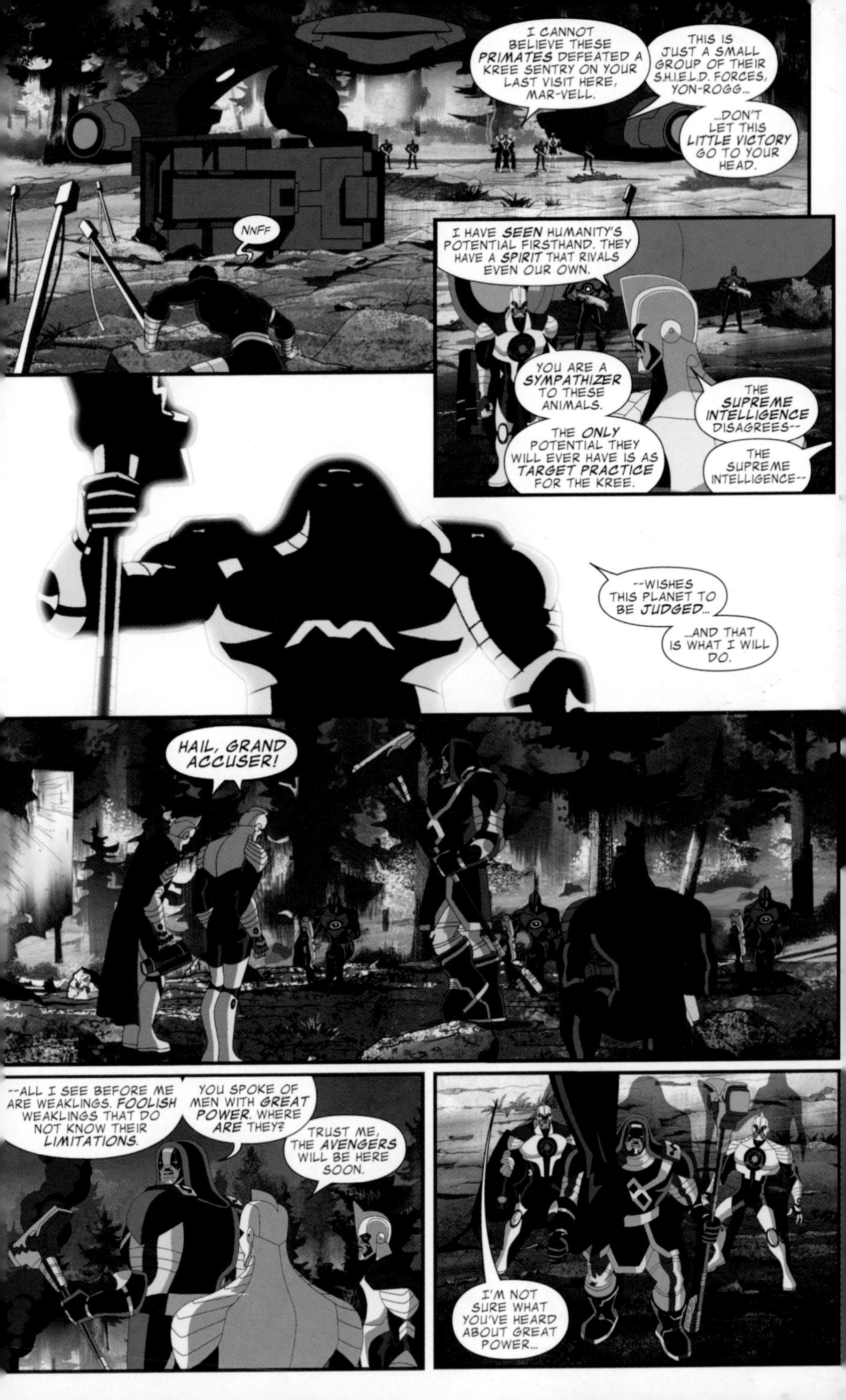
I CANNOT BELIEVE THESE PRIMATES DEFEATED A KREE SENTRY ON YOUR LAST VISIT HERE, MAR-VELL.
THIS IS JUST A SMALL GROUP OF THEIR S.H.I.E.L.D. FORCES, YON-ROGG...
...DON'T LET THIS LITTLE VICTORY GO TO YOUR HEAD.
NNFF
I HAVE SEEN HUMANITY'S POTENTIAL FIRSTHAND. THEY HAVE A SPIRIT THAT RIVALS EVEN OUR OWN.
YOU ARE A SYMPATHIZER TO THESE ANIMALS.
THE ONLY POTENTIAL THEY WILL EVER HAVE IS AS TARGET PRACTICE FOR THE KREE.
THE SUPREME INTELLIGENCE DISAGREES--
THE SUPREME INTELLIGENCE--
--WISHES THIS PLANET TO BE JUDGED...
...AND THAT IS WHAT I WILL DO.
HAIL, GRAND ACCUSER!
--ALL I SEE BEFORE ME ARE WEAKLINGS. FOOLISH WEAKLINGS THAT DO NOT KNOW THEIR LIMITATIONS.
YOU SPOKE OF MEN WITH GREAT POWER. WHERE ARE THEY?
TRUST ME, THE AVENGERS WILL BE HERE SOON.
I'M NOT SURE WHAT YOU'VE HEARD ABOUT GREAT POWER...

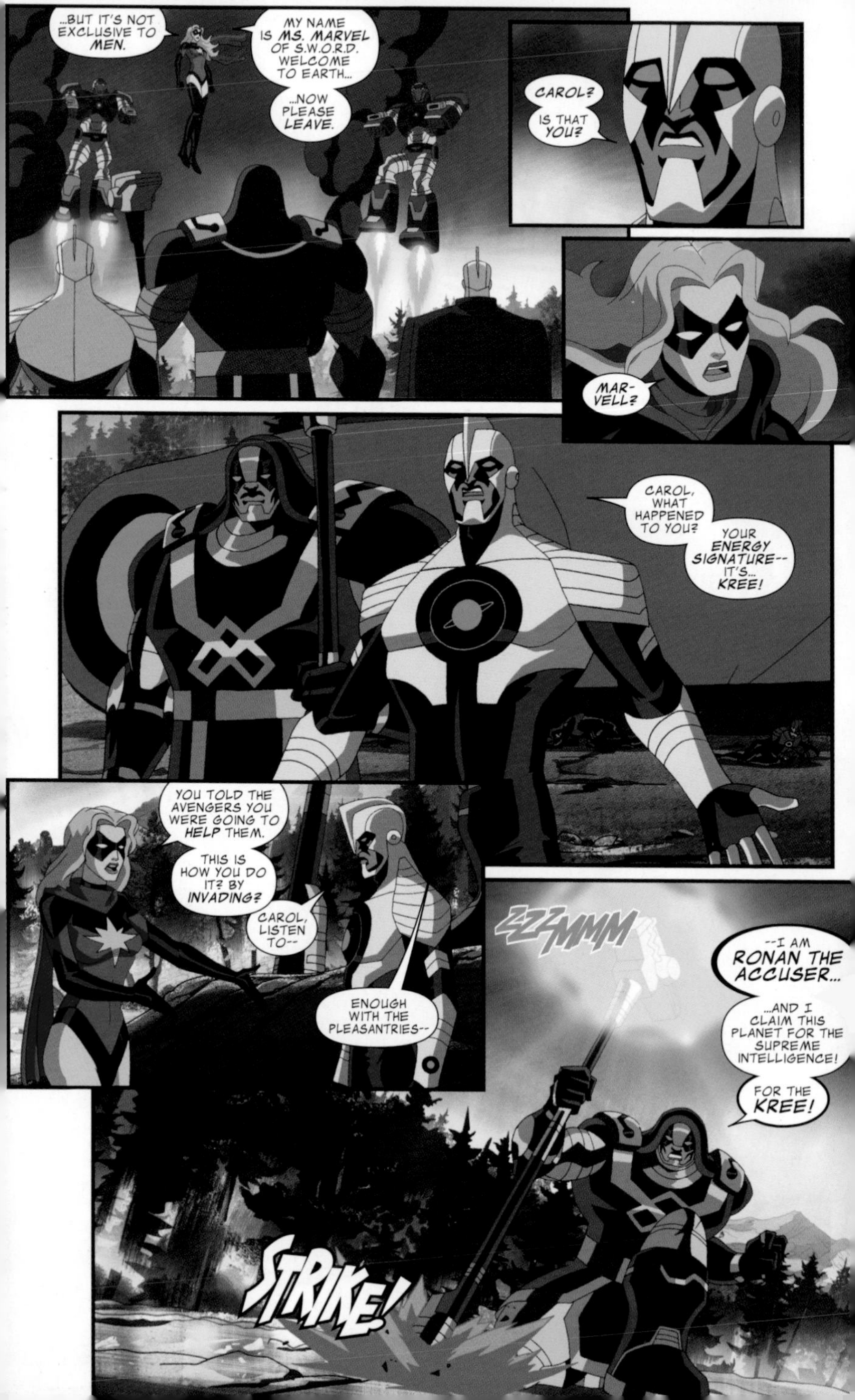

...BUT IT'S NOT EXCLUSIVE TO MEN.
MY NAME IS MS. MARVEL OF S.W.O.R.D. WELCOME TO EARTH...
...NOW PLEASE LEAVE.
CAROL?
IS THAT YOU?
MAR-VELL?
CAROL, WHAT HAPPENED TO YOU?
YOUR ENERGY SIGNATURE-- IT'S... KREE!
YOU TOLD THE AVENGERS YOU WERE GOING TO HELP THEM.
THIS IS HOW YOU DO IT? BY INVADING?
CAROL, LISTEN TO--
ENOUGH WITH THE PLEASANTRIES--
ZZZMMM
--I AM RONAN THE ACCUSER...
...AND I CLAIM THIS PLANET FOR THE SUPREME INTELLIGENCE!
FOR THE KREE!
STRIKE!

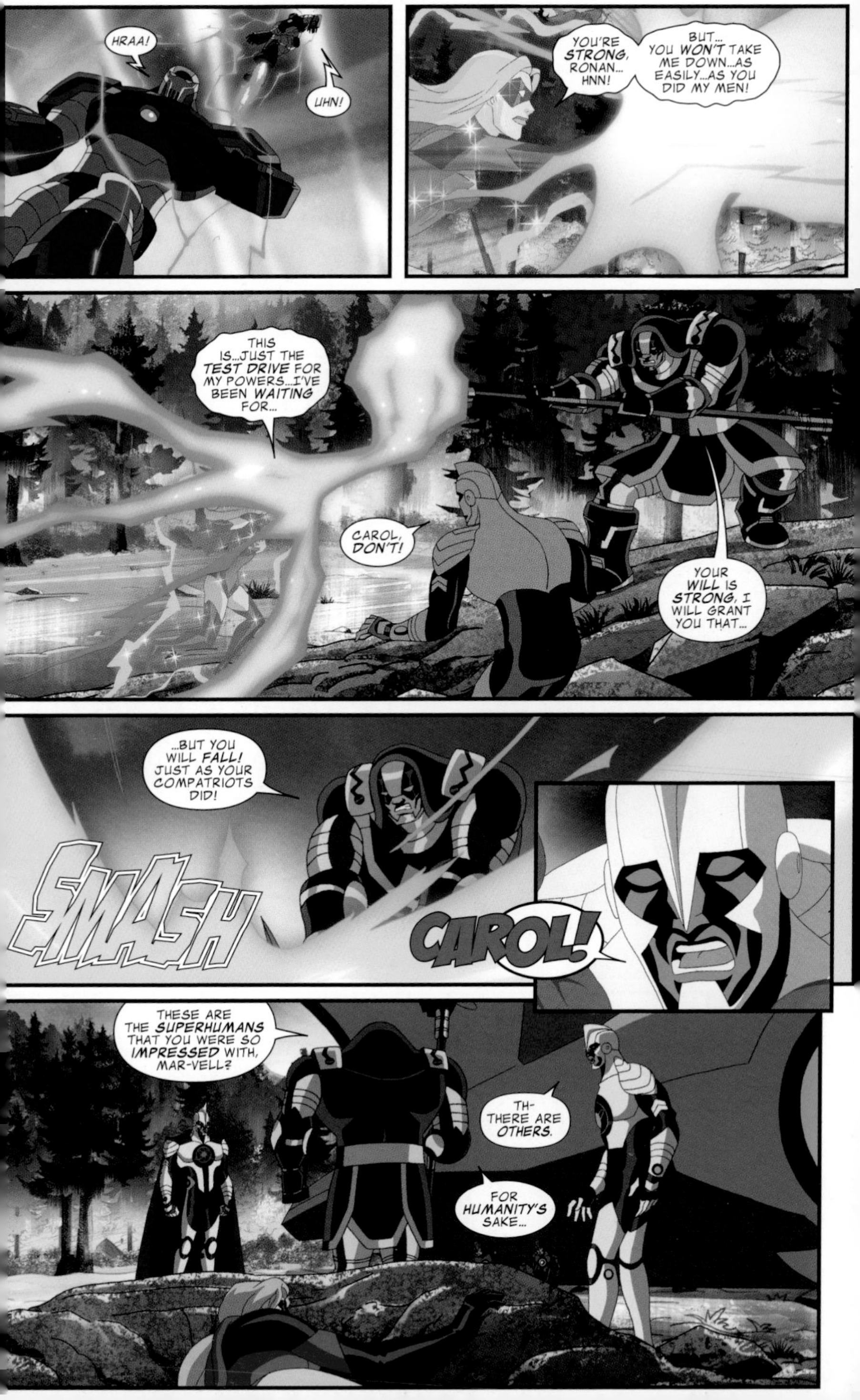
HRAA!
UHN!
YOU'RE STRONG, RONAN... HNN!
BUT... YOU WON'T TAKE ME DOWN...AS EASILY...AS YOU DID MY MEN!
THIS IS...JUST THE TEST DRIVE FOR MY POWERS...I'VE BEEN WAITING FOR...
CAROL, DON'T!
YOUR WILL IS STRONG, I WILL GRANT YOU THAT...
...BUT YOU WILL FALL! JUST AS YOUR COMPATRIOTS DID!
SMASH
CAROL!
THESE ARE THE SUPERHUMANS THAT YOU WERE SO IMPRESSED WITH, MAR-VELL?
TH- THERE ARE OTHERS.
FOR HUMANITY'S SAKE...

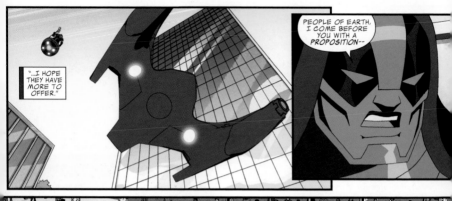

"...I HOPE THEY HAVE MORE TO OFFER."

PEOPLE OF EARTH, I COME BEFORE YOU WITH A PROPOSITION--

--EITHER SURRENDER YOUR PLANET *PEACEFULLY* AND JOIN THE KREE EMPIRE AS *DENEB IV* AND *TARSIS* HAVE BEFORE YOU--

--OR BE *DESTROYED.*

THE CHOICE IS YOURS.

CAN WE SEE WHAT'S BEHIND DOOR NUMBER THREE?

SO... YOU MUST BE ONE OF THE *"AVENGERS"* I WAS TOLD TO EXPECT.

ARE YOU THE LEADER?

WELL, I AM KINDA *POPULAR* BUT...

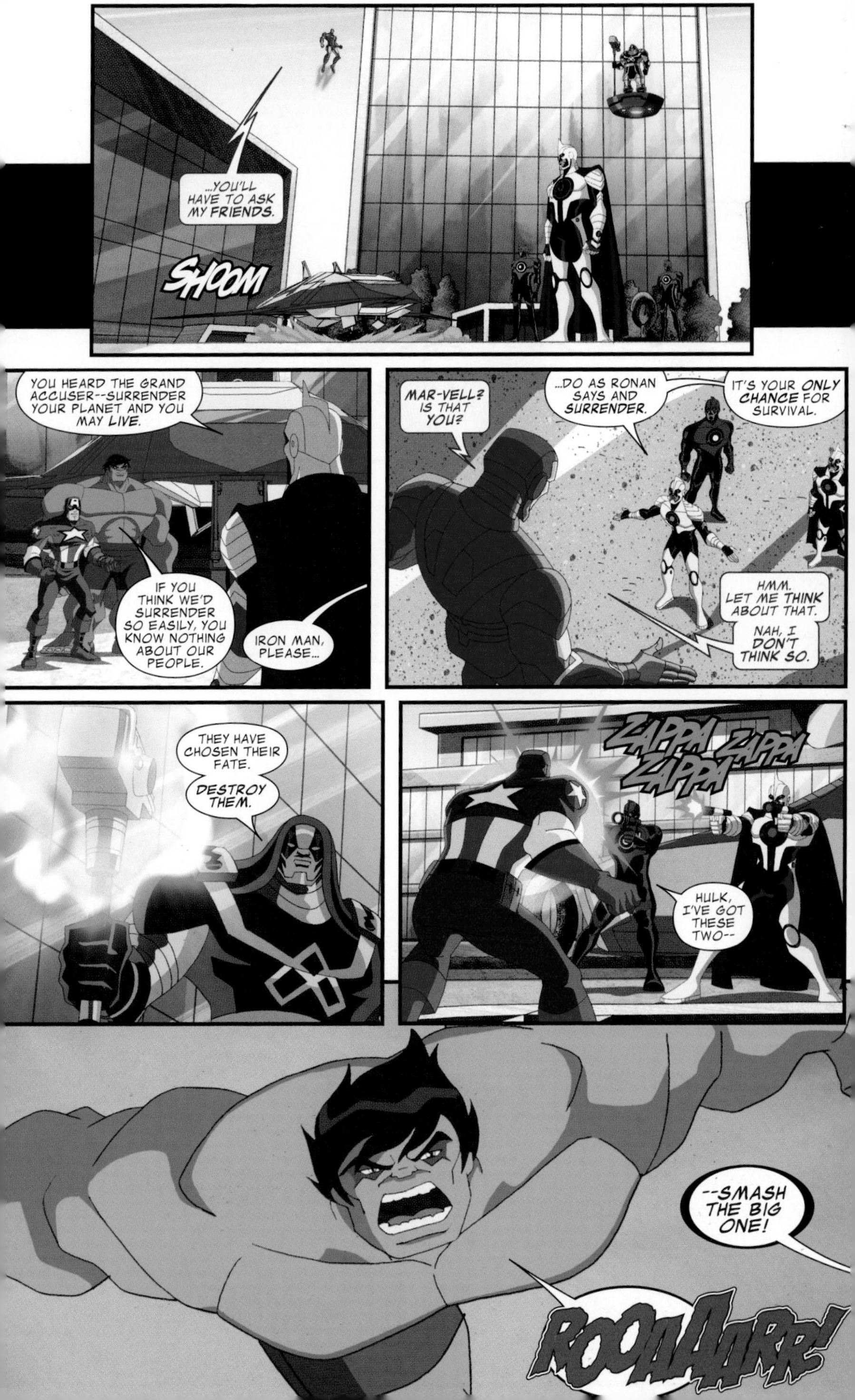
...YOU'LL HAVE TO ASK MY FRIENDS.
SHOOM
YOU HEARD THE GRAND ACCUSER--SURRENDER YOUR PLANET AND YOU MAY LIVE.
IF YOU THINK WE'D SURRENDER SO EASILY, YOU KNOW NOTHING ABOUT OUR PEOPLE.
IRON MAN, PLEASE...
MAR-VELL? IS THAT YOU?
...DO AS RONAN SAYS AND SURRENDER.
IT'S YOUR ONLY CHANCE FOR SURVIVAL.
HMM. LET ME THINK ABOUT THAT.
NAH, I DON'T THINK SO.
THEY HAVE CHOSEN THEIR FATE.
DESTROY THEM.
ZAPPA ZAPPA ZAPPA
HULK, I'VE GOT THESE TWO--
--SMASH THE BIG ONE!
ROOAAARR!

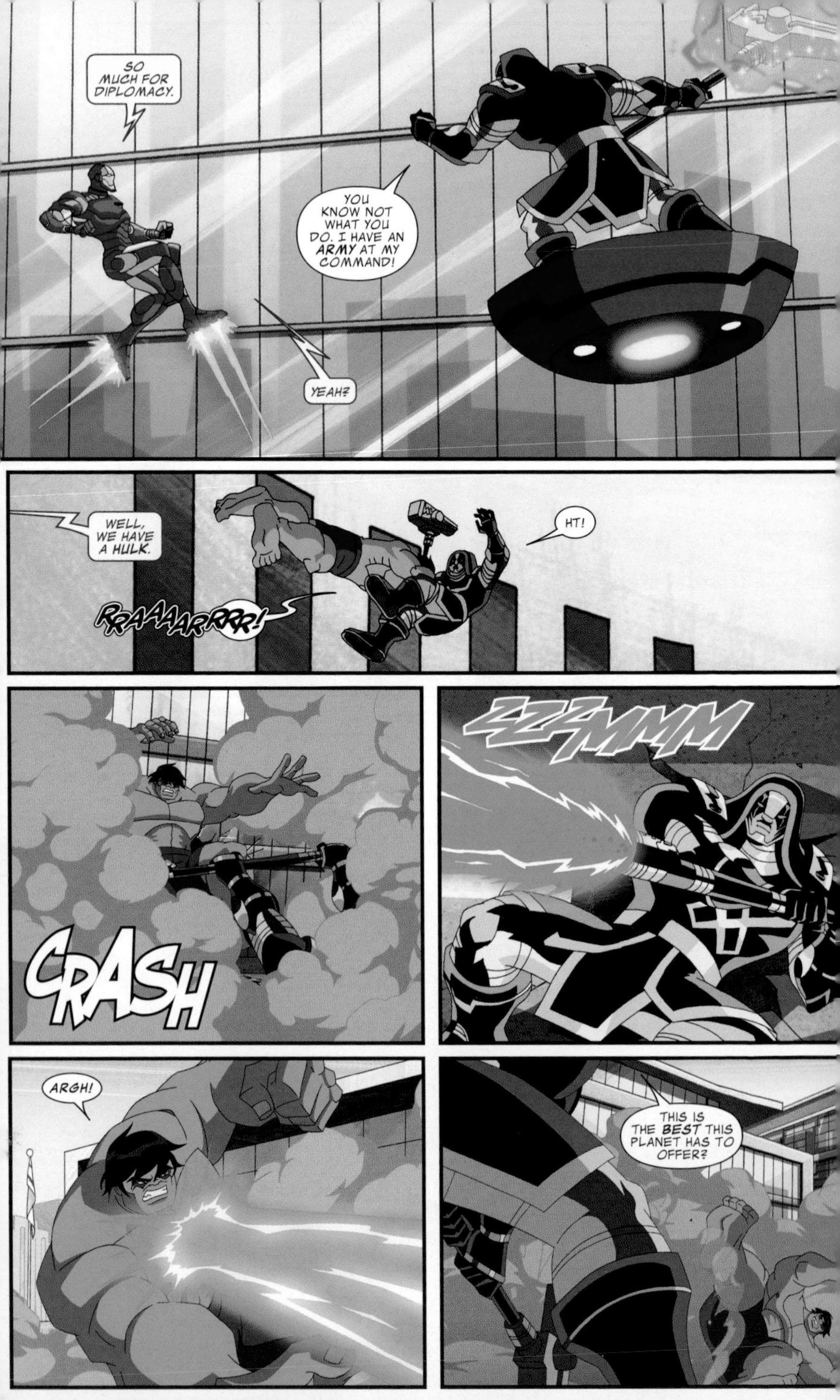
SO MUCH FOR DIPLOMACY.
YOU KNOW NOT WHAT YOU DO. I HAVE AN ARMY AT MY COMMAND!
YEAH?
WELL, WE HAVE A HULK.
HT!
RRAAAARRRR!
CRASH
ZZZMMMM
ARGH!
THIS IS THE BEST THIS PLANET HAS TO OFFER?

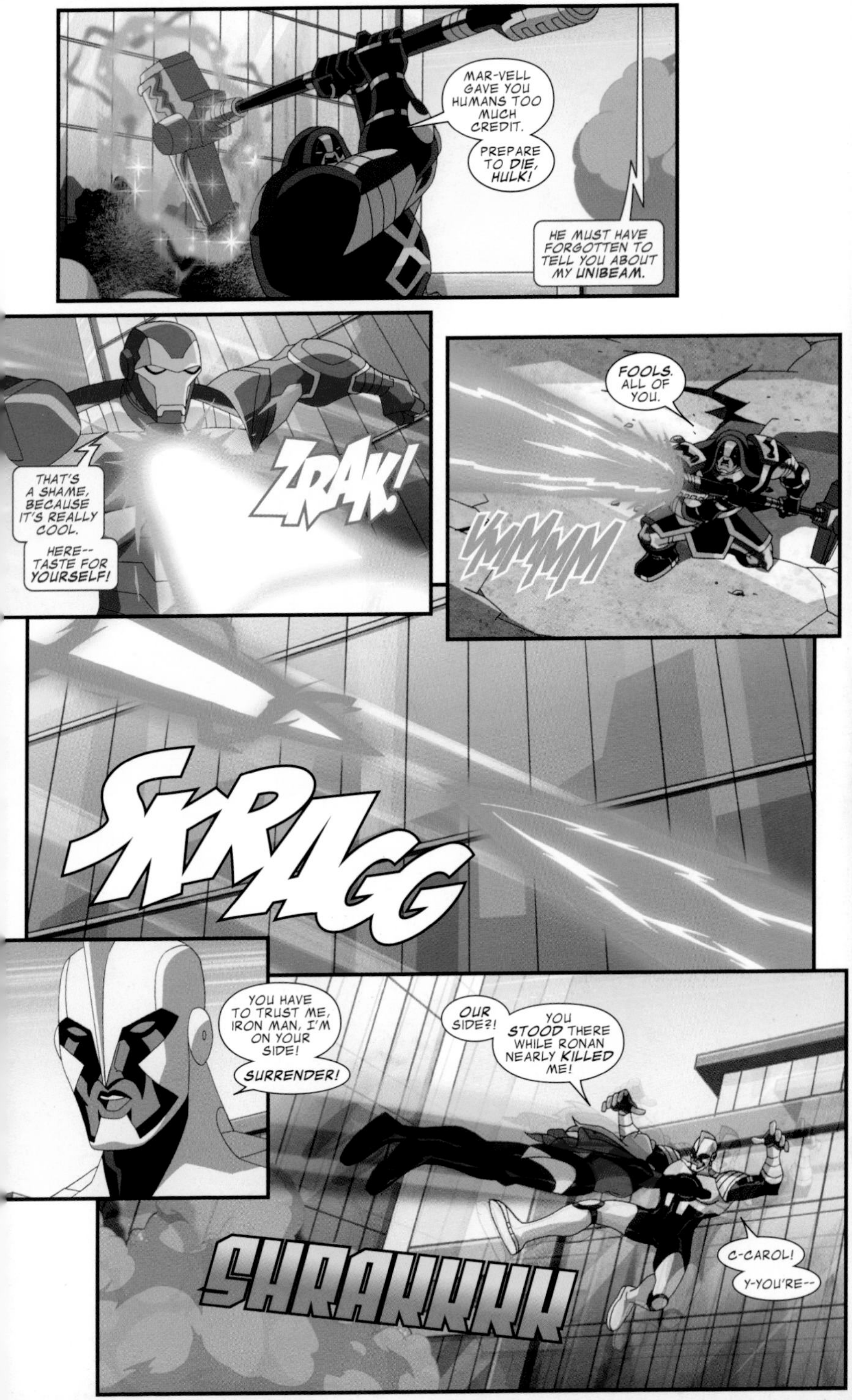
MAR-VELL GAVE YOU HUMANS TOO MUCH CREDIT.
PREPARE TO DIE, HULK!
HE MUST HAVE FORGOTTEN TO TELL YOU ABOUT MY UNIBEAM.
THAT'S A SHAME, BECAUSE IT'S REALLY COOL.
HERE--TASTE FOR YOURSELF!
ZRAK!
FOOLS. ALL OF YOU.
VMMMM
SKRAGG
YOU HAVE TO TRUST ME, IRON MAN, I'M ON YOUR SIDE!
SURRENDER!
OUR SIDE?!
YOU STOOD THERE WHILE RONAN NEARLY KILLED ME!
SHRAKKKK
C-CAROL!
Y-YOU'RE--

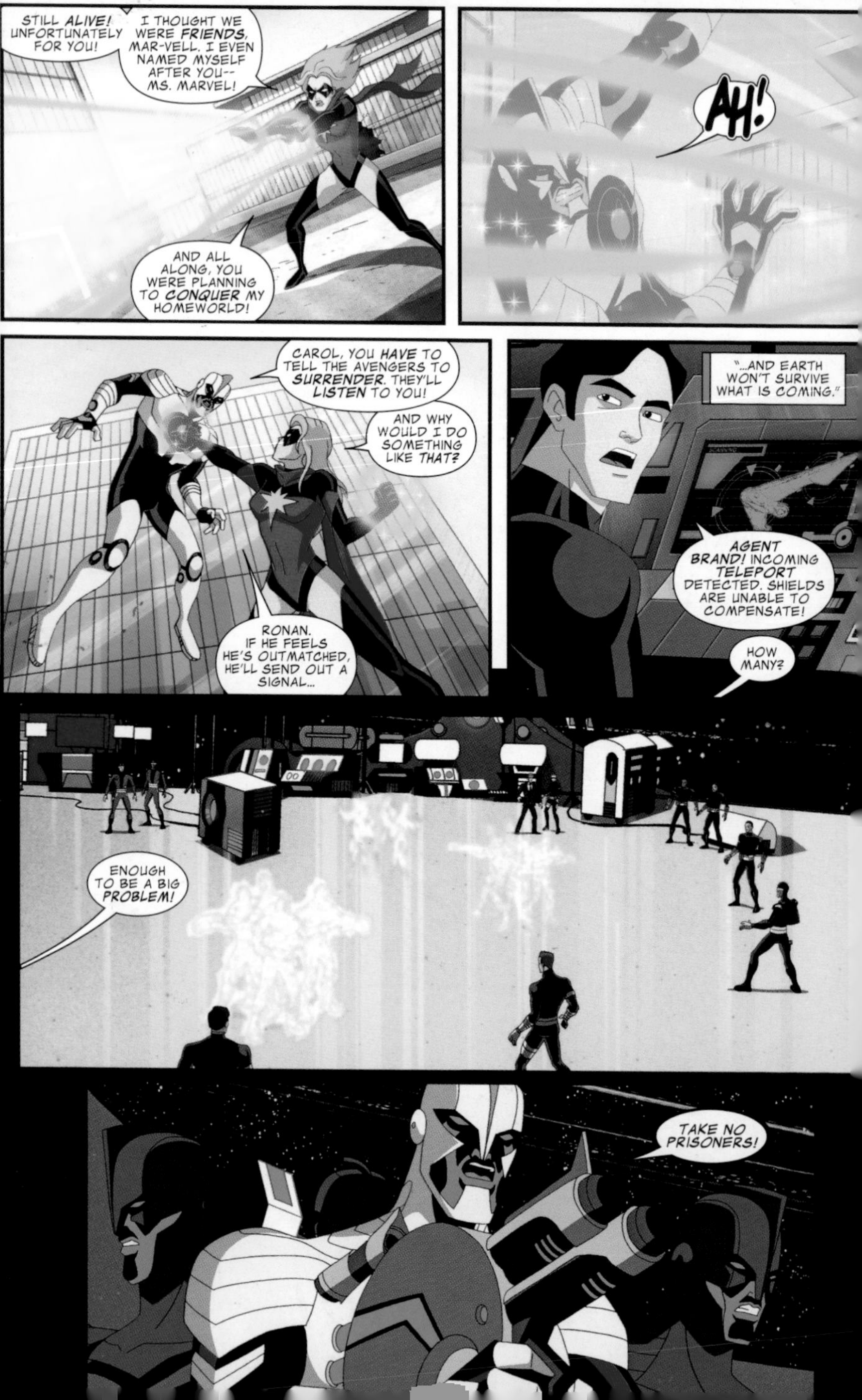
STILL ALIVE! UNFORTUNATELY FOR YOU!
I THOUGHT WE WERE FRIENDS, MAR-VELL. I EVEN NAMED MYSELF AFTER YOU-- MS. MARVEL!
AND ALL ALONG, YOU WERE PLANNING TO CONQUER MY HOMEWORLD!
AH!
CAROL, YOU HAVE TO TELL THE AVENGERS TO SURRENDER. THEY'LL LISTEN TO YOU!
AND WHY WOULD I DO SOMETHING LIKE THAT?
RONAN. IF HE FEELS HE'S OUTMATCHED, HE'LL SEND OUT A SIGNAL...
"...AND EARTH WON'T SURVIVE WHAT IS COMING."
AGENT BRAND! INCOMING TELEPORT DETECTED. SHIELDS ARE UNABLE TO COMPENSATE!
HOW MANY?
ENOUGH TO BE A BIG PROBLEM!
TAKE NO PRISONERS!

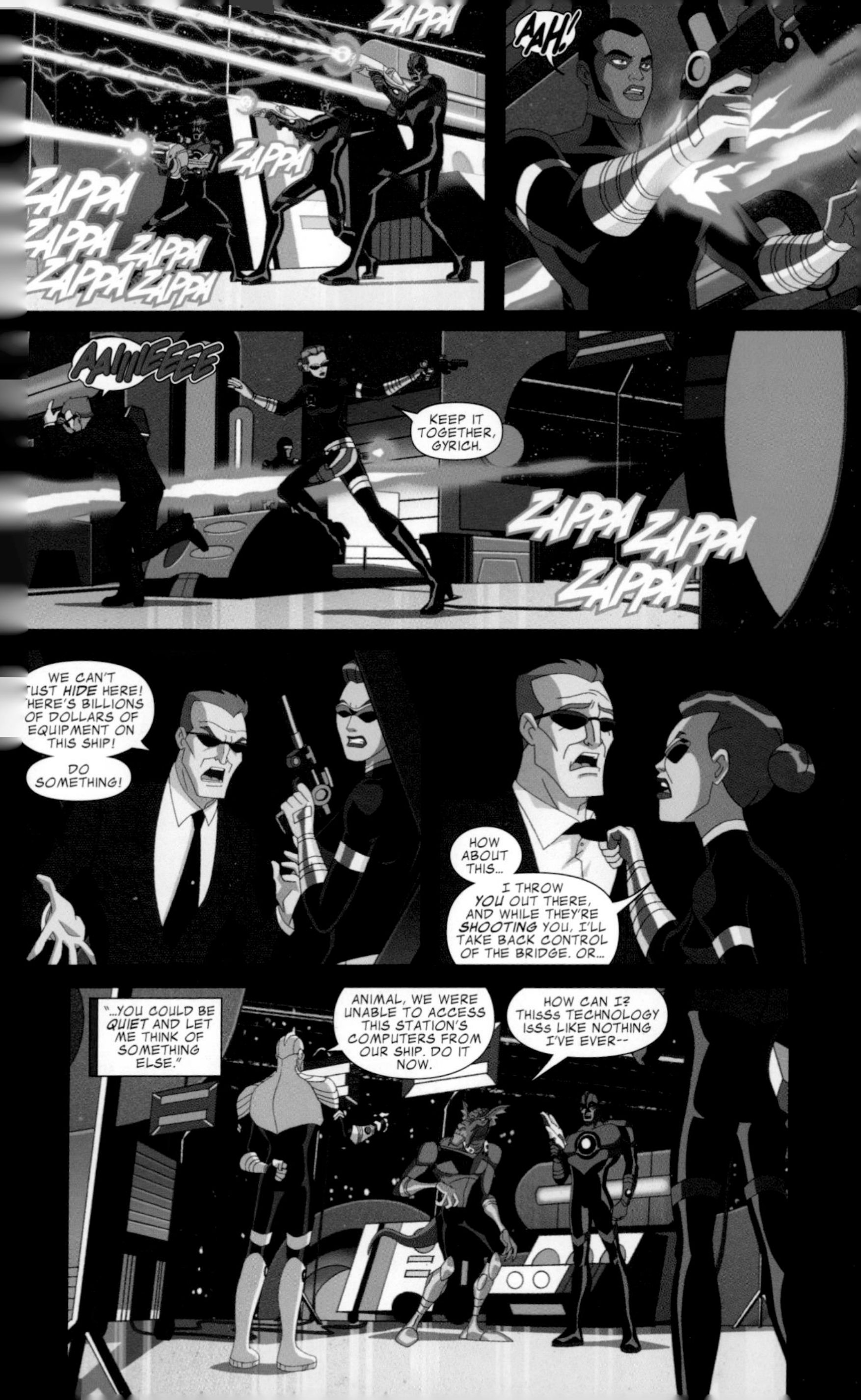
ZAPPA
ZAPPA
ZAPPA ZAPPA ZAPPA ZAPPA ZAPPA
AAH!
AAIIIIEEEE
KEEP IT TOGETHER, GYRICH.
ZAPPA ZAPPA ZAPPA
WE CAN'T JUST HIDE HERE! THERE'S BILLIONS OF DOLLARS OF EQUIPMENT ON THIS SHIP!
DO SOMETHING!
HOW ABOUT THIS...
I THROW YOU OUT THERE, AND WHILE THEY'RE SHOOTING YOU, I'LL TAKE BACK CONTROL OF THE BRIDGE. OR...
"...YOU COULD BE QUIET AND LET ME THINK OF SOMETHING ELSE."
ANIMAL, WE WERE UNABLE TO ACCESS THIS STATION'S COMPUTERS FROM OUR SHIP. DO IT NOW.
HOW CAN I? THISSS TECHNOLOGY ISSS LIKE NOTHING I'VE EVER--

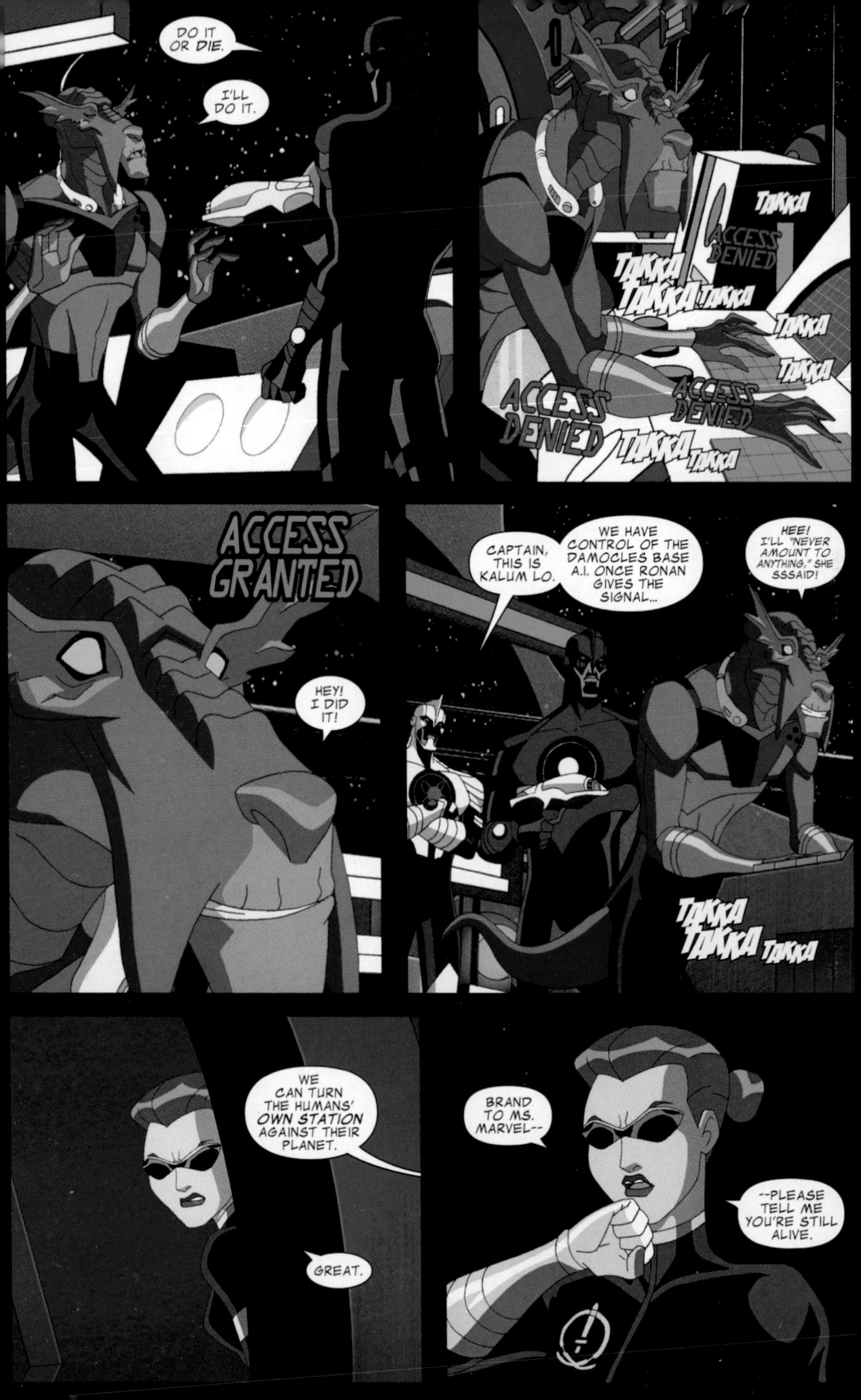
DO IT OR DIE.
I'LL DO IT.
TAKKA
ACCESS DENIED
TAKKA
TAKKA TAKKA
TAKKA
TAKKA
ACCESS DENIED
ACCESS DENIED
TAKKA TAKKA
ACCESS GRANTED
HEY! I DID IT!
CAPTAIN, THIS IS KALUM LO.
WE HAVE CONTROL OF THE DAMOCLES BASE A.I. ONCE RONAN GIVES THE SIGNAL...
HEE! I'LL "NEVER AMOUNT TO ANYTHING," SHE SSSAID!
TAKKA TAKKA TAKKA
WE CAN TURN THE HUMANS' OWN STATION AGAINST THEIR PLANET.
GREAT.
BRAND TO MS. MARVEL--
--PLEASE TELL ME YOU'RE STILL ALIVE.

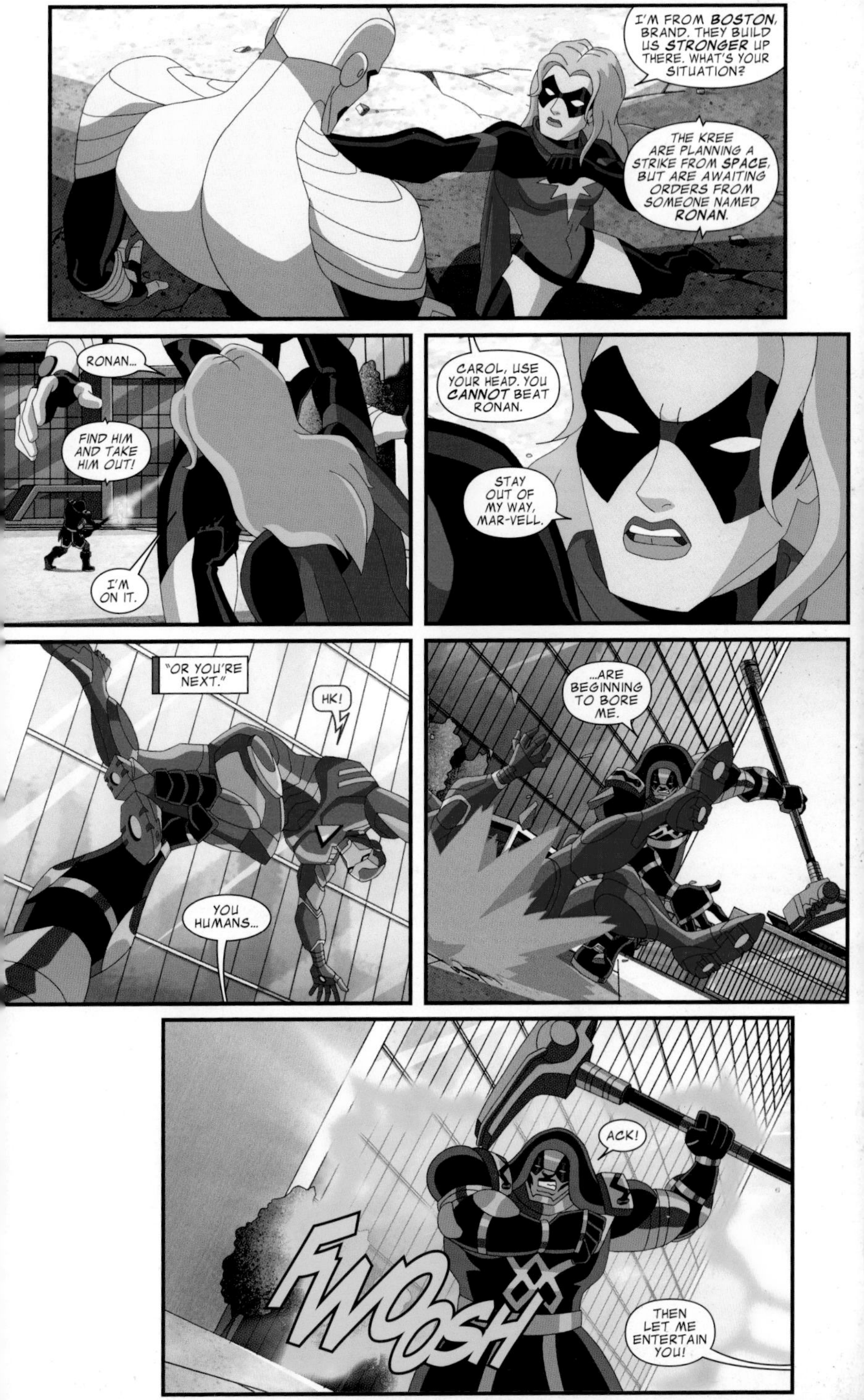
I'M FROM BOSTON, BRAND. THEY BUILD US STRONGER UP THERE. WHAT'S YOUR SITUATION?
THE KREE ARE PLANNING A STRIKE FROM SPACE, BUT ARE AWAITING ORDERS FROM SOMEONE NAMED RONAN.
RONAN...
FIND HIM AND TAKE HIM OUT!
I'M ON IT.
CAROL, USE YOUR HEAD. YOU CANNOT BEAT RONAN.
STAY OUT OF MY WAY, MAR-VELL.
"OR YOU'RE NEXT."
HK!
YOU HUMANS...
...ARE BEGINNING TO BORE ME.
ACK!
FWOOSH
THEN LET ME ENTERTAIN YOU!

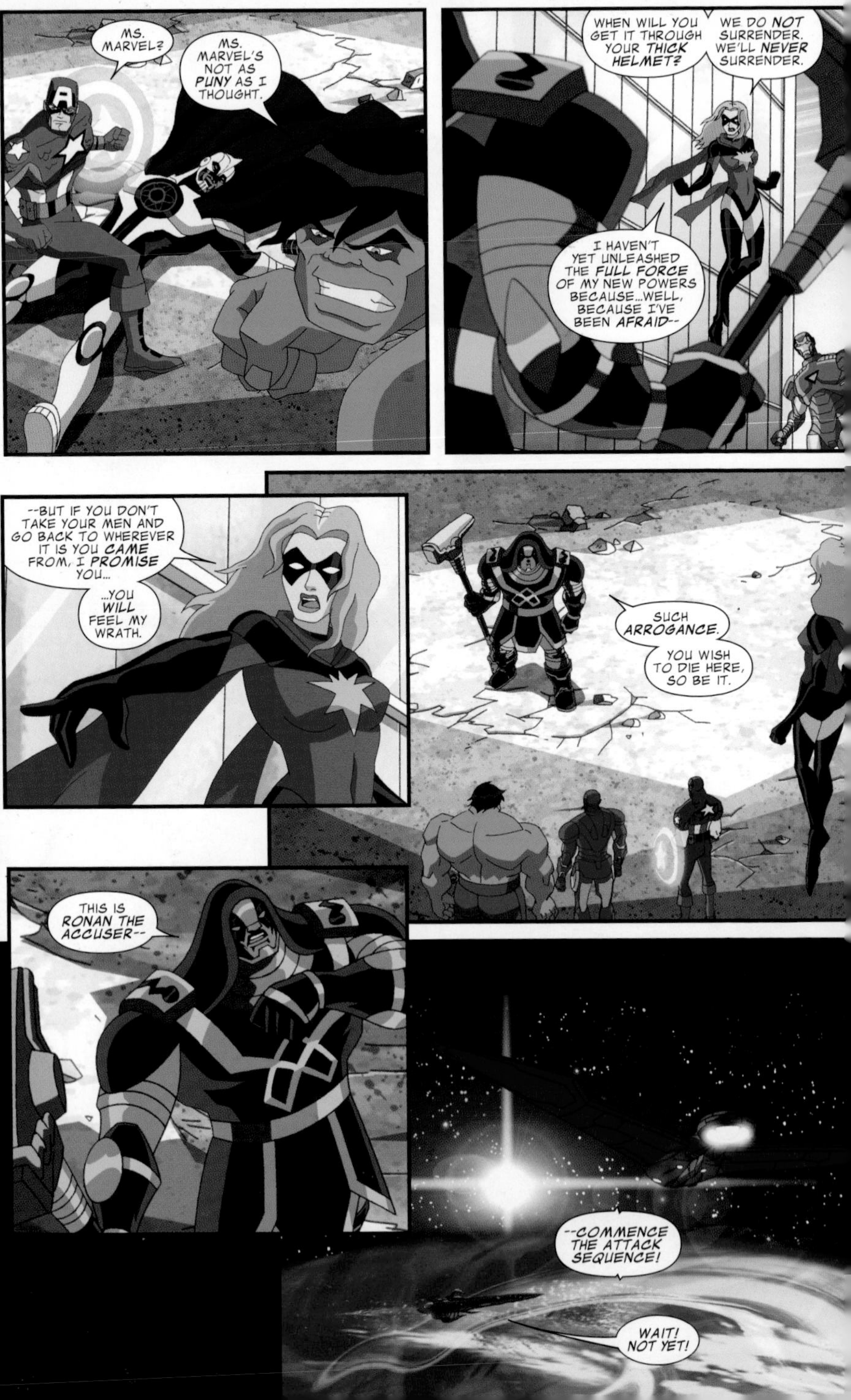
MS. MARVEL?
MS. MARVEL'S NOT AS PUNY AS I THOUGHT.
WHEN WILL YOU GET IT THROUGH YOUR THICK HELMET?
WE DO NOT SURRENDER. WE'LL NEVER SURRENDER.
I HAVEN'T YET UNLEASHED THE FULL FORCE OF MY NEW POWERS BECAUSE...WELL, BECAUSE I'VE BEEN AFRAID--
--BUT IF YOU DON'T TAKE YOUR MEN AND GO BACK TO WHEREVER IT IS YOU CAME FROM, I PROMISE YOU...
...YOU WILL FEEL MY WRATH.
SUCH ARROGANCE.
YOU WISH TO DIE HERE, SO BE IT.
THIS IS RONAN THE ACCUSER--
--COMMENCE THE ATTACK SEQUENCE!
WAIT! NOT YET!

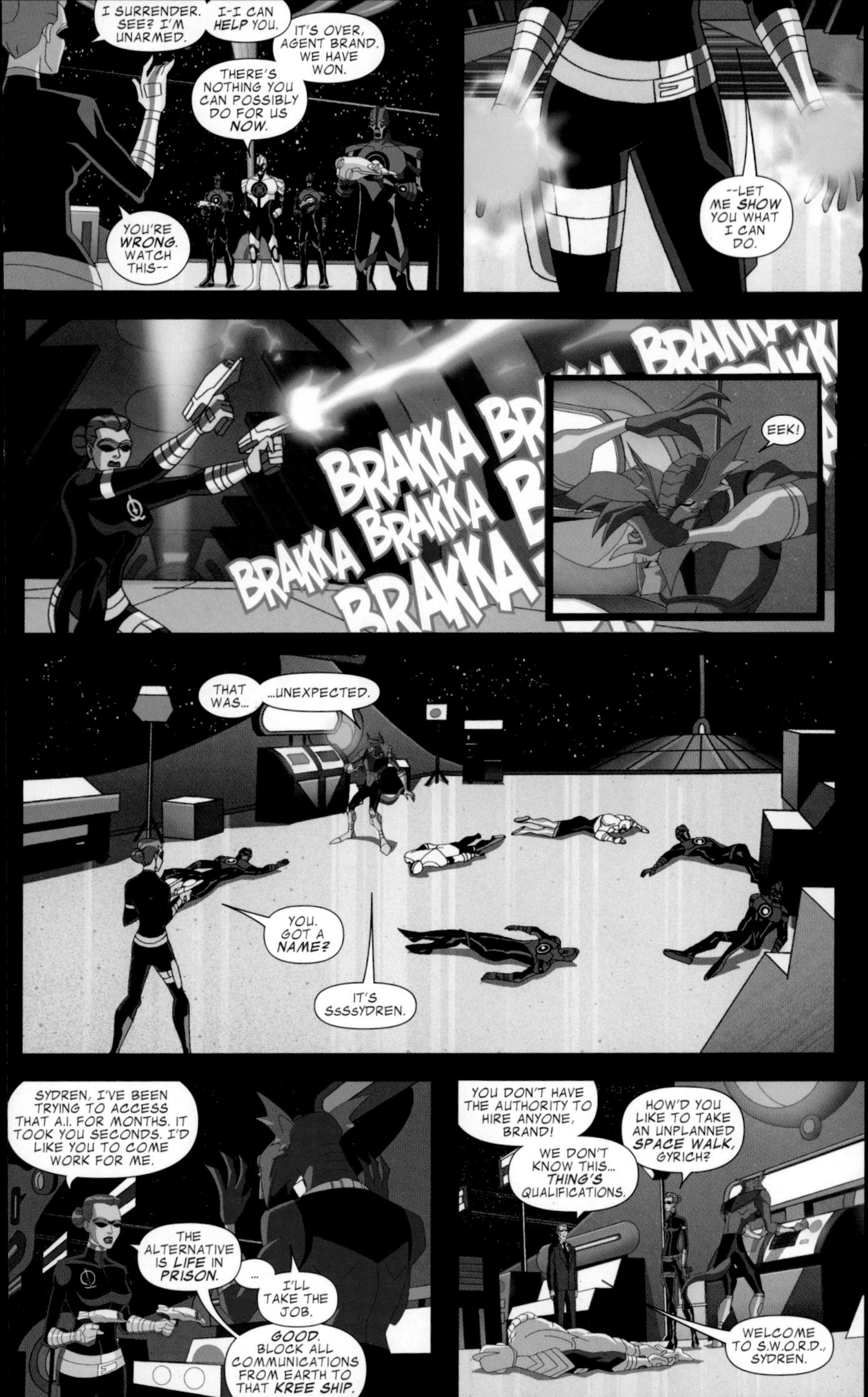
I SURRENDER. SEE? I'M UNARMED.
I-I CAN HELP YOU.
IT'S OVER, AGENT BRAND. WE HAVE WON.
THERE'S NOTHING YOU CAN POSSIBLY DO FOR US NOW.
YOU'RE WRONG. WATCH THIS--
--LET ME SHOW YOU WHAT I CAN DO.
BRAKKA BRAKKA BRAKKA BRAKKA BRAKKA
EEK!
THAT WAS...
...UNEXPECTED.
YOU. GOT A NAME?
IT'S SSSSYDREN.
SYDREN, I'VE BEEN TRYING TO ACCESS THAT A.I. FOR MONTHS. IT TOOK YOU SECONDS. I'D LIKE YOU TO COME WORK FOR ME.
THE ALTERNATIVE IS LIFE IN PRISON.
...
I'LL TAKE THE JOB.
GOOD. BLOCK ALL COMMUNICATIONS FROM EARTH TO THAT KREE SHIP.
YOU DON'T HAVE THE AUTHORITY TO HIRE ANYONE, BRAND!
WE DON'T KNOW THIS... THING'S QUALIFICATIONS.
HOW'D YOU LIKE TO TAKE AN UNPLANNED SPACE WALK, GYRICH?
WELCOME TO S.W.O.R.D., SYDREN.

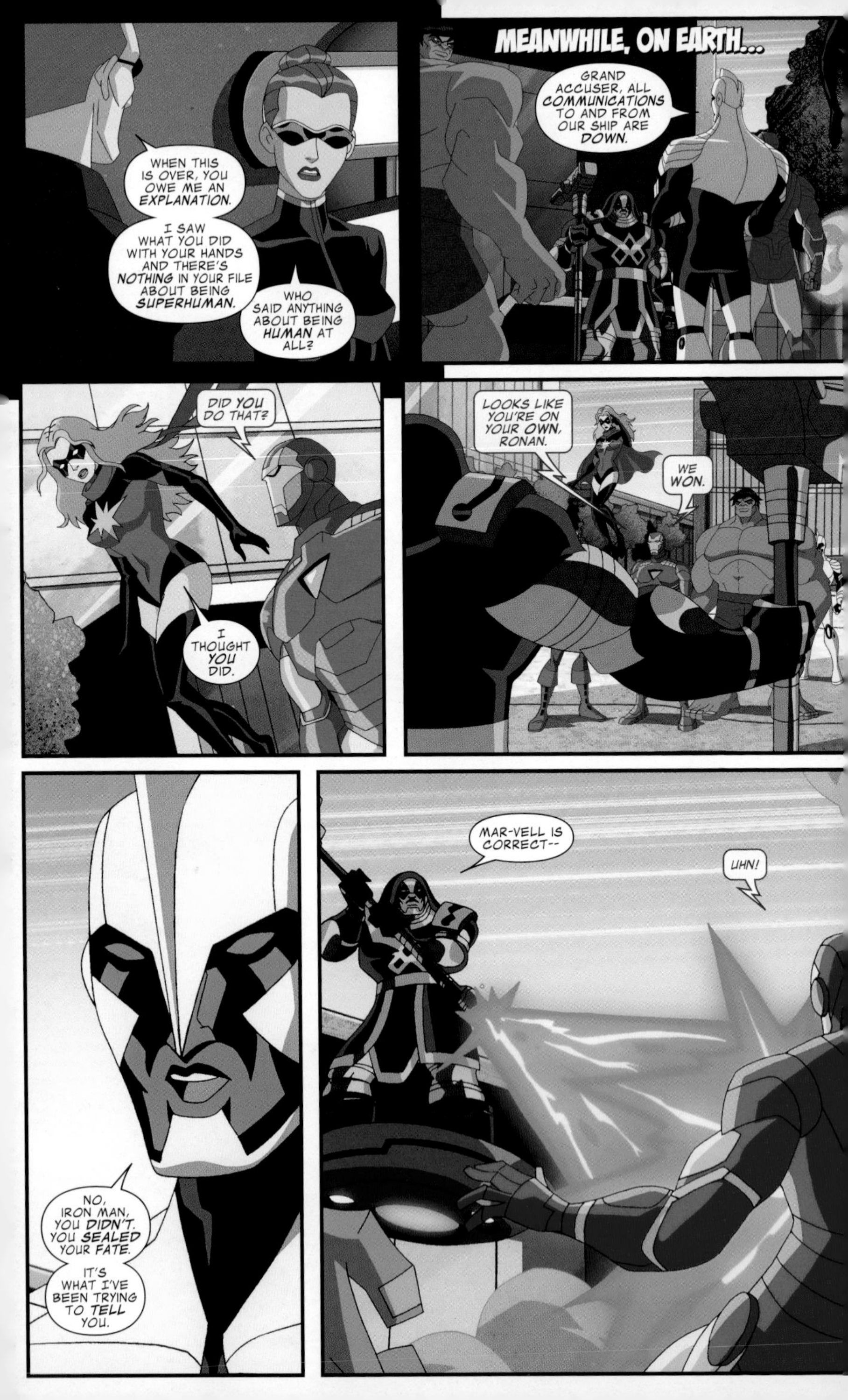

WHEN THIS IS OVER, YOU OWE ME AN EXPLANATION.
I SAW WHAT YOU DID WITH YOUR HANDS AND THERE'S NOTHING IN YOUR FILE ABOUT BEING SUPERHUMAN.
WHO SAID ANYTHING ABOUT BEING HUMAN AT ALL?
MEANWHILE, ON EARTH...
GRAND ACCUSER, ALL COMMUNICATIONS TO AND FROM OUR SHIP ARE DOWN.
DID YOU DO THAT?
I THOUGHT YOU DID.
LOOKS LIKE YOU'RE ON YOUR OWN, RONAN.
WE WON.
NO, IRON MAN, YOU DIDN'T. YOU SEALED YOUR FATE.
IT'S WHAT I'VE BEEN TRYING TO TELL YOU.
MAR-VELL IS CORRECT--
UHN!

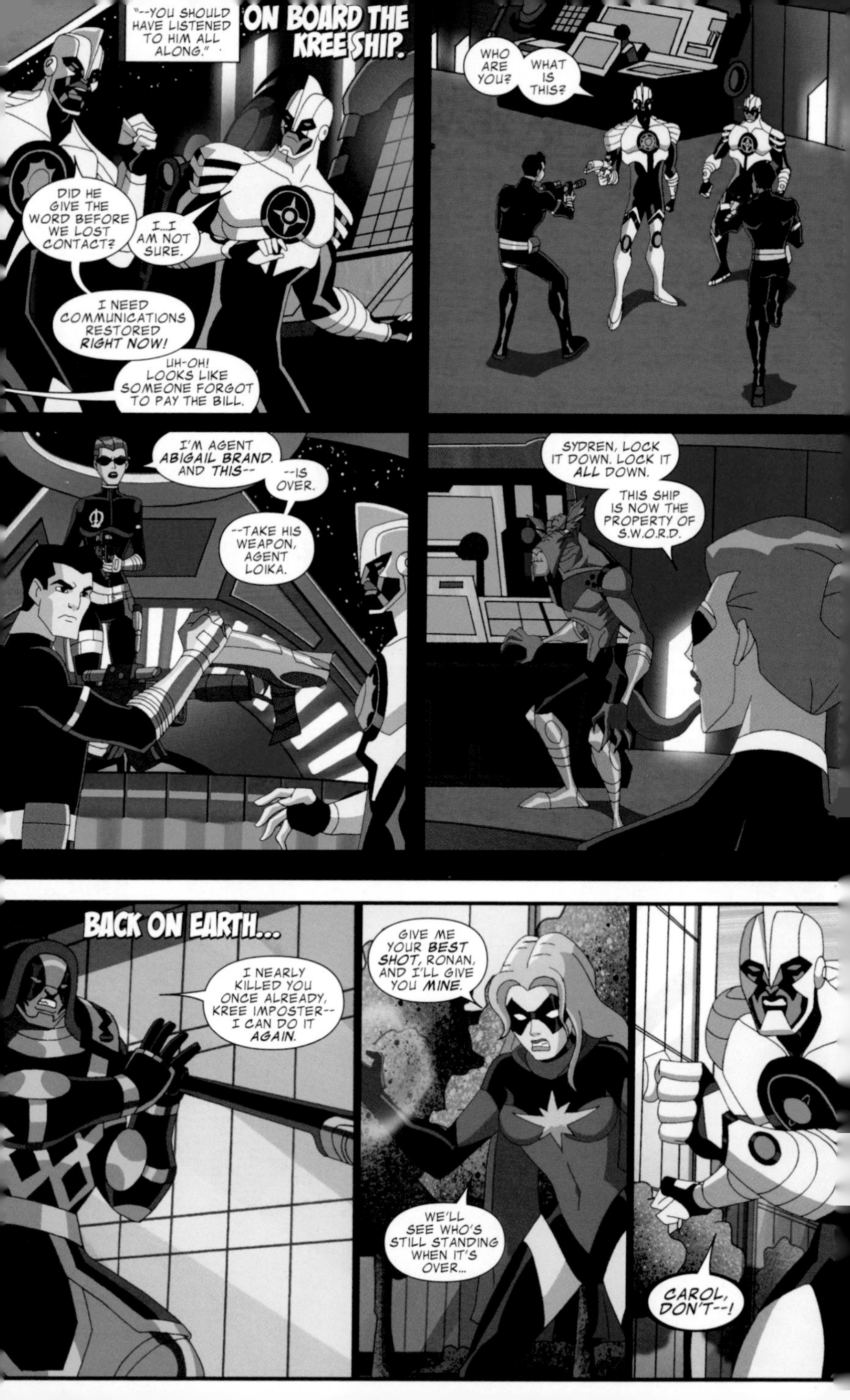
"--YOU SHOULD HAVE LISTENED TO HIM ALL ALONG."
ON BOARD THE KREE SHIP.
DID HE GIVE THE WORD BEFORE WE LOST CONTACT?
I...I AM NOT SURE.
I NEED COMMUNICATIONS RESTORED RIGHT NOW!
UH-OH! LOOKS LIKE SOMEONE FORGOT TO PAY THE BILL.
WHO ARE YOU?
WHAT IS THIS?
I'M AGENT ABIGAIL BRAND. AND THIS--
--IS OVER.
--TAKE HIS WEAPON, AGENT LOIKA.
SYDREN, LOCK IT DOWN. LOCK IT ALL DOWN.
THIS SHIP IS NOW THE PROPERTY OF S.W.O.R.D.
BACK ON EARTH...
I NEARLY KILLED YOU ONCE ALREADY, KREE IMPOSTER-- I CAN DO IT AGAIN.
GIVE ME YOUR BEST SHOT, RONAN, AND I'LL GIVE YOU MINE.
WE'LL SEE WHO'S STILL STANDING WHEN IT'S OVER...
CAROL, DON'T--!

AAAAHH!

MAR-VELL-- NO!

HNN...

WHY?

WHY DID YOU PUT YOURSELF BETWEEN OUR BLASTS?

I...HAD TO PROVE TO YOU...MY FRIENDSHIP IS TRUE...

YOU WON'T LISTEN TO ME OTHERWISE.

IF RONAN WINS...THERE'S A CHANCE THAT HUMANITY WILL SURVIVE.

IF HE LOSES--WELL, THE KREE EMPIRE IS...A HUNDRED STAR SYSTEMS STRONG...

I'M SORRY, BUT I CAN'T DO WHAT YOU'RE ASKING ME TO DO.

GIVING U IS AGAIN HUMAN NATURE

IT IS YOUR FAT FLAW. TH TIME...

VMMMM

...YOU WILL NOT GET BACK UP!

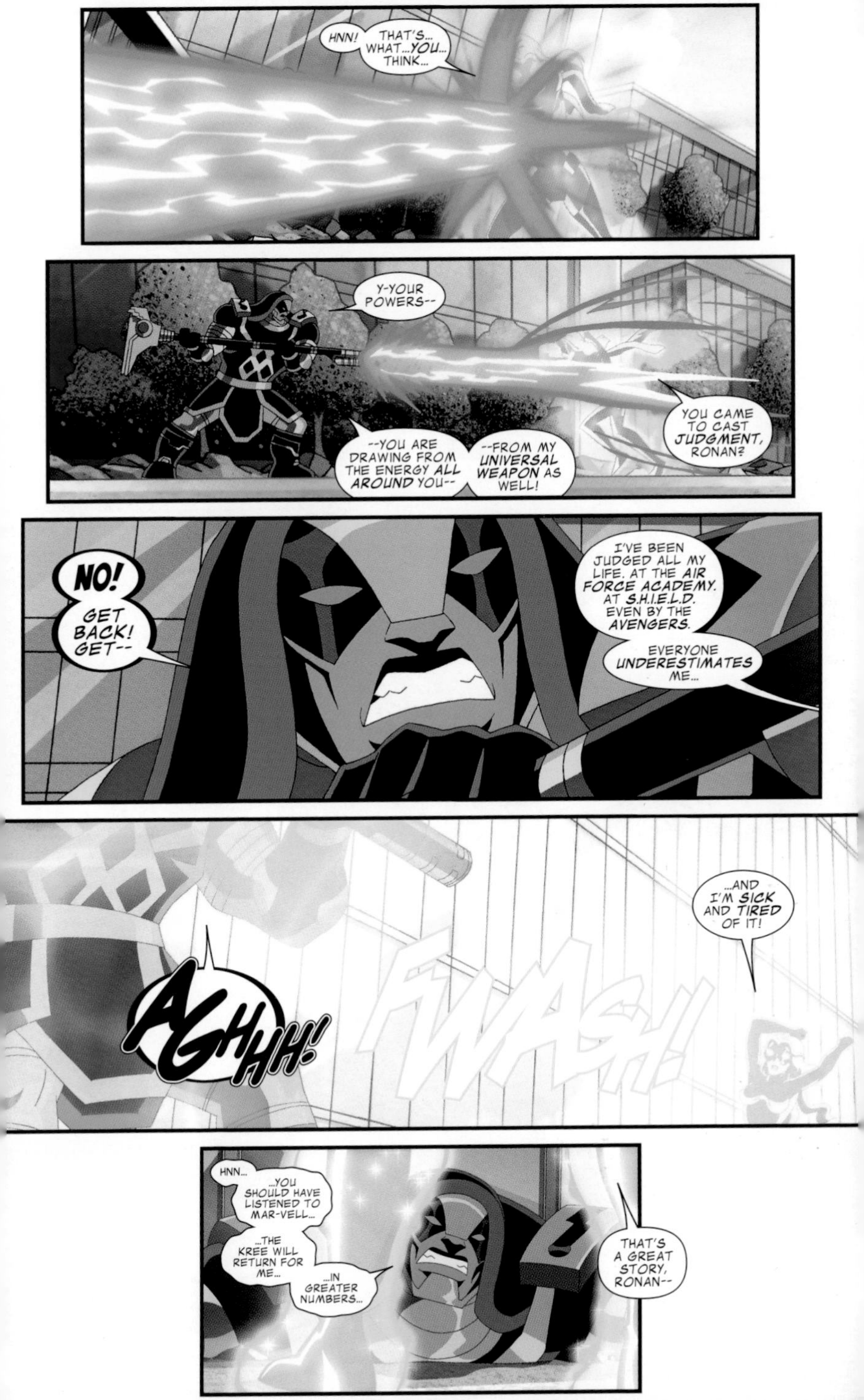
HNN!
THAT'S... WHAT...YOU... THINK...
Y-YOUR POWERS--
--YOU ARE DRAWING FROM THE ENERGY ALL AROUND YOU--
--FROM MY UNIVERSAL WEAPON AS WELL!
YOU CAME TO CAST JUDGMENT, RONAN?
NO! GET BACK! GET--
I'VE BEEN JUDGED ALL MY LIFE. AT THE AIR FORCE ACADEMY. AT S.H.I.E.L.D. EVEN BY THE AVENGERS.
EVERYONE UNDERESTIMATES ME...
...AND I'M SICK AND TIRED OF IT!
AGHHH!
FWASH!
HNN...
...YOU SHOULD HAVE LISTENED TO MAR-VELL...
...THE KREE WILL RETURN FOR ME...
...IN GREATER NUMBERS...
THAT'S A GREAT STORY, RONAN--

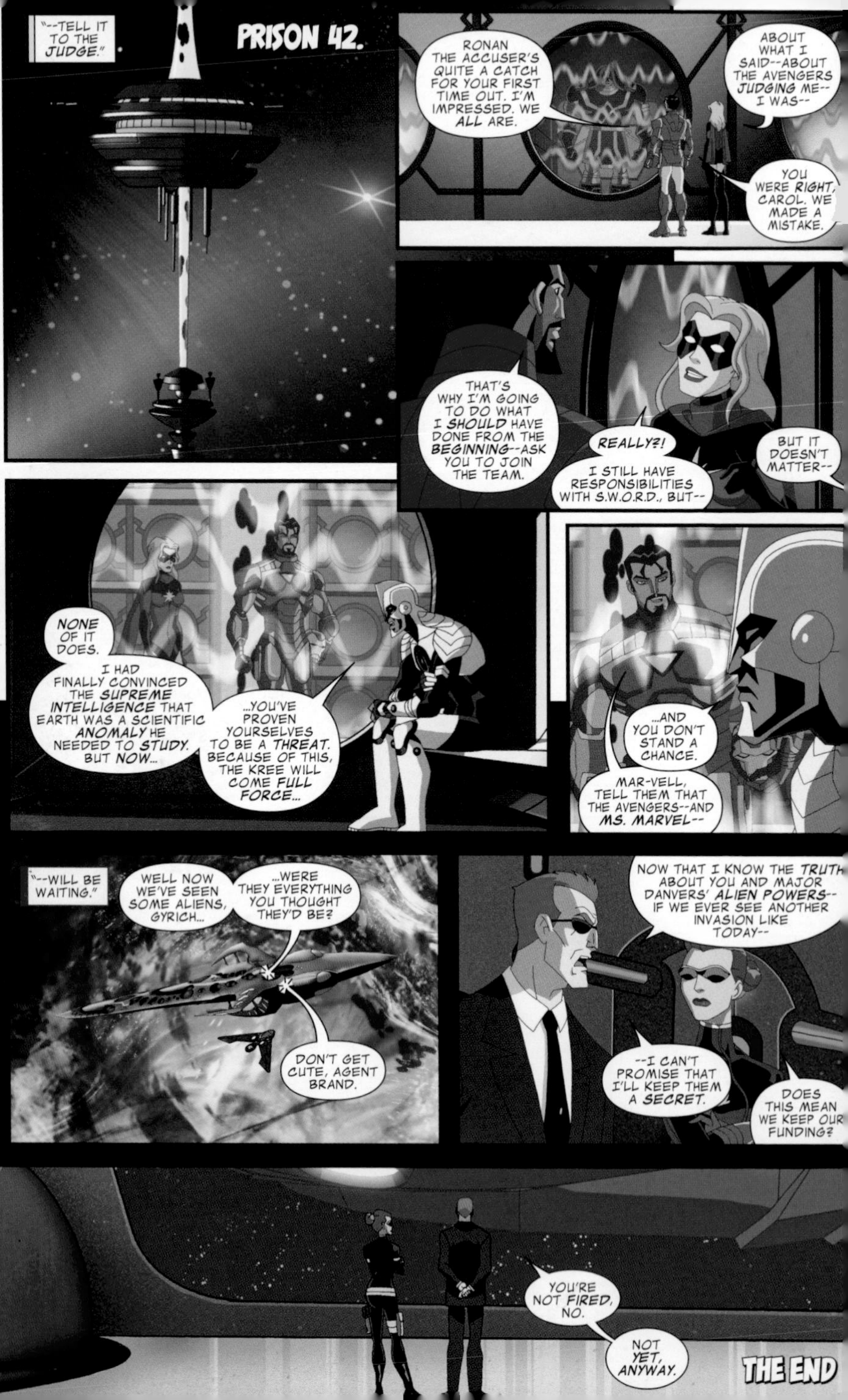
"--TELL IT TO THE JUDGE."
PRISON 42.
RONAN THE ACCUSER'S QUITE A CATCH FOR YOUR FIRST TIME OUT. I'M IMPRESSED. WE ALL ARE.
ABOUT WHAT I SAID--ABOUT THE AVENGERS JUDGING ME--I WAS--
YOU WERE RIGHT, CAROL. WE MADE A MISTAKE.
THAT'S WHY I'M GOING TO DO WHAT I SHOULD HAVE DONE FROM THE BEGINNING--ASK YOU TO JOIN THE TEAM.
REALLY?!
I STILL HAVE RESPONSIBILITIES WITH S.W.O.R.D., BUT--
BUT IT DOESN'T MATTER--
NONE OF IT DOES.
I HAD FINALLY CONVINCED THE SUPREME INTELLIGENCE THAT EARTH WAS A SCIENTIFIC ANOMALY HE NEEDED TO STUDY. BUT NOW...
...YOU'VE PROVEN YOURSELVES TO BE A THREAT. BECAUSE OF THIS, THE KREE WILL COME FULL FORCE...
...AND YOU DON'T STAND A CHANCE.
MAR-VELL, TELL THEM THAT THE AVENGERS--AND MS. MARVEL--
"--WILL BE WAITING."
WELL NOW WE'VE SEEN SOME ALIENS, GYRICH...
...WERE THEY EVERYTHING YOU THOUGHT THEY'D BE?
DON'T GET CUTE, AGENT BRAND.
NOW THAT I KNOW THE TRUTH ABOUT YOU AND MAJOR DANVERS' ALIEN POWERS--IF WE EVER SEE ANOTHER INVASION LIKE TODAY--
--I CAN'T PROMISE THAT I'LL KEEP THEM A SECRET.
DOES THIS MEAN WE KEEP OUR FUNDING?
YOU'RE NOT FIRED, NO.
NOT YET, ANYWAY.
THE END

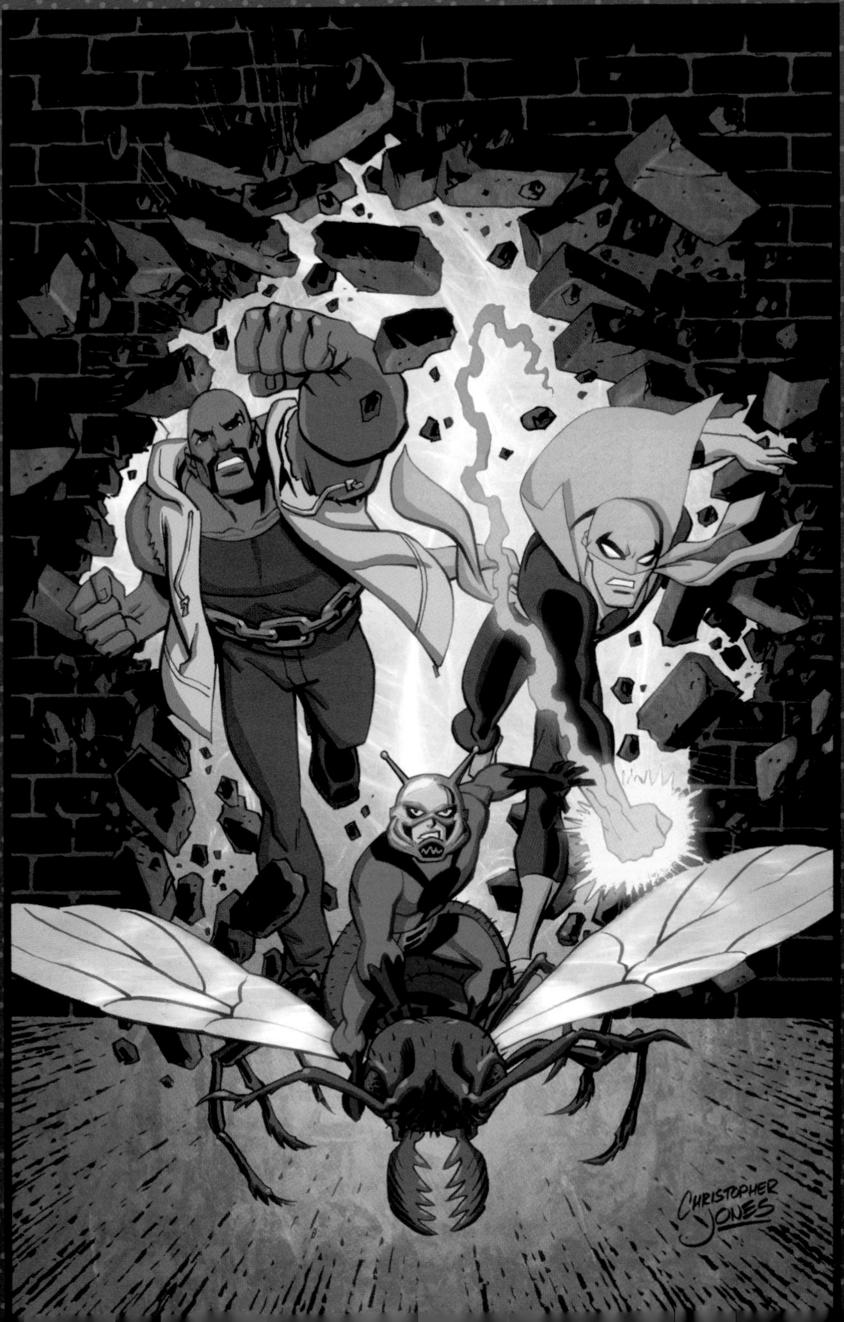
CHRISTOPHER JONES

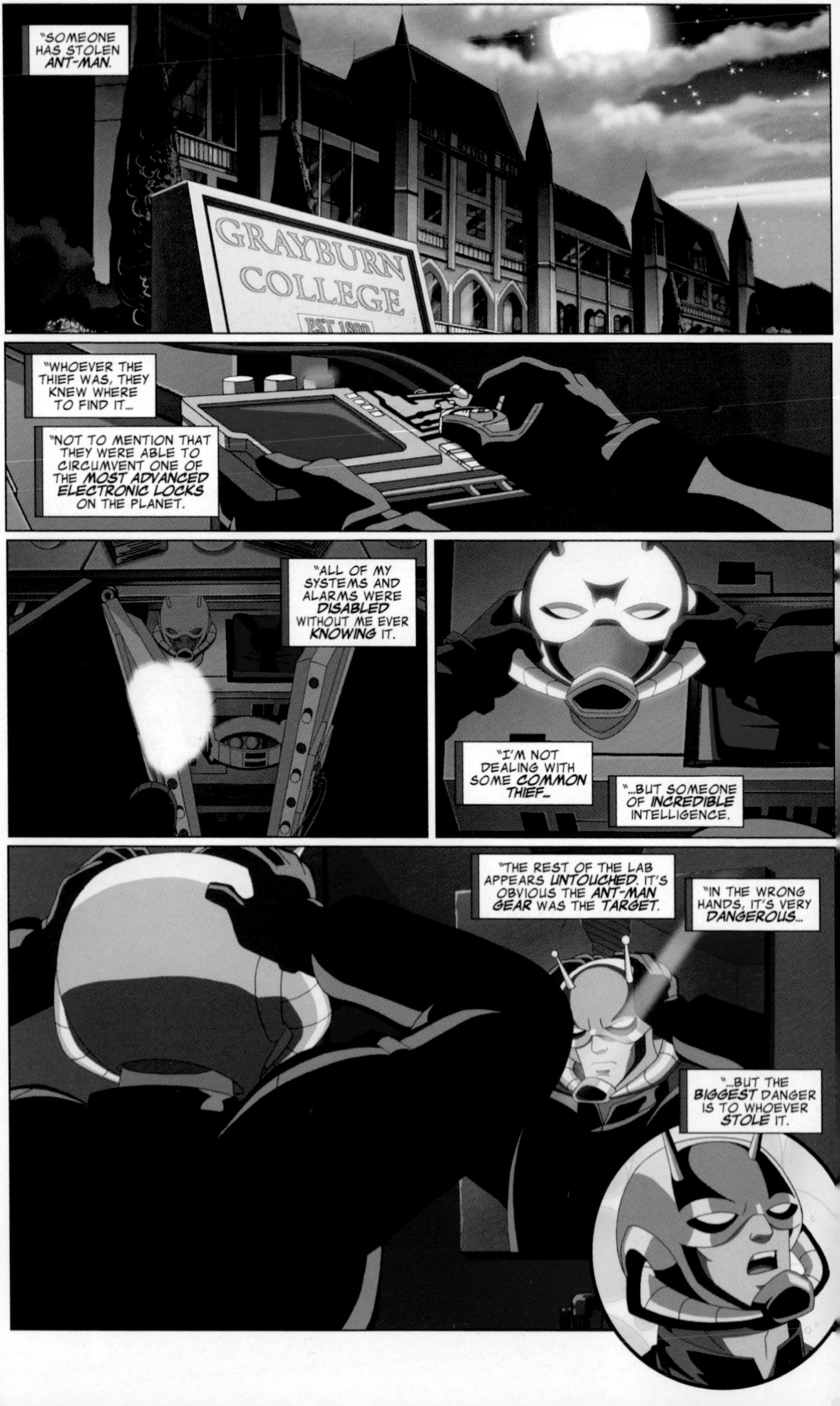

"SOMEONE HAS STOLEN ANT-MAN.
GRAYBURN COLLEGE
EST 1800
"WHOEVER THE THIEF WAS, THEY KNEW WHERE TO FIND IT...
"NOT TO MENTION THAT THEY WERE ABLE TO CIRCUMVENT ONE OF THE MOST ADVANCED ELECTRONIC LOCKS ON THE PLANET.
"ALL OF MY SYSTEMS AND ALARMS WERE DISABLED WITHOUT ME EVER KNOWING IT.
"I'M NOT DEALING WITH SOME COMMON THIEF...
"...BUT SOMEONE OF INCREDIBLE INTELLIGENCE.
"THE REST OF THE LAB APPEARS UNTOUCHED. IT'S OBVIOUS THE ANT-MAN GEAR WAS THE TARGET.
"IN THE WRONG HANDS, IT'S VERY DANGEROUS...
"...BUT THE BIGGEST DANGER IS TO WHOEVER STOLE IT.

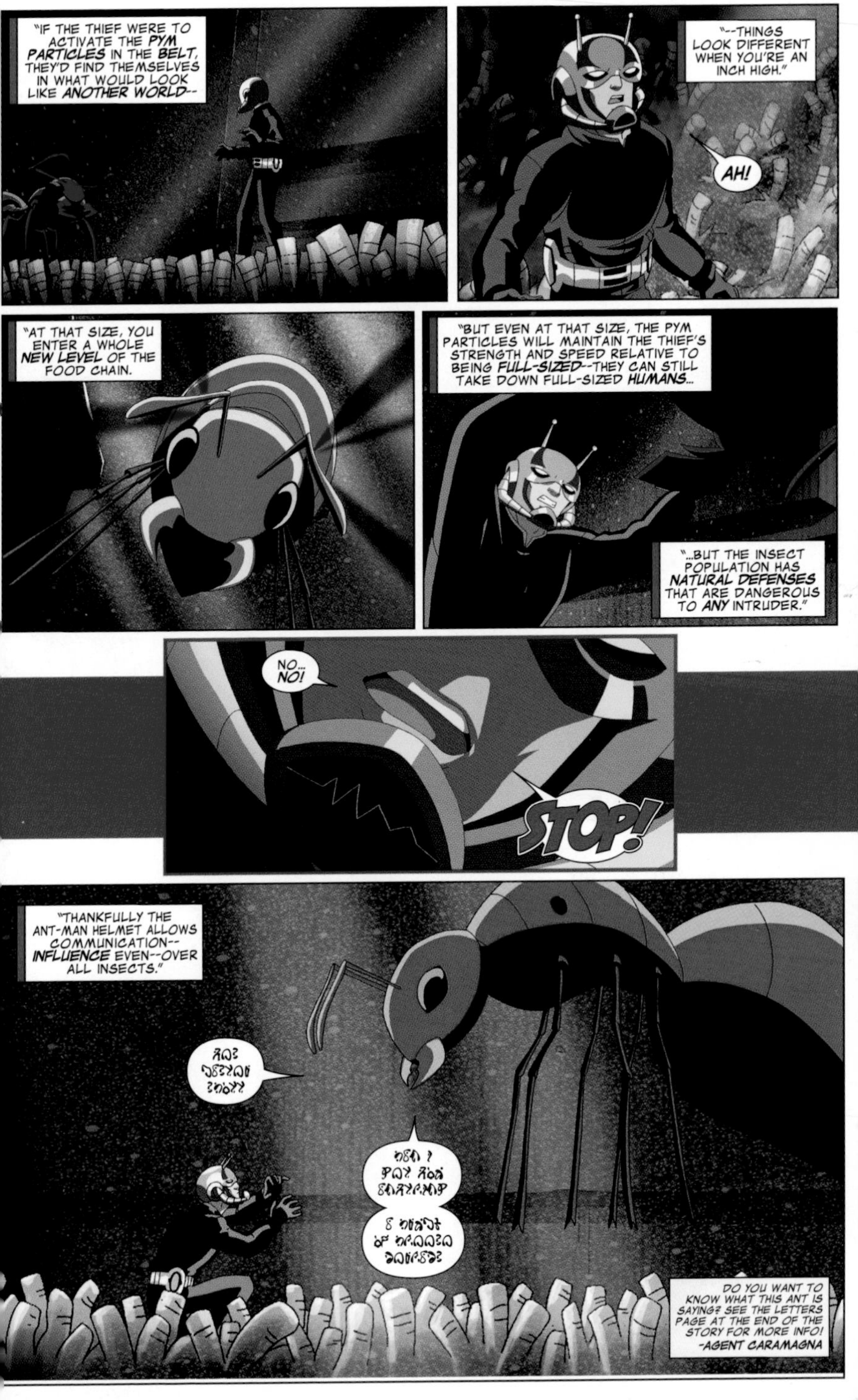
"IF THE THIEF WERE TO ACTIVATE THE PYM PARTICLES IN THE BELT, THEY'D FIND THEMSELVES IN WHAT WOULD LOOK LIKE ANOTHER WORLD--
"--THINGS LOOK DIFFERENT WHEN YOU'RE AN INCH HIGH."
AH!
"AT THAT SIZE, YOU ENTER A WHOLE NEW LEVEL OF THE FOOD CHAIN.
"BUT EVEN AT THAT SIZE, THE PYM PARTICLES WILL MAINTAIN THE THIEF'S STRENGTH AND SPEED RELATIVE TO BEING FULL-SIZED--THEY CAN STILL TAKE DOWN FULL-SIZED HUMANS...
"...BUT THE INSECT POPULATION HAS NATURAL DEFENSES THAT ARE DANGEROUS TO ANY INTRUDER."
NO... NO!
STOP!
"THANKFULLY THE ANT-MAN HELMET ALLOWS COMMUNICATION-- INFLUENCE EVEN--OVER ALL INSECTS."
DO YOU WANT TO KNOW WHAT THIS ANT IS SAYING? SEE THE LETTERS PAGE AT THE END OF THE STORY FOR MORE INFO! -AGENT CARAMAGNA

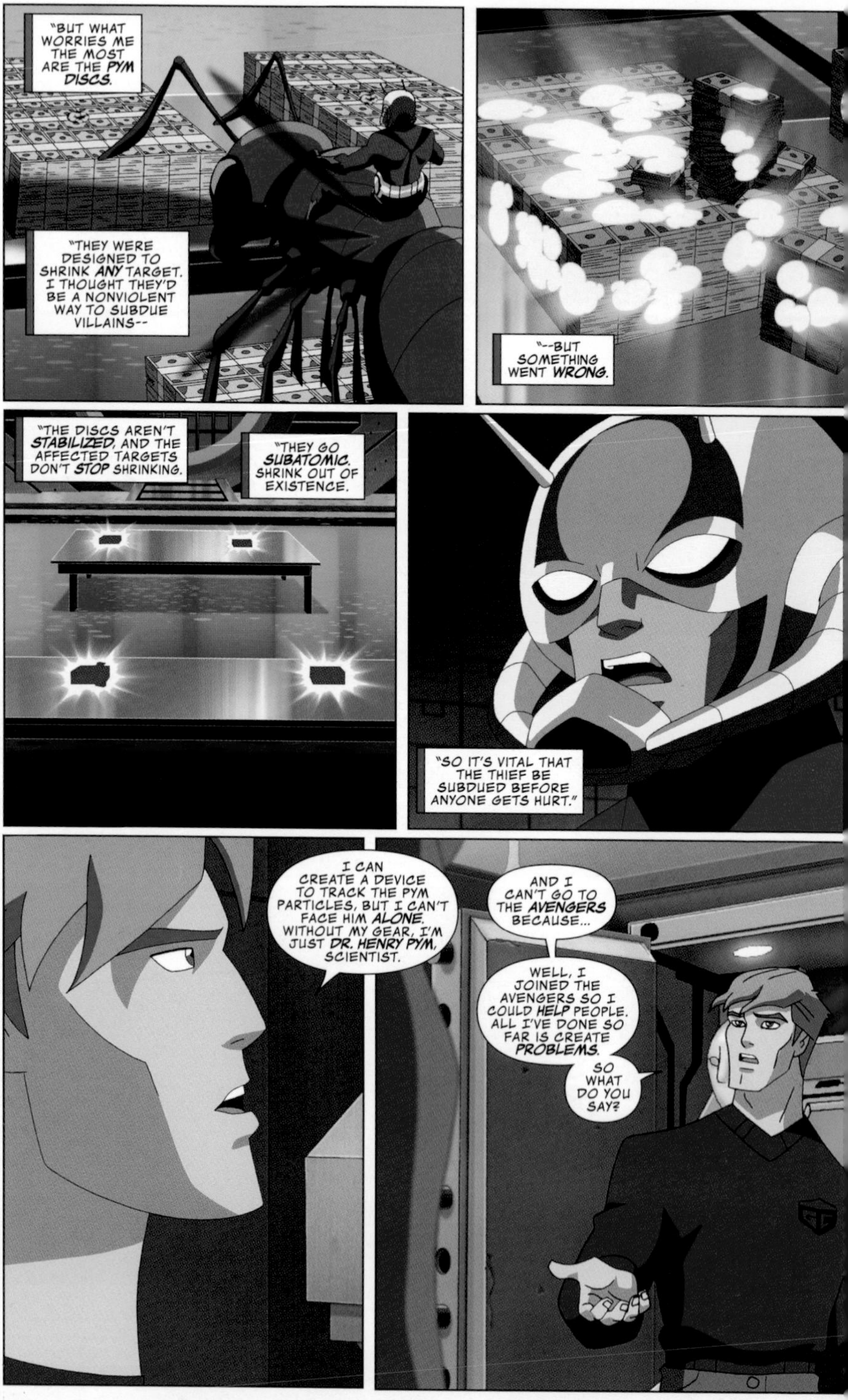
"BUT WHAT WORRIES ME THE MOST ARE THE PYM DISCS.
"THEY WERE DESIGNED TO SHRINK ANY TARGET. I THOUGHT THEY'D BE A NONVIOLENT WAY TO SUBDUE VILLAINS--
"--BUT SOMETHING WENT WRONG.
"THE DISCS AREN'T STABILIZED, AND THE AFFECTED TARGETS DON'T STOP SHRINKING.
"THEY GO SUBATOMIC. SHRINK OUT OF EXISTENCE.
"SO IT'S VITAL THAT THE THIEF BE SUBDUED BEFORE ANYONE GETS HURT."
I CAN CREATE A DEVICE TO TRACK THE PYM PARTICLES, BUT I CAN'T FACE HIM ALONE. WITHOUT MY GEAR, I'M JUST DR. HENRY PYM, SCIENTIST.
AND I CAN'T GO TO THE AVENGERS BECAUSE...
WELL, I JOINED THE AVENGERS SO I COULD HELP PEOPLE. ALL I'VE DONE SO FAR IS CREATE PROBLEMS.
SO WHAT DO YOU SAY?

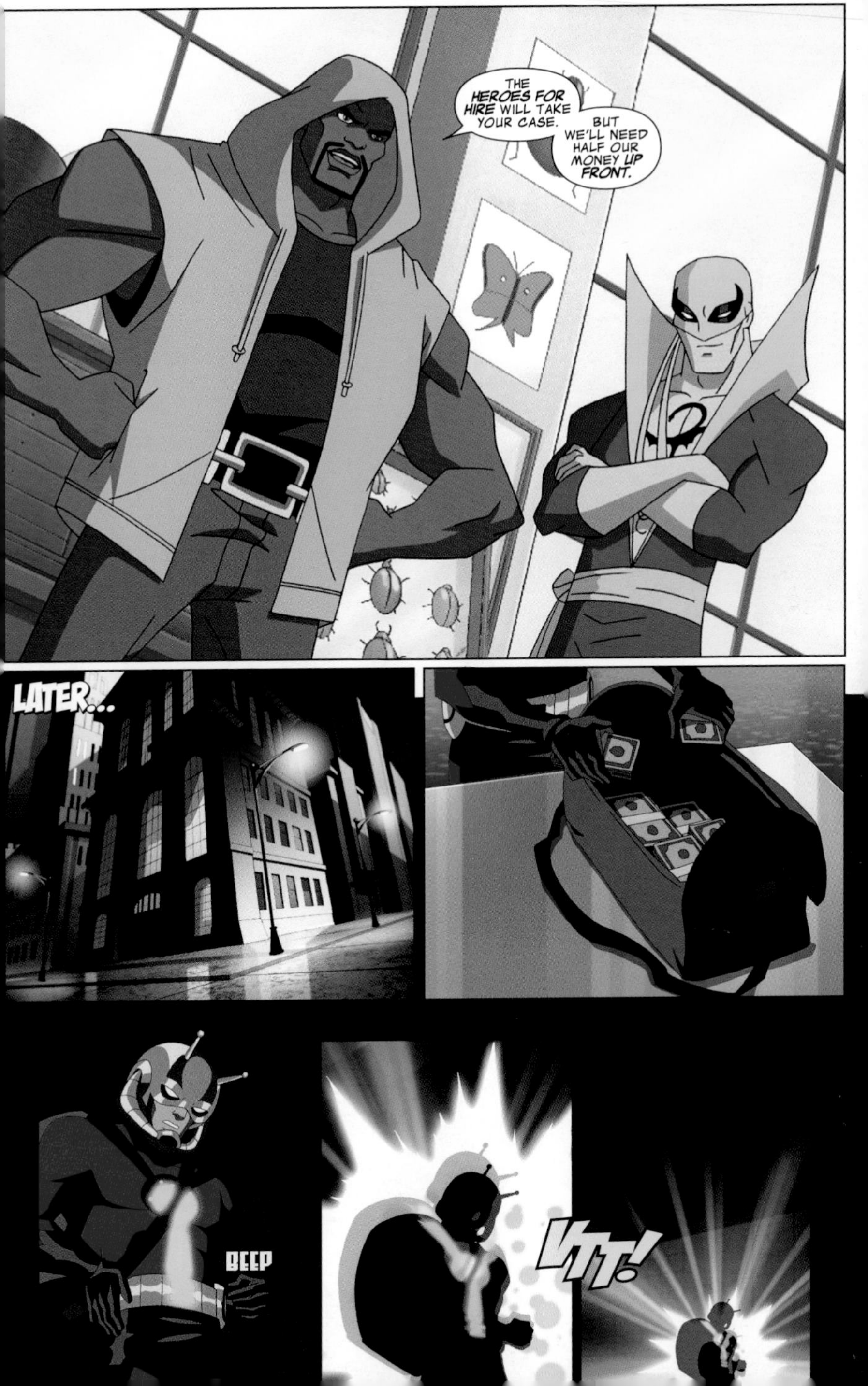
THE HEROES FOR HIRE WILL TAKE YOUR CASE.
BUT WE'LL NEED HALF OUR MONEY UP FRONT.
LATER...
BEEP
VTT!

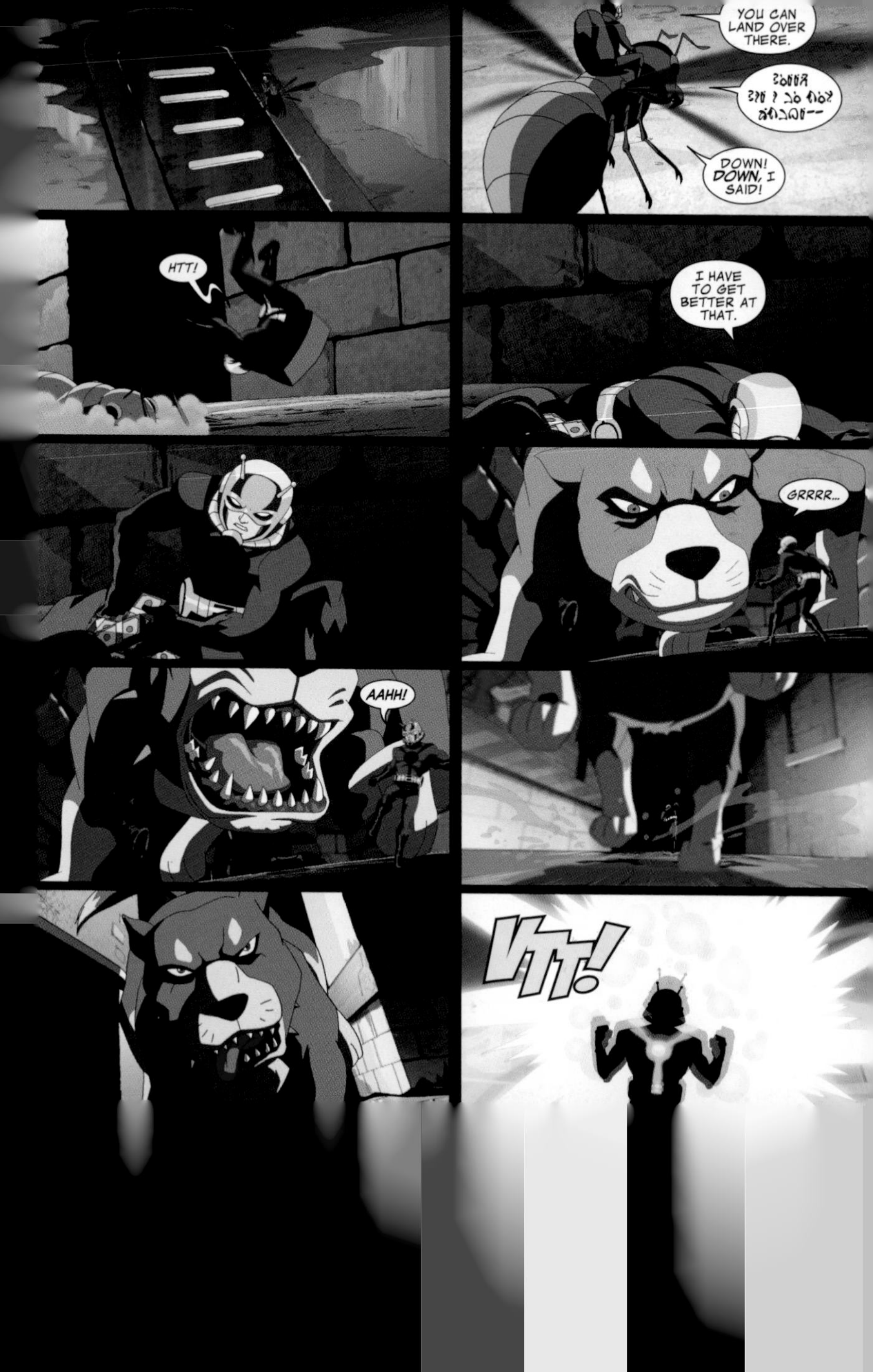
YOU CAN LAND OVER THERE.
DOWN! DOWN, I SAID!
HTT!
I HAVE TO GET BETTER AT THAT.
GRRRR...
AAHH!
VTT!

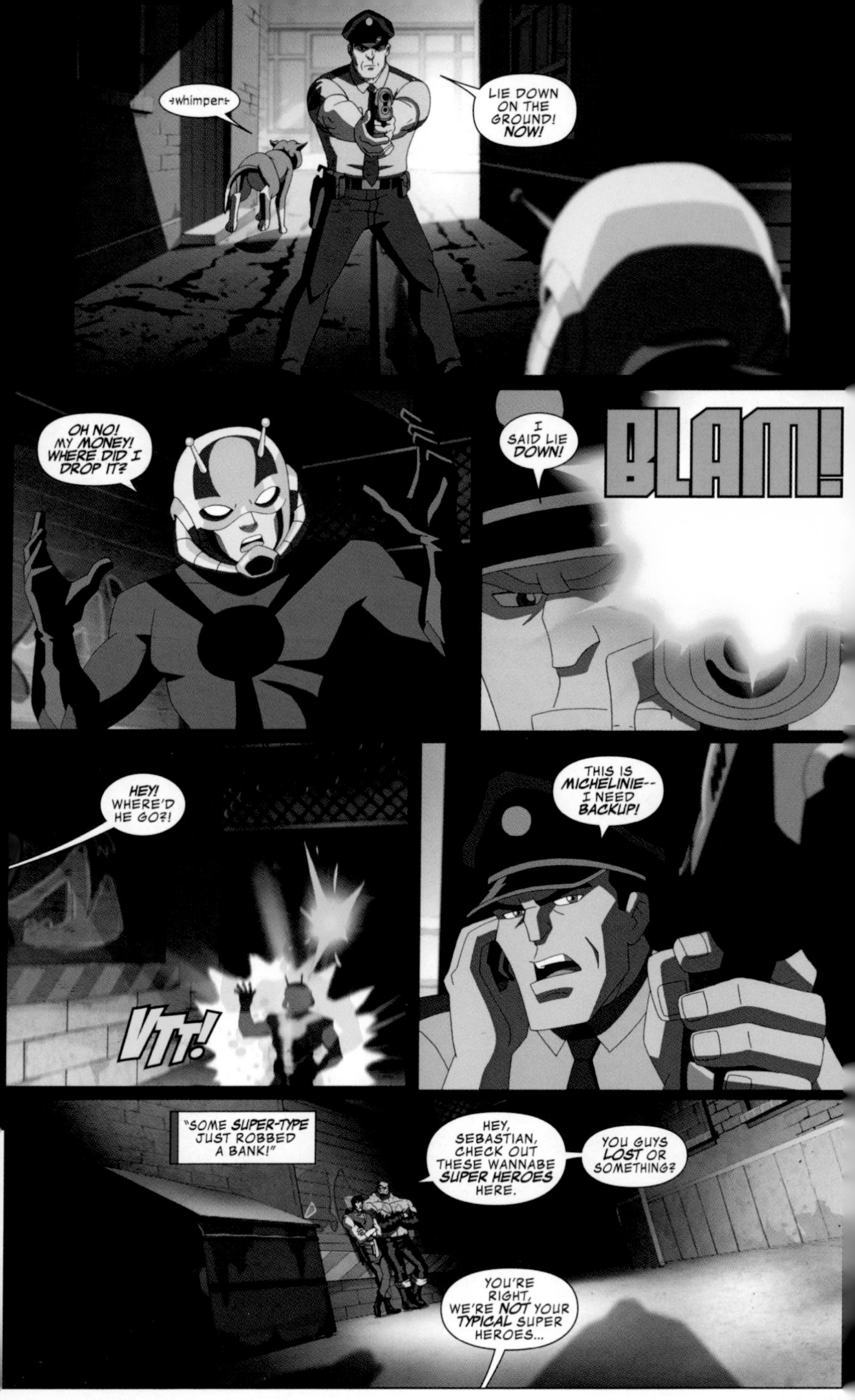

-whimper-
LIE DOWN ON THE GROUND! NOW!
OH NO! MY MONEY! WHERE DID I DROP IT?
I SAID LIE DOWN!
BLAM!
HEY! WHERE'D HE GO?!
VTT!
THIS IS MICHELINIE-- I NEED BACKUP!
"SOME SUPER-TYPE JUST ROBBED A BANK!"
HEY, SEBASTIAN, CHECK OUT THESE WANNABE SUPER HEROES HERE.
YOU GUYS LOST OR SOMETHING?
YOU'RE RIGHT, WE'RE NOT YOUR TYPICAL SUPER HEROES...

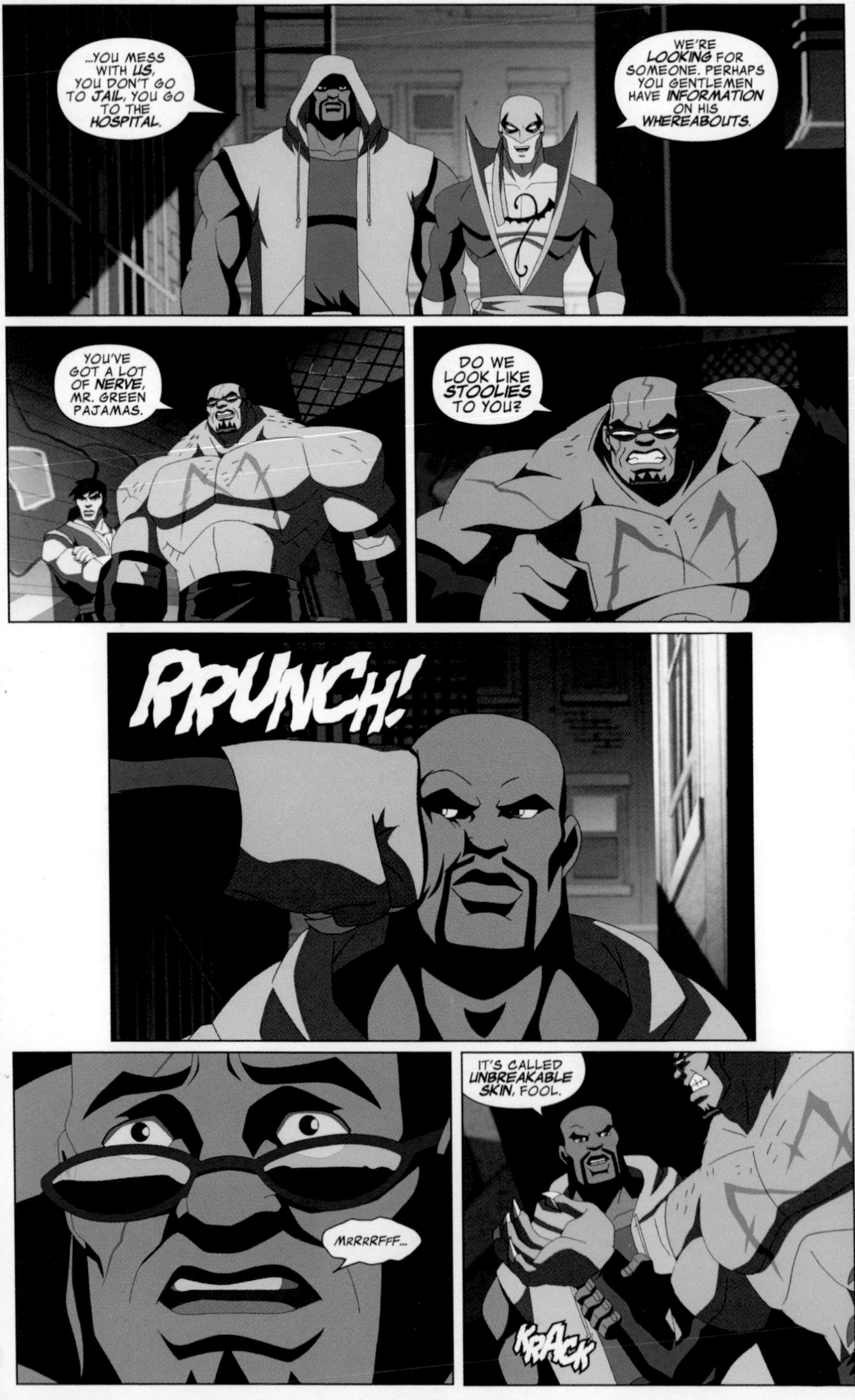
...YOU MESS WITH US, YOU DON'T GO TO JAIL, YOU GO TO THE HOSPITAL.
WE'RE LOOKING FOR SOMEONE. PERHAPS YOU GENTLEMEN HAVE INFORMATION ON HIS WHEREABOUTS.
YOU'VE GOT A LOT OF NERVE, MR. GREEN PAJAMAS.
DO WE LOOK LIKE STOOLIES TO YOU?
RRUNCH!
MRRRRFFF...
IT'S CALLED UNBREAKABLE SKIN, FOOL.
KRACK

WOOSH!

POW!

YOU'RE FAST...

...BUT I'VE SPENT YEARS STUDYING IN K'UN-LUN...

...SO I'M JUST A LITTLE BIT *FASTER*.

WHAM!

CRUNCH!

TOUGH GUYS, EH, *IRON FIST*?

I GUESS WE WON'T BE GETTING MUCH INFO OUT OF THEM *NOW*, LUKE.

WHAT ARE YOU DOING THIS IS NO TIME TO FOCUS YOUR *FENG SHUI*.

YOU MEAN MY *CHI*.

AND *FOCUSING MY ENERGY* WILL DO *MORE* FOR US NOW THAN YOUR *HARDEST* PUNCH.

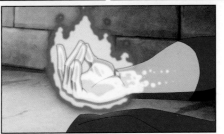

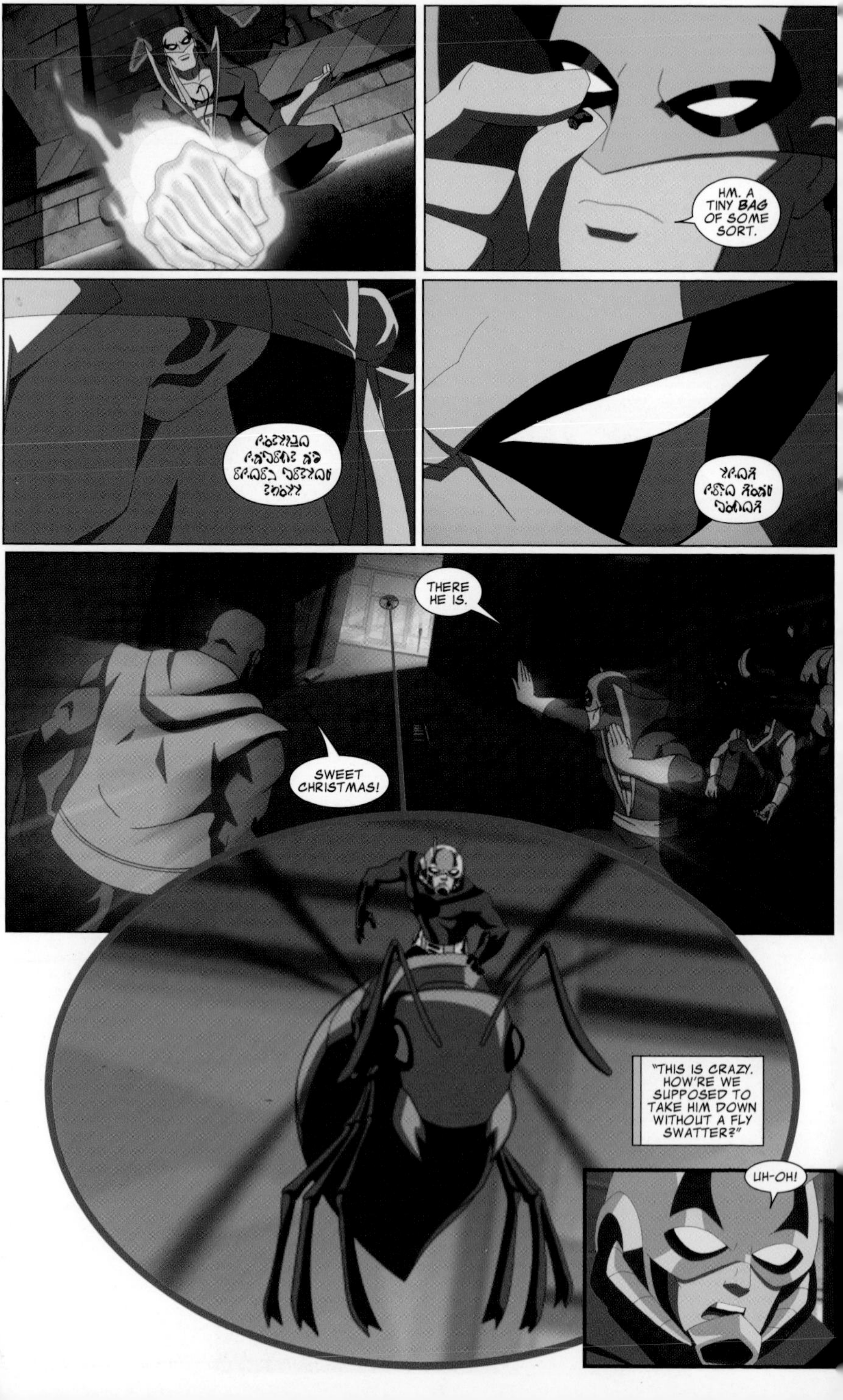
HM. A TINY BAG OF SOME SORT.
THERE HE IS.
SWEET CHRISTMAS!
"THIS IS CRAZY. HOW'RE WE SUPPOSED TO TAKE HIM DOWN WITHOUT A FLY SWATTER?"
UH-OH!

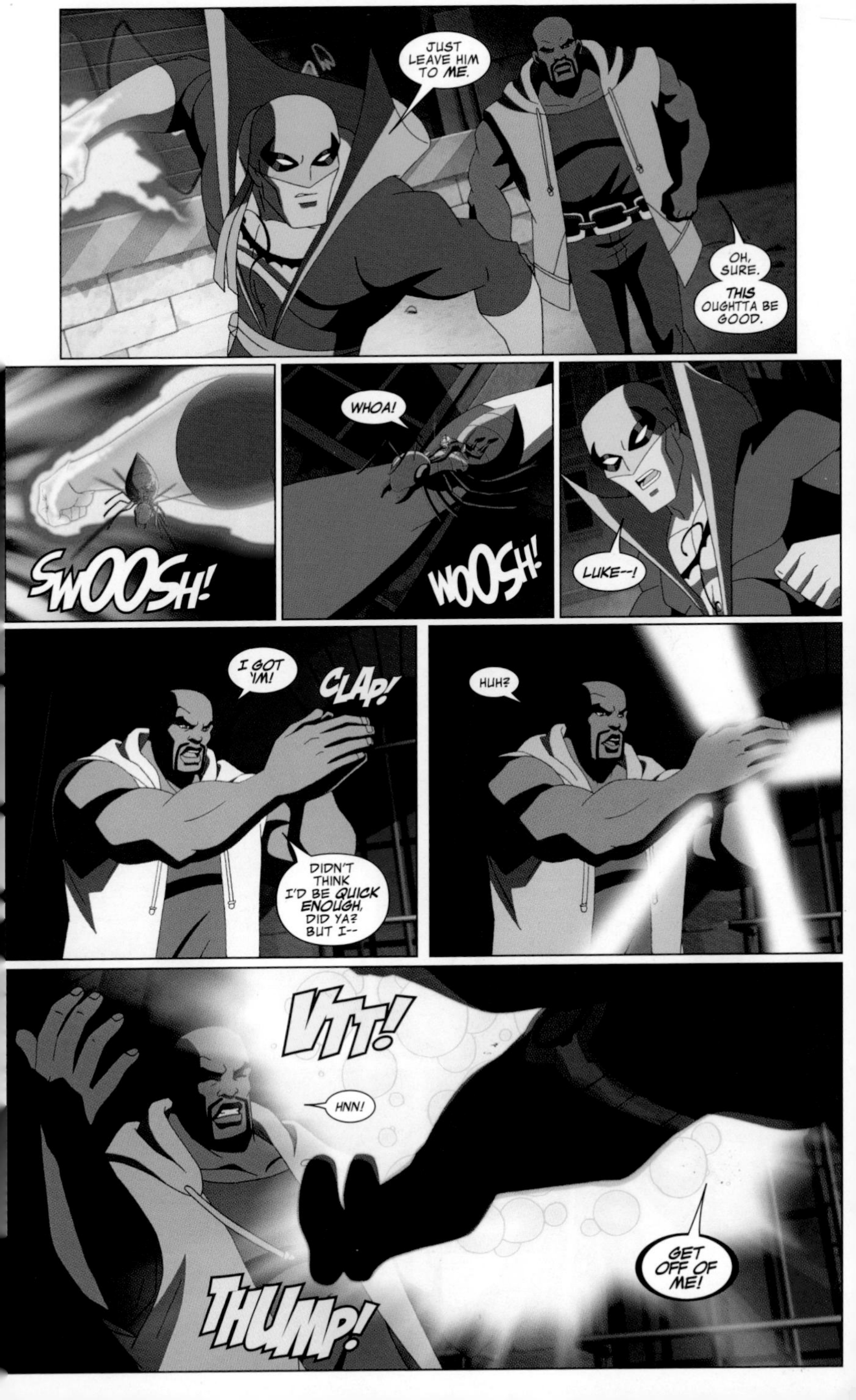
JUST LEAVE HIM TO ME.
OH, SURE. THIS OUGHTTA BE GOOD.
SWOOSH!
WHOA!
WOOSH!
LUKE--!
I GOT 'IM!
CLAP!
DIDN'T THINK I'D BE QUICK ENOUGH, DID YA? BUT I--
HUH?
VTT!
HNN!
GET OFF OF ME!
THUMP!

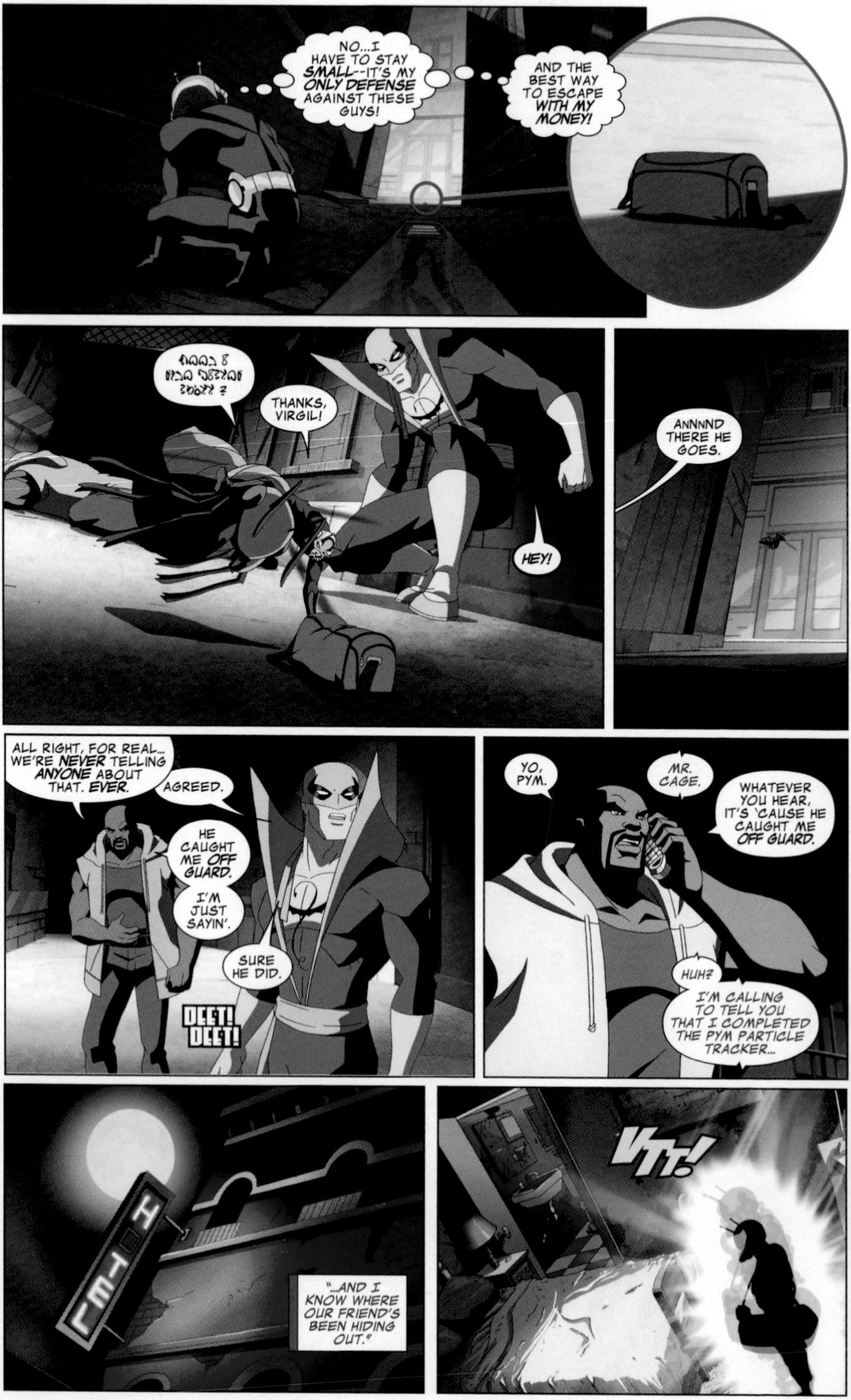
NO...I HAVE TO STAY SMALL--IT'S MY ONLY DEFENSE AGAINST THESE GUYS!
AND THE BEST WAY TO ESCAPE WITH MY MONEY!
THANKS, VIRGIL!
HEY!
ANNNND THERE HE GOES.
ALL RIGHT, FOR REAL... WE'RE NEVER TELLING ANYONE ABOUT THAT. EVER.
AGREED.
HE CAUGHT ME OFF GUARD.
I'M JUST SAYIN'.
SURE HE DID.
DEET! DEET!
YO, PYM.
MR. CAGE.
WHATEVER YOU HEAR, IT'S 'CAUSE HE CAUGHT ME OFF GUARD.
HUH?
I'M CALLING TO TELL YOU THAT I COMPLETED THE PYM PARTICLE TRACKER...
HOTEL
"...AND I KNOW WHERE OUR FRIEND'S BEEN HIDING OUT."
VTT!

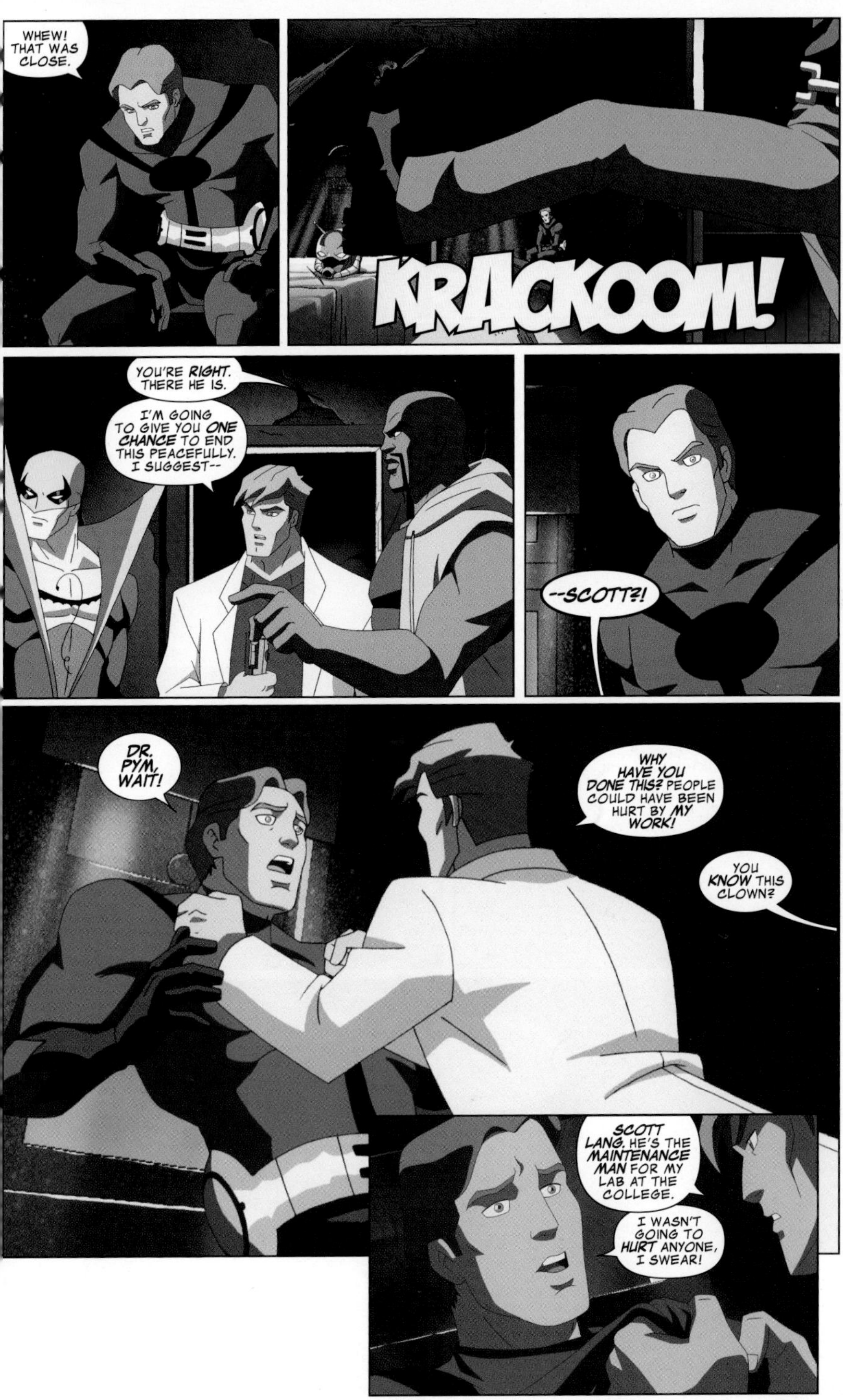
WHEW! THAT WAS CLOSE.
KRACKOOM!
YOU'RE RIGHT. THERE HE IS.
I'M GOING TO GIVE YOU ONE CHANCE TO END THIS PEACEFULLY. I SUGGEST--
--SCOTT?!
DR. PYM, WAIT!
WHY HAVE YOU DONE THIS? PEOPLE COULD HAVE BEEN HURT BY MY WORK!
YOU KNOW THIS CLOWN?
SCOTT LANG. HE'S THE MAINTENANCE MAN FOR MY LAB AT THE COLLEGE.
I WASN'T GOING TO HURT ANYONE, I SWEAR!

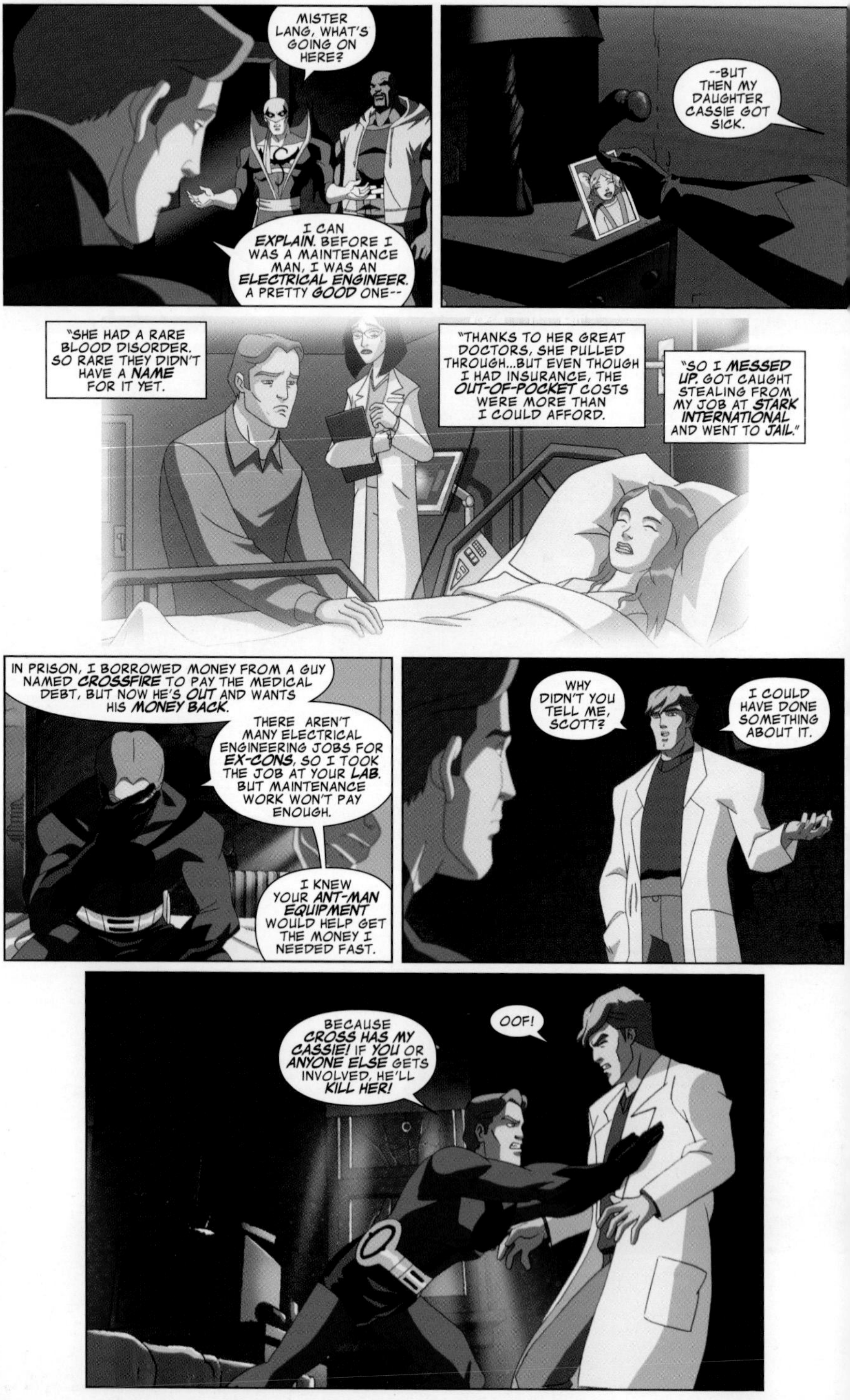
MISTER LANG, WHAT'S GOING ON HERE?
I CAN EXPLAIN. BEFORE I WAS A MAINTENANCE MAN, I WAS AN ELECTRICAL ENGINEER. A PRETTY GOOD ONE--
--BUT THEN MY DAUGHTER CASSIE GOT SICK.
"SHE HAD A RARE BLOOD DISORDER. SO RARE THEY DIDN'T HAVE A NAME FOR IT YET.
"THANKS TO HER GREAT DOCTORS, SHE PULLED THROUGH...BUT EVEN THOUGH I HAD INSURANCE, THE OUT-OF-POCKET COSTS WERE MORE THAN I COULD AFFORD.
"SO I MESSED UP. GOT CAUGHT STEALING FROM MY JOB AT STARK INTERNATIONAL AND WENT TO JAIL."
IN PRISON, I BORROWED MONEY FROM A GUY NAMED CROSSFIRE TO PAY THE MEDICAL DEBT, BUT NOW HE'S OUT AND WANTS HIS MONEY BACK.
THERE AREN'T MANY ELECTRICAL ENGINEERING JOBS FOR EX-CONS, SO I TOOK THE JOB AT YOUR LAB. BUT MAINTENANCE WORK WON'T PAY ENOUGH.
I KNEW YOUR ANT-MAN EQUIPMENT WOULD HELP GET THE MONEY I NEEDED FAST.
WHY DIDN'T YOU TELL ME, SCOTT?
I COULD HAVE DONE SOMETHING ABOUT IT.
BECAUSE CROSS HAS MY CASSIE! IF YOU OR ANYONE ELSE GETS INVOLVED, HE'LL KILL HER!
OOF!

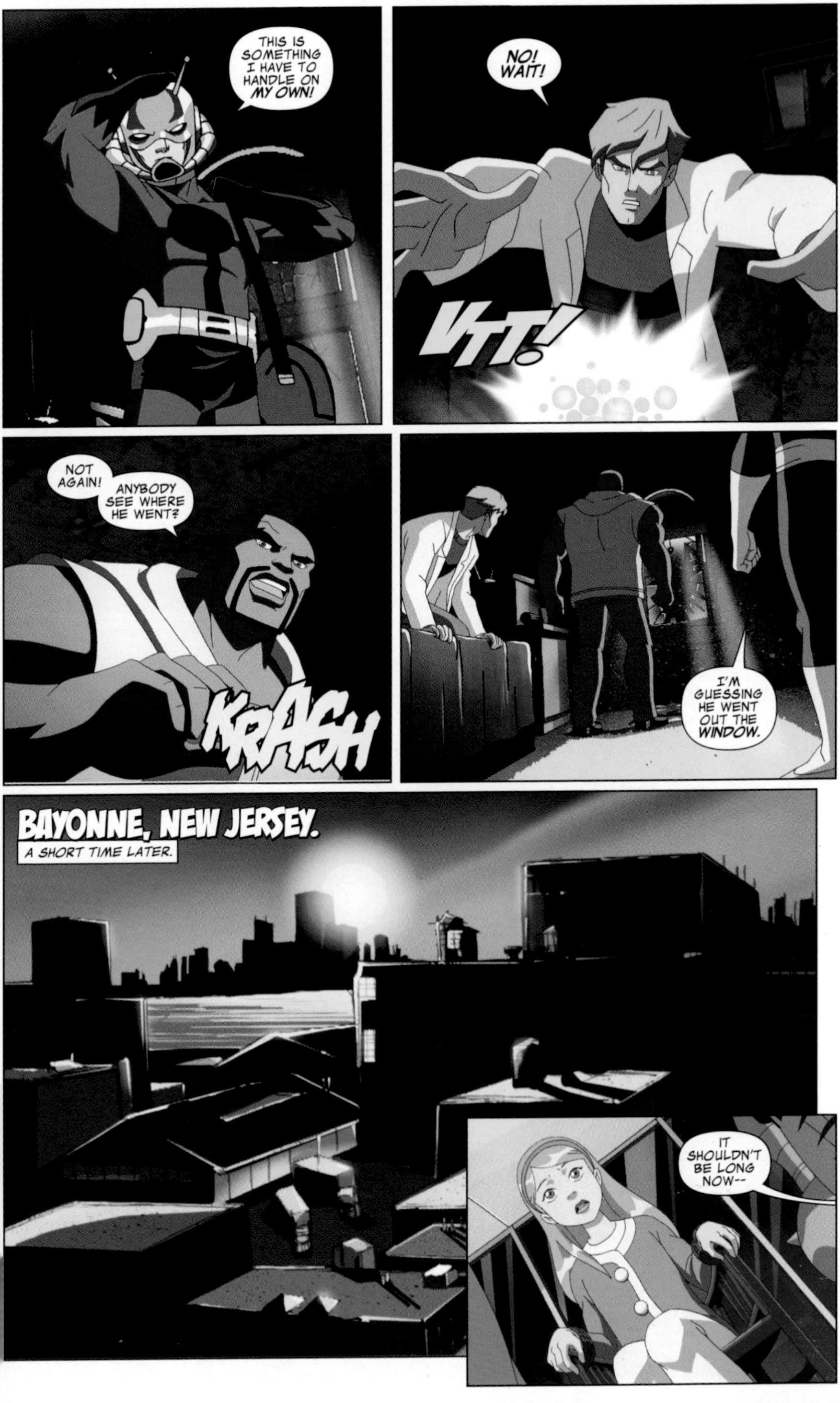
THIS IS SOMETHING I HAVE TO HANDLE ON MY OWN!
NO! WAIT!
VTT!
NOT AGAIN!
ANYBODY SEE WHERE HE WENT?
KRASH
I'M GUESSING HE WENT OUT THE WINDOW.
BAYONNE, NEW JERSEY.
A SHORT TIME LATER.
IT SHOULDN'T BE LONG NOW--

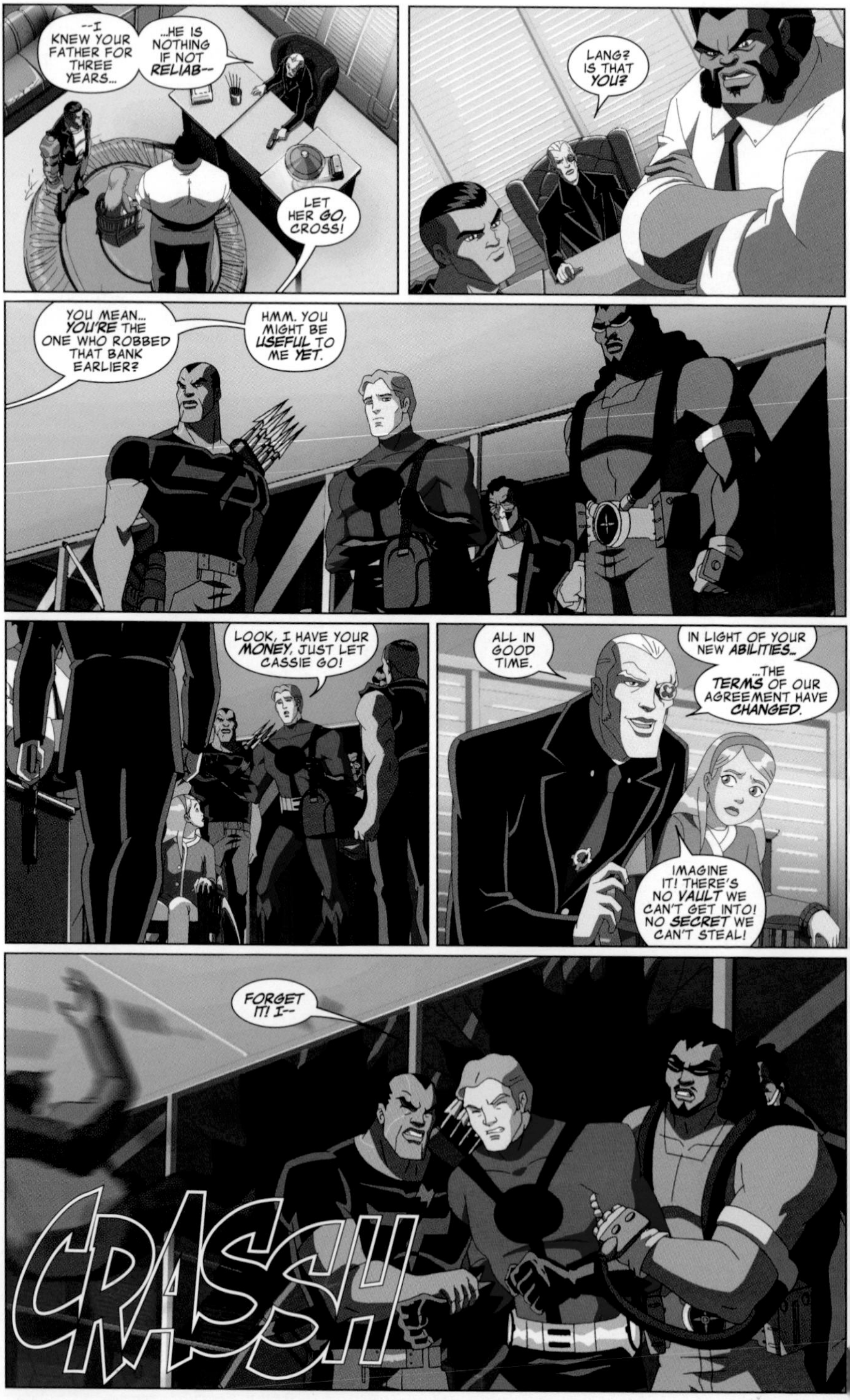
--I KNEW YOUR FATHER FOR THREE YEARS...
...HE IS NOTHING IF NOT RELIAB--
LET HER GO, CROSS!
LANG? IS THAT YOU?
YOU MEAN... YOU'RE THE ONE WHO ROBBED THAT BANK EARLIER?
HMM. YOU MIGHT BE USEFUL TO ME YET.
LOOK, I HAVE YOUR MONEY, JUST LET CASSIE GO!
ALL IN GOOD TIME.
IN LIGHT OF YOUR NEW ABILITIES...
...THE TERMS OF OUR AGREEMENT HAVE CHANGED.
IMAGINE IT! THERE'S NO VAULT WE CAN'T GET INTO! NO SECRET WE CAN'T STEAL!
FORGET IT! I--
CRASSH

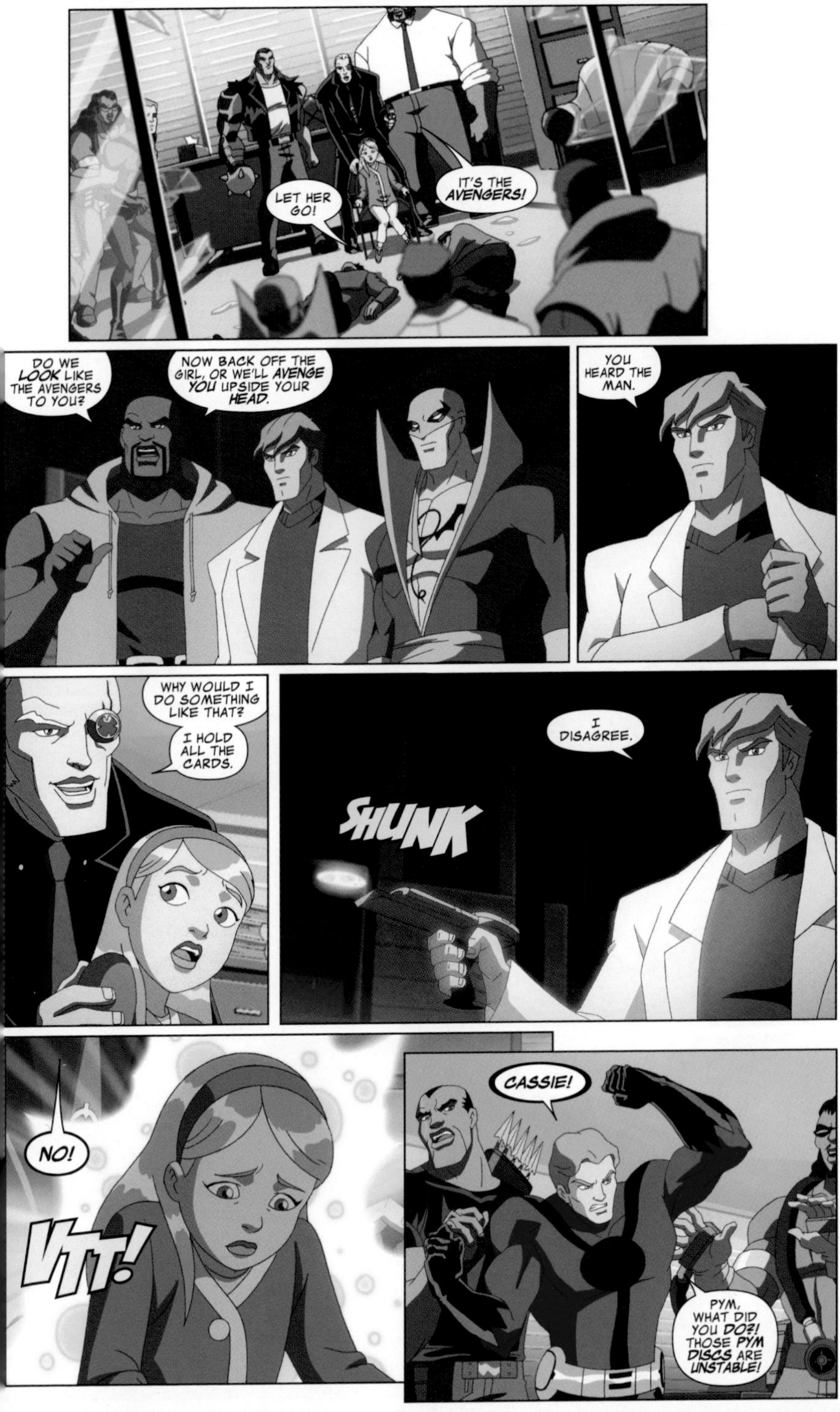
LET HER GO!
IT'S THE AVENGERS!
DO WE LOOK LIKE THE AVENGERS TO YOU?
NOW BACK OFF THE GIRL, OR WE'LL AVENGE YOU UPSIDE YOUR HEAD.
YOU HEARD THE MAN.
WHY WOULD I DO SOMETHING LIKE THAT?
I HOLD ALL THE CARDS.
I DISAGREE.
SHUNK
NO!
VTT!
CASSIE!
PYM, WHAT DID YOU DO?! THOSE PYM DISCS ARE UNSTABLE!

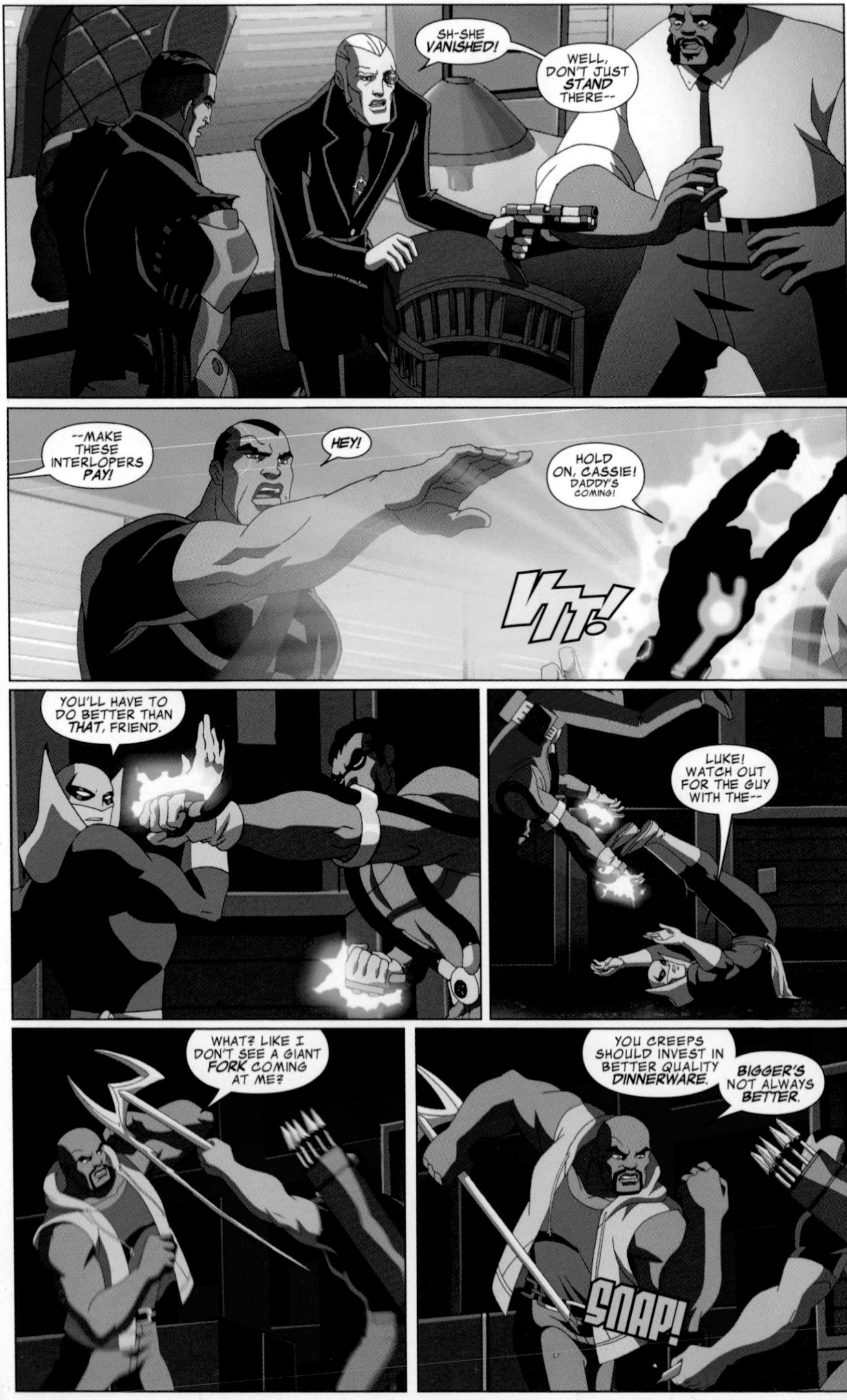
SH-SHE VANISHED!
WELL, DON'T JUST STAND THERE--
--MAKE THESE INTERLOPERS PAY!
HEY!
HOLD ON, CASSIE! DADDY'S COMING!
YOU'LL HAVE TO DO BETTER THAN THAT, FRIEND.
LUKE! WATCH OUT FOR THE GUY WITH THE--
WHAT? LIKE I DON'T SEE A GIANT FORK COMING AT ME?
YOU CREEPS SHOULD INVEST IN BETTER QUALITY DINNERWARE.
BIGGER'S NOT ALWAYS BETTER.
SNAP!

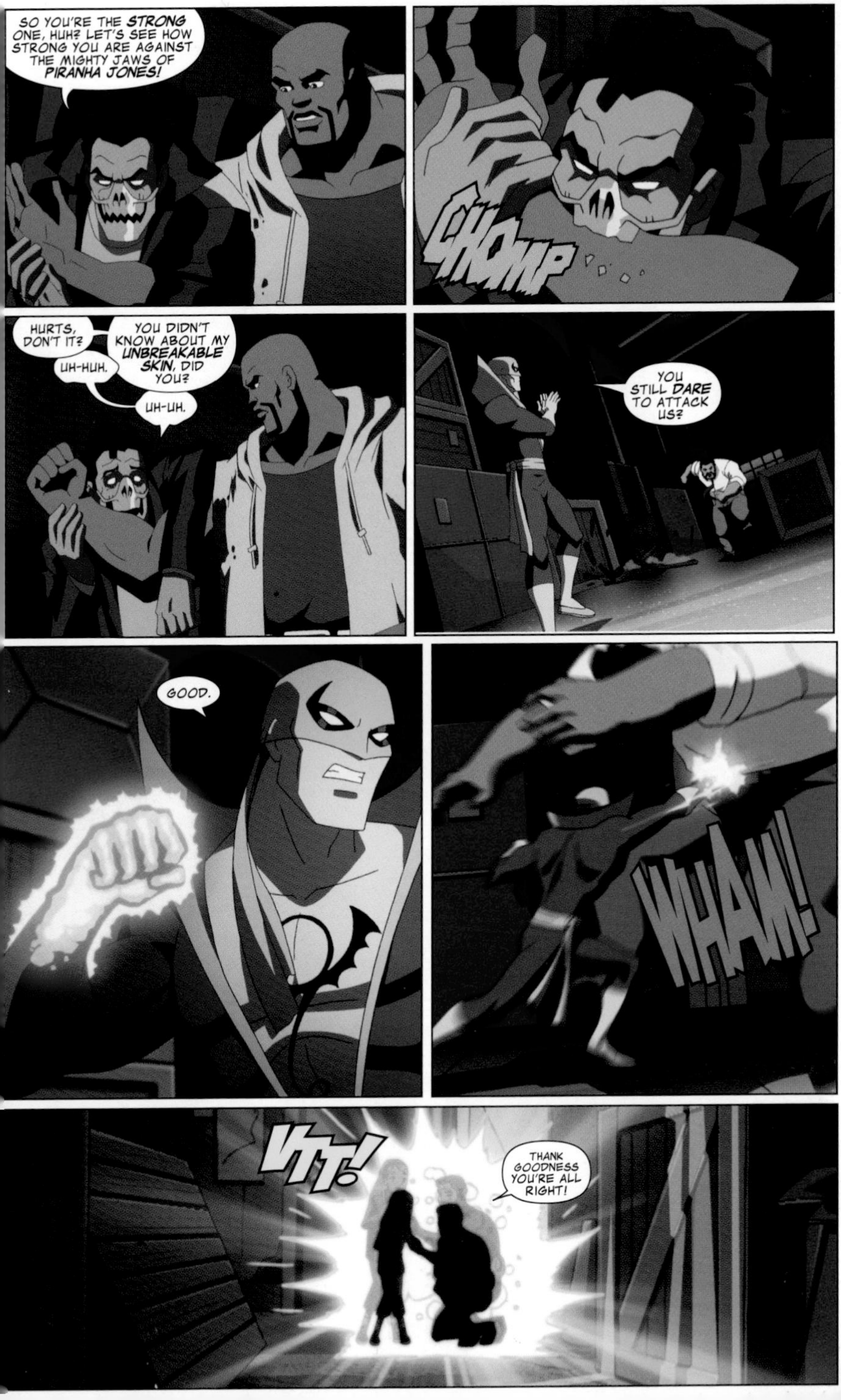
SO YOU'RE THE STRONG ONE, HUH? LET'S SEE HOW STRONG YOU ARE AGAINST THE MIGHTY JAWS OF PIRANHA JONES!
CHOMP
HURTS, DON'T IT?
UH-HUH.
YOU DIDN'T KNOW ABOUT MY UNBREAKABLE SKIN, DID YOU?
UH-UH.
YOU STILL DARE TO ATTACK US?
GOOD.
WHAM!
VTT!
THANK GOODNESS YOU'RE ALL RIGHT!

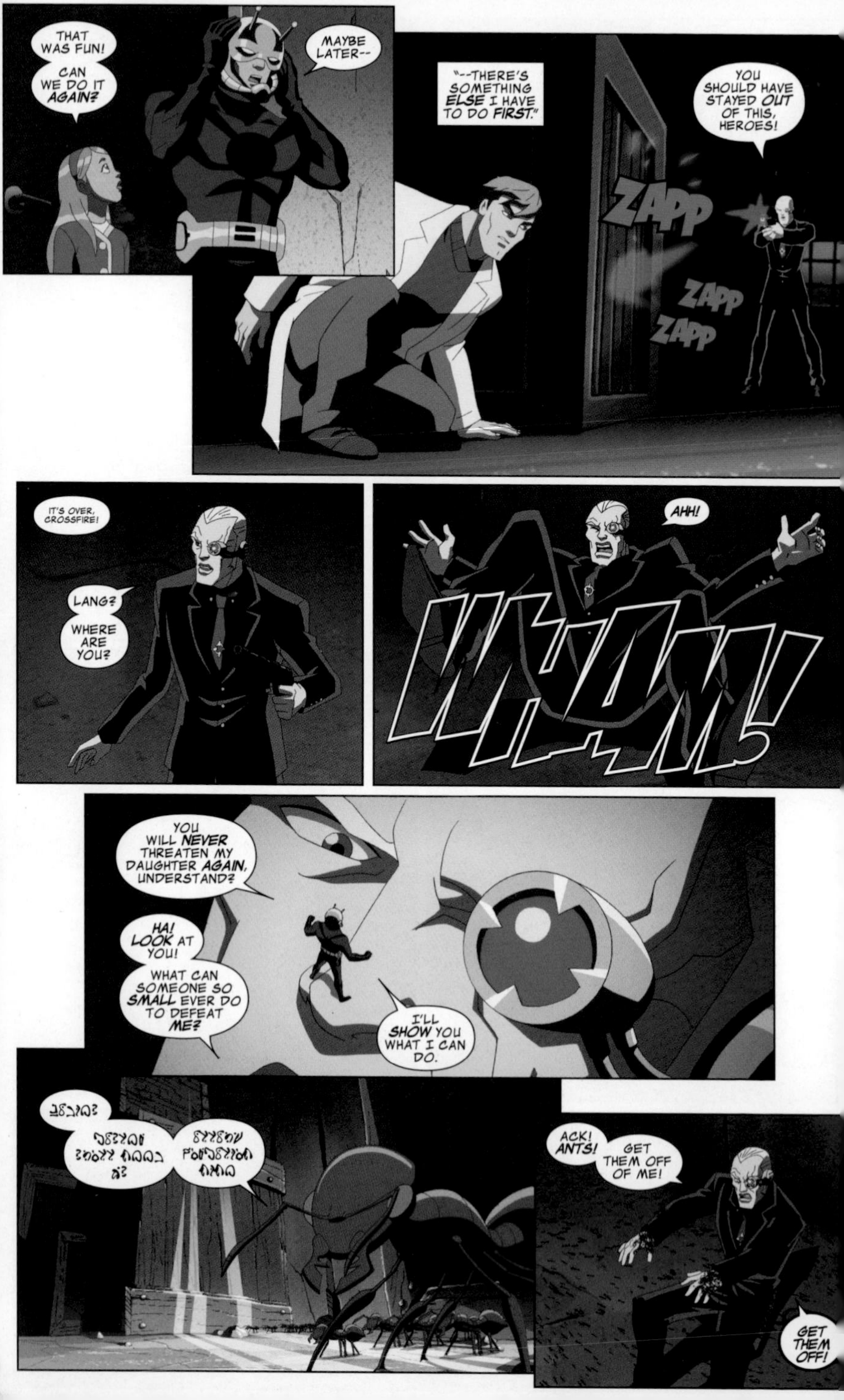

THAT WAS FUN!
CAN WE DO IT AGAIN?
MAYBE LATER--
"--THERE'S SOMETHING ELSE I HAVE TO DO FIRST."
YOU SHOULD HAVE STAYED OUT OF THIS, HEROES!
ZAPP
ZAPP
ZAPP
IT'S OVER, CROSSFIRE!
LANG?
WHERE ARE YOU?
AHH!
WHOM!
YOU WILL NEVER THREATEN MY DAUGHTER AGAIN, UNDERSTAND?
HA! LOOK AT YOU!
WHAT CAN SOMEONE SO SMALL EVER DO TO DEFEAT ME?
I'LL SHOW YOU WHAT I CAN DO.
ACK! ANTS!
GET THEM OFF OF ME!
GET THEM OFF!

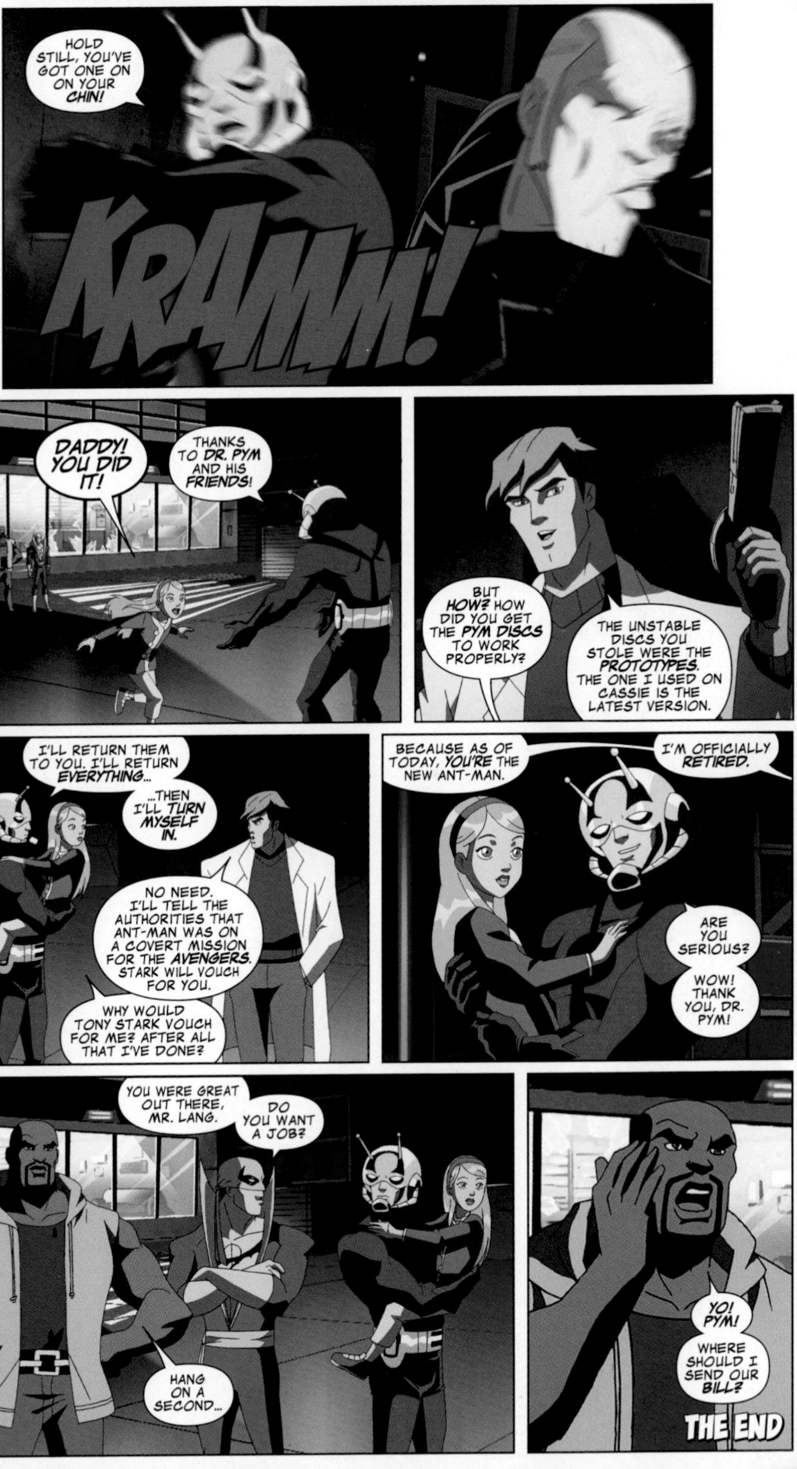

HOLD STILL, YOU'VE GOT ONE ON ON YOUR CHIN!
KRAMM!
DADDY! YOU DID IT!
THANKS TO DR. PYM AND HIS FRIENDS!
BUT HOW? HOW DID YOU GET THE PYM DISCS TO WORK PROPERLY?
THE UNSTABLE DISCS YOU STOLE WERE THE PROTOTYPES. THE ONE I USED ON CASSIE IS THE LATEST VERSION.
I'LL RETURN THEM TO YOU. I'LL RETURN EVERYTHING...
...THEN I'LL TURN MYSELF IN.
NO NEED. I'LL TELL THE AUTHORITIES THAT ANT-MAN WAS ON A COVERT MISSION FOR THE AVENGERS. STARK WILL VOUCH FOR YOU.
WHY WOULD TONY STARK VOUCH FOR ME? AFTER ALL THAT I'VE DONE?
BECAUSE AS OF TODAY, YOU'RE THE NEW ANT-MAN.
I'M OFFICIALLY RETIRED.
ARE YOU SERIOUS?
WOW! THANK YOU, DR. PYM!
YOU WERE GREAT OUT THERE, MR. LANG.
DO YOU WANT A JOB?
HANG ON A SECOND...
YO! PYM!
WHERE SHOULD I SEND OUR BILL?
THE END